THE ALCHEMY OF SUPREME COMPASSION

THE ULTIMATE PATH

TO HIGHER CONSCIOUSNESS AND
DEATHLESS LIFE

As Revealed By
Ramalinga Vallalar
Aruludaiyaar

Copyright © Aruludaiyaar

All rights reserved. No part of this publication may be reproduced, distributed, or transmitted in any form or by any means, including photocopying, recording, or other electronic or mechanical methods, without the prior written permission of the author, except in the case of brief quotations embodied in critical reviews and certain other non-commercial uses permitted by copyright law.

THE SACRED - HALL OF TRUE AND
PURE KNOWLEDGE
"SATHYA GNANA SABHAI"
VADALUR, TAMIL NADU - INDIA

THE GRACE LIGHT PATH
"SUDDHA SANMARGA"

AS PER THE TEACHING OF HIS HOLINESS
RAMALINGA VALLALAR

HIS HOLINESS
RAMALINGA VALLALAR

Contents

I – FOREWORD 1

II – PREFACE 5

III – INTRODUCTION 23

IV - AN AUTO BIOGRAPHICAL JOURNEY FROM DARKNESS TO LIGHT 33

V -THE DIVINE LIFE OF RAMALINGA VALLALAR AND HIS MESSAGE 61

VI - THE SUPREME AND ULTIMATE SPIRITUAL PATH 97

VII - THE SEVEN VEILS OF THE SOUL - THE 7 MAYA SHAKTI 136

VIII - DIET PROTOCOL OF SUDDHA SANMARGA 140

IX- VEGETARIANISM AND COMPASSION 201

X - VALLALAR'S DIVINE REVELATION OF SACRED HERBALS 214

XI - THE STORY OF CREATION – THE EVOLUTION OF THE SOULS – FROM ATOM TO SOUL 224

XII - STATES OF CONCIOUSNESS - PLANES OF ASCENT OF THE SOUL THROUGH THE 17 STATES OF CONSCIOUSNESS 260

XIII - SCIENCE OF DEATHLESSNESS – TRIPLE SIDDHI & TRIPLE BODY ..280

XIV - COMPASSION PART I 296

XV - COMPASSION – PART 2 328

XVI - COMPASSION – PART 3 340

XVII –RAMALINGAM VALLALAR'S DEATHLESS LIFE & CHARITABLE TRUST 352

ACKNOWLEDGEMENTS

I wish to express my deepest gratitude and my heartfelt thanks and deep appreciation to His Holiness **RAMALINGA VALLALAR**, who inspired me to write this treatise on the "Alchemy of Supreme Compassion" and has guided me at each stage of its preparation.

Also, I would like to express my deepest love and thanks to the brothers and sisters who have facilitated the writing and publication of this opuscule:

- To my Dearest spiritual Mother, Maji for her unbounded inspiration, love and full support on my spiritual journey.
- To his Honourable Babu Sadhu and Yoga Pria from "Arutperunjoti Vallalar Charitable Trust" from Thiruvannamalai, for his unconditional love, His guidance and support.
- To the most honourable members of the "Arutperunjyothi" Ramalingam Vallalar's Deathless Life & Charitable Trust" at Chennai – Tamil Nadu – Mr. Vinothkumar Raju, Mrs. ChithraVinothkumar and Mr. Balachander for their limitless kindness, compassion, advices, invaluable suggestions and full support facilitating the publication of the book.
- To Tamil Chemmal Vijayarangan Ayya – Tamil Professor who reveals to me the secrets of the Tamil language and the nectar hidden within the most sublime and divine verses written by Saint Ramalinga Vallalar.
- To the Countess Marina von Kamarowsky for her precious support, understanding, advice and unconditional love
- To Mrs Patricia Dubois for her unconditional love, generosity and support, and Sam Fortescue for his precious help, advice and skills in English which permit the writing of this opuscule.
- To Octavian Nicodim, Mr. Vasile, Mrs. Elena Nicodim and Iulia Taban for their love and invaluable support.

I - FOREWORD

ARUTPERUNJOTHI - ARUTPERUNJOTHI
THANIPPERUNKARUNAI - ARUTPERUNJOTHI

Oh God! The Vast Supreme Grace Light!
Oh God! The Vast Supreme Grace Light!
The embodiment of Supreme Mercy!
Oh God! The Vast Supreme Grace light!

By Vinothkumar Raju & Chithra
Samarasa Suddha Sanmarka Sathya Sangam, Treasurer,
Padiyanallur, Chennai-52, Tamil Nadu, India

I am grateful to be able to write a foreword to the fine book of **Thiru. Aruludaiyaar (Alain Legras)**, from Nancy - Eastern part of France, entitled "**The Alchemy of Supreme Compassion**". From the very moment I met Aruludaiyaar, in December 2017, this instant marked a great turning point in my spiritual journey. I was astonished to realize, how much he was already rooted into the experience and understanding of **Vallalar's Suddha Sanmargam**. I came to realise that he has most probably been prepared for this journey since his childhood. In fact, he told me that, since a very young age, he was paying attention to the needy. He inherited this kind of compassion from his grand-parents and his mother. Over the past four decades, he has been living a life in constant search for God and truth. His meeting with Vallalar's philosophy changed his life to a point that his outside search stopped and found God in himself. He realised that he had to incorporate all living beings in his spiritual journey to God realization; as Vallalar told, the highest spiritual practice is to see every living being as an extension of oneself, oneself being nothing but God. Based on that realisation, he felt the inner call to dedicate his life to the suffering and poor people to contribute to the eradication of ignorance, sicknesses, suffering and poverty.

Since we came into contact, there was an inner call to launch a pilgrim in the footsteps of Thiru Arut Prakasa Ramalingam Vallalar and the Greatest Saints and Siddhas of Tamil Nadu. There was a need to merge into the life and teaching of these great beings, especially Ramalingam Vallalar. We started from Ramalingam's birthplace Maruthur, then Vallalar Nagar in Chennai, **Nataraja Temple in Chithambaram (Poorva Gyana Sithipuram).**, Siva Temples in Thanjai, Siva Temples in Madurai, Manikavasagar's Siva Temple in Thiruperunthurai, Manikavasgar's birthplace, Thirugyanasambandar's Sattinathar Temple in Sirkali, and his marriage place where he mingled with the light of Arutperunjothi in Thiruperumana Nallur temple, Achalapuram, Thiruvettriyoor, Kandakottam, Patinathar Temple, Veera Ragaver Temple, Kathirkamam Murgan Temple's Bogar and Maha Avathar Babaji Nagaraj Temple in Sri Lanka, Maha Avathar Babaji (Nagaraj) birthplace in Parangipetai, Saint Thirumoolar Temple where he wrote Thirumanthiram 3000, Thiruvaduthurai Atheenam Saints called Nambiyar Thevar and Thirumaaligai Thevar in Thiruvaduthurai, Sirkali Chitrambalanadigal Temple in Sidharkadu where 63 Saints with Guru Chitrambalanadigal attained Enlightenment (Jeeva Samathi) and wrote Thugalarubootham book etc. including all Samaya Kuravargal places and Santhana Kuravargal places, Kanchipuam's Siva Temples, Thiruporur Murgan Temple, etc…, to arrive **at the very seat of the Suddha Sanmargam Path for all mankind in Vadalur (Uthra Gyana Sithipuram).**

All along these highly spiritual places, **Aruludaiyaar** felt that beside feeding the poor, there was a call to educate the needy and the poor people in the art of Deathlessness. From there came the inspiration to educate the poor people in the art of deathlessness and to write a book in English on the Alchemy of Supreme Compassion "**Jeevakarunyam**"; an opuscule that should contain the very essence of Ramalingam Vallalar's education for deathlessness, which should be as simple, practical and comprehensive as possible. Thus, all the people in the world could have access to **Ramalingam Vallalar' Suddha Sanmargam**, the True and Pure Path, leading them to the complete union with God in the state of Supreme Bliss.

The essence of "**The Alchemy of Supreme Compassion**" is all about Mercy, the Boundless Benevolent Effulgence which is known as "**Arutperunjothi**", the Vast Supreme Grace Light. Benevolence, Mercy or Karunai is the innate nature of the Almighty. This compassion emanates in a fivefold expression: (1) matter, (2) energy, (3) intellect; (4) spirit; (5) Grace. When man attains perfection, he realizes that the Compassionate Effulgence or Mercy is the source of all that is manifest and non-manifest.

The seat of "**Arutperunjyothi**" in man and in all living beings, is in the soul in man. The presence of God in the soul manifests as a spark of effulgent Light; the All Merciful Lord exists in every soul in the form of a guiding light. Hitherto, man, so far, has thought that he was separated from God, and that he had to reach Him through his own individual efforts. Having forgotten his divine identity, man has been searching everywhere except within himself.

The question now is, how this divine Effulgence is going to grow and flourish again in the soul of man?

Man has first to realize, that he must discard the believe that he is the physical body, and surrender himself to the source of Life, the Vast Supreme Grace Light, for his climbing into the Light of its own true self. To realize it, man has to live a life of compassion towards all beings and be always thinking how small man is, in the scale of the universe, and at the foot of the vastness and greatness of the Almighty God. By doing so, one will certainly find that little by little, the Divine grace will fill up one's entire being.

Thus, one is brought to realize that the abode (of the Lord), the Soul and the Effulgence are one and the same, namely the mid portion of the forehead "**Ajna**", the seat of Fire and direct entrance to the soul. By having constantly, one's own attention there, one will find that the Effulgent Grace will spread through one's entire being. This will bring one to the understanding that the search for peace and happiness outside of oneself, through the mere realization of desires, has no end, and will stop playing the game of the compulsive nature of thoughts and desires, by surrendering them back to the All Merciful Lord.

Slowly man will find that Grace in the form of Supreme Bliss will engulf him, this without losing his consciousness. Thus, man is coming to the realization that he has mingled with God and God has mingled with him, both remaining an inseparable Oneness. Now he has found himself to be that Effulgence and lives forever at Thy command. In this process nothing is lost, everything is gained.

This Lord of Infinite Light, "**Arutperunjothi**", has been completely realized by Vallalar, (**Thiruarutprakasa Ramalingam Vallalar from Vadalur**), which he has expressed so divinely, into thousands of devotional songs, addressed to the Almighty Lord with a heartfelt of pure devotion and love; thousands of verses of "**Thiru Arutpa**" and "**Arutperunjothi Agaval**" contain the essence of all his teachings, and are considered as the most valuable jewel in the crown of the Lord.

On this highly inspirational spiritual journey with Thiru. Aruludaiyaar, I am very pleased to say that **Thiruarutprakasa Ramalingam Vallalar** has certainly chosen a great soul in the form of Thiru. Aruludaiyaar, to spread the Supreme Teaching of Suddha Sanmargam to the Western Countries. I feel sincerely uplifted being in contact with Thiru. Aruludaiyar's sincerity, dedication and determination towards learning the true essence of Tamil language and Sanmargam Disciplines; this theoretically as well practically through direct experience. I am very grateful and thankful to **Thiruarutprakasa Ramalingam Vallalar** for meeting with such a great soul, and for giving me the great opportunity to write a foreword on this opuscule "**The Alchemy of Supreme Compassion**". I am very confident that this book will make a huge impact in Western Countries, and I wish that this Journey with Thiru. Aruludaiyaar be continued.

It is my earnest desire that through the publication of this book "**The Alchemy of Supreme Compassion**", the ideals of Ramalingam Vallalar will spread all over the World, wishing that "**Ahimsa**", non-violence, and Universal Brotherhood's ideals will find an honourable place in the heart and mind of all human beings, irrespective of caste, creed, religion or nationality. When actively practiced, the coming generations will find on earth – a place where peace, harmony, happiness, longevity and prosperity have become a living reality among all people everywhere.

II - PREFACE

Since time immemorial, great sages have made elaborated research by way of yoga, meditation, prier and contemplation in order to find the origin, the reason and the goal of existence. They have undertaken great penance and sacrifice in their endeavour to find the basis for Truth. They have dedicated their all life in studying, observing and analysing the laws of nature which administrate the all universe and the eternal power behind all movements and principles which are forming the foundation of life as a whole.

They revealed that the universe could not just have come on its own. They saw that it could not just have come out of nothing, and that, there should be a power that lay behind which create and manifest itself eternally, through all the forms at all level of creation.

The origin of creation and humanity could be traced up to this power alone. This divine power is complete in itself. Though, the all creation has come from this divine power, our universe takes or adds nothing from this power. This divine power remains ever the same. The Isa Upanishad says:

"That is complete, and this is complete. The completeness comes out of completeness because this power is complete in itself and this alone remains."

(Poornamadah, poornamidam, poornathpoornamudachyate. Poo-nasyapoornamadaya, poornamevavasishyate).

The seers and saints scripted all they realised through direct cognition of the all story of creation in Sanskrit verses which came to be known as Vedas and Upanishads. These scriptures traced the origin of creation and underlined eternal principles that form the very basis of life. Considered as the enlightened collective wisdom of a long tradition of sages, throughout time, these principles have come to be known as "Sanatana Dharma", the Cosmic or Eternal Order.

Since the universe has originated from the divine source, all lives in the universe are sacred. The divine is manifested in human form, in plants, animals, stones, mountains and rivers. As the Upanishad says:

"Having created, God enters into his creation."

"Sanatana Dharma" is the Natural Laws of Nature that govern the entire creation. It sets the standard of conducts and seeks to achieve human excellence in all fields. It shows the way to truth and righteousness. It calls upon humanity to take a universal view and aim a new world order where the whole human race lives in peace, in a spirit of good will and tolerance. This human body as well as the all creation is made of the five elements: earth, sky, fire, water, air and the 96 tattvas, life principles or basic constituents.

"As is the human body, so is the cosmic body;
As is the human mind, so is the cosmic mind;
As is the microcosm, so is the macrocosm;
As is the atom, so is the universe."
- The Upanishads

As seen and demonstrated by ancient sages from time immemorial, everything at every level of creation, from the smallest particle to the greatest manifestation in nature, is the natural expressions of Thy Merciful Nature. Thus, "Sanatana Dharma", the Cosmic Law, inherent within every human being, is naturally calling everyone to live in perfect harmony and peace with the all of nature and all living beings.

Tamil Nadu, situated in the extreme south-east of India, witnessed intense religious activity since a very ancient time. According to legend, Lord Siva, the Supreme Grace Light, deputed saint Agasthiar, the greatest of the seven rishis. Blessed by Lord Muruga, the son of Lord Siva, Agasthiar established a healthy tradition of art, astronomy, medicine, alchemy…etc, establishing the foundation for the Tamil culture and language. The Tamil is the oldest of all languages; Ramalinga said that it is the language of Lord Siva

Himself. In Tamil Nadu, the people consider the Tamil language as being sacred and divine. It is compared as the Love and Merciful nature of Lord Siva. The word Tamil means sweetness; nowhere else, the language influences the people as deeply as in Tamil Nadu. TholKapiyam, which date back to many centuries ago, was the first systematic attempt at development of Tamil. The term "TholKapiyam" derives from the word "Tholkapiyar", a disciple of saint Agasthiyar who framed the rules of grammar and classified the entire area of human activity as subjective "Akam" and objective "Puram". This study marked the dawn of a new era of Tamil literature. Silappadhikaram by Ilango Adigal was noted for the woman's dignity it sought to establish and Thirukkural remains the greatest work ever undertaken in Tamil on ethics and human values. Appearing around the 2nd century, they contributed to establish a divine culture on the Tamil soil. Tamil literature reached its pinnacle of glory during the "Sangam" period. Nakkeerar and many other scholars of reputation, have laid a solid foundation for the full blossoming of the Tamil culture. The Pandya, Chola and Chera Kings who were great connoisseurs of art and science from the great Siddhas and saints of this blessed land, helped the tradition to flourish. In fact, the Sangam period is considered as the golden period of the Tamil literature and culture. It is difficult to study the growth of Tamil literature in isolation. Tamil literature has flourished in the light of intense spiritual movements. Every important Tamil literature is an expression of the profound love and devotion to the Supreme Grace Light, Lord Siva.

Tamil Nadu is a land of immense wealth, exquisite beauty, compassion and charm. It is not a land where just paddy is grown. Along the rich Kaveri river belt, transcending the lush green paddy field, one would find the majestic Brahadeeswar temple leaping towards the sky. There are many temples in Tamil Nadu, whose magnificence and opulence defy description, which stand as living testimony of a glorious past. Every temple is an architecture marvel, a fitting expression of devotion and a poetry in stone. They stand as a witness to the great devotion of the people and the rulers. The inscriptions on the temple speak of a rich cultural heritage that existed many hundred years, thousand years before. Apart for being a place of worship, the temple also served as a forum for the promotion of art and culture. The magnificent Siva temple of Arunachalesvara temple of Thiruvannamalai, Brihadeswarar temple of Tajore, Jalakandeswarar temple of Vellore, Sundareswarar temple of

Kovur, suburb of Chennai, Thillai Nataraja temple of Chidambaram, Sangameshwarar temple of Erode, Ardhanaareeswaraa temple of Tiruchengode, Nellappar temple of Tirunelveli, Vaithteeswaran temple near Sirkali, Kapaleeshwarar temple of Mylapore, Perur Pateeswarar temple of Coimbatore etc…, speak volumes about Shaivite tradition, the tradition of Lord Siva. There are also great temples of Vaishnava tradition, the tradition of Lord Vishnou at Srirangam, Srivalliputhur, Kancheepuram, Sholingar, Srivalliputhur, Kumbakonam and Triplicane etc…

The medieval period witnessed new faiths exerting their influence on the Indian psyche. The new faiths promised a new order of religion based on a liberal system of worship. The Pandya Kings too, gave their support to these faiths and even saint Appar was no exception. But the Hindu philosophy is Eternal and unchangeable. It would survive on its own strength and grow on its own, even if some transitory clouds overshadow it. As Lord Krishna himself said in the Bhagavad Gita, whenever the need arises, He would manifest Himself in some form or other to provide the necessary correction, guidance and direction.

The community getting distracted by other faiths needed a spiritual leader who could clear their doubts, fulfil their aspirations and guide them to the right path. The need of the hour was to assimilate the various thoughts contained in the Vedas and Upanishads to present them in a logical, rational and cohesive way. In the 8th century, a dynamic spiritual leader, Shankaracharya, who believed to be Siva Himself, emerged with his philosophy of Adwaita. He established the four mutts, four seats occupied by well-chosen realised beings, who were serving as custodian of the Vedic tradition in the four directions of India and rejuvenated the all Hindu philosophy. He said that Brahman, the One Almighty God, alone was real, one without a second, who is self-effulgent, self-existing, who is omnipresent, omnipotent and omniscient. He said that "Brahman reveals itself through the self by itself alone.

Saiva Sidhantam came up with the theory that the Eternal Supreme Power, Siva, is the cause and effect and that He causes the creation and causes the ends. It is said that the soul and the world originated from Lord Siva and ultimately get absorbed into Him. Like water in the ocean evaporates, forms into clouds and rains, all lives originated from Him and are reaching back to Him. Ranked as one of the highest systems of human thought, the philosophy of Saiva Sidhanta, though originated in Kashmir region around 250 BC, it appeared later in south India where it got spread and flourished. Sidhanta speaks about three entities: "Pathi" (Siva), Pasu (the soul) and "Pasa", representing the impediment that restrains the soul; that which binds the souls is pasa. Pasa is said to be of three specific coloration: aanava, karma and Maya. Of these three, aanava is the ignorance called egoism; Maya is the material cause of all that has created the universe; karma, which is divided into two – good and bad – is that which causes birth. Sidhanta believes that when death occurs, the soul which is free from karma (past actions) ascends to heaven and attains the union with "Paramathma" (God). The body disintegrates and whatever remains of it goes to the earth. The soul tainted by past karmas is getting rebirth. The soul perceives through self-consciousness, intellect and mind while the body perceives through sensory organs. Though the soul remains dormant, by the practice of meditation and grace, it gets the inner vision and the light within the soul brightens up. By meditation, one gets the power to discriminate from the real and unreal and attains the stage of divinity. The enlightened soul realises through direct experience that Siva is the ultimate Truth, the ultimate refuge and that Siva, the Supreme Father, alone is granting ultimate liberation through which one is free from the cycle of life and death.

The Periya Puranam, unlike other Puranas, narrates the life stories of people who lived in more recent period between BCE 300 an CE 865. It covers the life sketch of sixty-three ardent devotees of Lord Siva called the 63 Nayanmars which through 4286 verses exemplifies their remarkable power, love and intense devotion to Lord Siva. These very profound and touching devotional verses are reflecting on their power and their own experience of complete union with Lord Siva, lived in a perfected body of light which forms the basic foundation of Saiva Sidhanta.

Among the 63 great saints, servants and admirers of Lord Siva, we count: Jnana Sambhandar, Manikkavachakar, Sundaramoorthy Nayanar and appar. They delight the heart of the true seeker of Truth, enlighten the devotees, elevating and leading them to salvation.

In sharp contrast to medieval period, between 800 to 1500, which witnessed intense religious activity, the modern age saw development on different fronts and gradually drifted towards materialism. The world was ushering into a new era of modernisation. As it is, the Hindu way of life was marred by irrational customs and dogmas. The caste system made matters worse. There was no unity of thought or unity of action. It casted a big dark spell of gloom all over Tamil Nadu. Despite, its rich cultural heritage, during this period, Tamil Nadu witnessed a crisis of identity.

It was in this scenario that Ramalingam Chidambaram (1823 – 1874) appeared like a brilliant star with his vision of universal brotherhood and universal God. He saw mankind as one single family, bond by love and compassion.

Ramaliga's Supreme Compassion path to deathlessness about which this book is the essence, comes on the line of the great thinkers and saints of Tamil Nadu with a distinct individuality of his own. Ramalingam was a great philosopher, poet and mystic. He demonstrated that his Cosmogonic view of Truth was not a dream or a fantasy of unpractical thinkers or idlers. His very life was a record of his philosophy and spiritual experiences. He was a living embodiment of love, sincerity, purity, spirituality and godliness. His spotless character, the indescribable glow of blessedness with which he was endowed by His grace, the divine wisdom he displayed, his unabating universal compassion for all suffering creatures, his all-absorbing love of God, had bestowed on him a unique position among the saints and philosophers of the Land. In addition to these, he was a profound scholar in Tamil. The numerous verses and songs poured out of his molten heart that wept for the attainment of spiritual eminence are remarkable for their literary excellence, melting rhythm, entrancing melody and great lucidity of expression. They inspired and moved not only the literate but also illiterate masses into tears. The wealth of his thought, his basic approach to spirituality which was not far from common human comprehension, and the lucidity with which he expounded the great mystic heights of spiritual experiences, have offered solace and guidance to many seekers after truth and true spirituality. His approach was simple and direct not baffling even a person of common understanding. Ramalinga had thus, by his thoughts, poetry verses, his conduct and spiritual achievements, found a sacred niche in the heart of almost every Tamilian who aspires to ascend the glorious heights of spiritual attainment. Without any propaganda, the fame and popularity of

Ramalingam Chidambaram had been growing year by year spontaneously in intensity all these years, after Ramalingam's body melted into the Almighty Lord. He is now worshipped as the chosen one of the Lord, sent into the world to guide humanity to the attainment of Eternal Bliss.

The advent of Ramalinga was marked by an awakening of spiritual revival all over the world. He was born in the 19th century, when mankind all over the world tired of materialism, were eager to turn their gaze towards the ultimate truth and the real purpose of human existence. Madam Blavatsky, Col. Olcot, Lead beater and Annie Besant led the spiritual renaissance in the west through the theosophical society movement. Ma Anandamayi Ma, Saint Ramakrishna and his disciple Swami Vivekananda and others led this revival in North India. Ramalingam was the sole representative of the spiritual movement in Tamil Nadu. He was the first to proclaim the universality and equality of all religious truth and the equality of all men and women in spiritual unity. He was thus, the forerunner of the theosophical movement and this was admitted by Madam H .P. Blavatsky herself in The Theosophist, July 1882.

It is interesting to note that Ramalingam evolved no new pet theory of his own, he realized the spiritual basis of the ancient ideals of life of the Tamil land and was well acquainted with the ancient thoughts on philosophy and spirituality and their practical aspects.

Ramalinga called his philosophy, the ancient philosophic thoughts and practices of Tamil Nadu which he has elucidated in terms and methods suitable to his times. The very name of his philosophy "Suddha Sanmarga" the good path of Truth and Purity.

His basic approach to spirituality was not laid in any remote spiritual conduct or practice or in any mystic yoga modes, but it is based on an active universal love and compassion approach for all creatures.

To understand the full significance of this active universal love, preached by Ramalinga, it is necessary to comprehend the nature and scope of the concept of love advocated by Jainism and Buddhism the two great philosophic systems of the world which had exploited the philosophic and spiritual value of love.

It was the negative aspect of love which these two systems emphasized. Jainism adopted ahimsa, not to kill or not to harm any living creatures as its basic doctrine. Ahimsa means renunciation of the mind to kill or harm anything. This is different from the feeling of active love or active compassion. Ahimsa arises from the idea of keeping unattached to the world. Active love implies activity in the world and brings in attachment to those who suffer "himsa", misery or suffering. Jainism, which aimed at non-activity and non-attachment, rejected active love and adopted ahimsa as its main doctrine. This ahimsa thus keeps itself within the limits of non-activity and neglects the helpful activity to relieve the distressed.

Buddhism is also advocating compassion within the limits of non-activity and non-attachment. According to Buddhism suffering could be ended only by its Eight-fold principles, right knowledge etc. Unless the Eight-fold path is followed and release from the world, the suffering continued and recurred even if relieved. The suffering and misery could never be relieved or wiped out by renouncing to the world and the attachment to it which are the root cause of the suffering and misery in the world. Buddhist philosophy, therefore, do not preach active compassion, as it creates attachment with the persons suffering. The compassion developed in Buddhism is thus an ethic of thought not of action. What Buddha advocated was the ethical activity of the mind and spirit in the ethical aspect of love and compassion. This aspect of love or compassion has its own importance. It generates a spiritual power, which goes out to transform the persons who come under its sway. This was the secret of the powerful personality of the great Buddha. The radiation of kindness issuing from him is said to have affected not only human beings but also animals. ("A wild elephant which his hostile cousin Devadatta let loose on him in a narrow lane stopped in its course, so the story relates, struck by the force of his kindness, and lowered the trunk it had already raised to strike."). Similar incidents happened, we are told, in the life of Ramalinga as well.

The love for mankind which Ramalinga developed and adopted was an active universal love which not only comprised ahimsa and the mental love of Buddhism but went far beyond them and reached a stage far higher and nobler and more beneficial to humanity.

Even this basic approach was nothing new introduced by Ramalinga. From time immemorial the Tamil land had been the home of this universal compassion and active help. They believed that the world exists because of men who live for others and are ready to sacrifice anything for the cause of humanity.

Their love was a universal love which knew no bounds or the limitation of caste, creed, color or country. "All countries are yours and all men are your kith and kin declared Kanian Pookundranar. He exemplified this selfless devotion and service to humanity by the simile of a raft put into a ferry"

The raft is of no use to itself. It has lost itself and is there only to serve humanity without any discrimination of caste, creed, color or country. The raft cannot escape, from the responsibility into which it has been pushed into. Similarly, man cannot escape from the responsibility into which he has been ushered into this world and should serve humanity even as the raft does. The ancient Tamilians explored the value and meaning of human existence. They found that active universal compassion and active help for all the creatures of the world in distress had the greatest ethical and spiritual value.

Their compassion did not stop with selfless devotion to humanity and active help to men, beasts and birds but extended even to the vegetable kingdom.

Nearly two thousand years ago long before Jagadish Chandra Bose, the great son of Bengal, demonstrated the unseen agonies of the vegetable kingdom which thrilled the European world, Chieftain Pary of the Tamil land felt the agonies of the Mullai Creeper Jasminum indicum tossed about by untruly wind and tortured by careless passers. Pary had the vulture to visualize its distress which the creeper could not speak out. He was deeply moved by its wretched condition, left the chariot in which he rode, so that the creeper as a support to spread on, and walked back home. This is no mythology or poetic exaggeration but a plain historical fact. Authors after authors have spoken and praised the tenderness and nobility of Pary's heart. It was a glorious day in the human thought to be recorded in golden letters that for the first time in the history of the world a human being notorious for his selfishness, rose to the level of being disturbed in heart by the distress of a mute plant and went to the length of sacrificing his own comfort and convenience for the sake of a trivial plant life.

Ramalinga is the inheritor of this noble heritage of boundless compassion and active help. How much of this unique culture was in the blood of Ramalinga! He knew the spiritual value of this unbounded compassion and insisted on it as the first step to be taken even before the love of God and placed his Jeevakarunya Olukkam, Compassion towards all living beings as the first rung in the ladder of spirituality.

Ramalingam is the legatee of this noble heritage of active compassion without limit. This precious culture flows in the veins of his Holiness Ramalinga.

"This is my desire, oh my Father, to consider all lives of the crowds that surround me as my life, to bring them joy, to remove their distress and to put an end to their fear and I wish to become immaculate in the heart, to sing to your Sacred Feet, to dance in singing – Siva Siva - and with an uncontained joy of being able to remain eternal on earth ".

Thus, he introduced a new angle of vision and a new practical approach to access the realization of God hitherto unknown to the philosophies and religions of the world. These are the great physical transformations that occur in the aspirant's body. These transformations vary according to the intensity of the spiritual fire generated in the body of the aspirant. These transformations were reported by the holy poet Nackirar. His famous poem *"Tiromurugattruppadai"* is well known in the Tamil world and we are far from having discovered all the philosophical wisdom that is hidden there.

Nackirar was the first to describe the divine radiance of the Almighty as the Light unfolding all the Majesty and the Greatness of His Divine Grace and called it "The Sun that manifests His Divine Grace".

Anurachalam Pillai, a great scholar in the lineage of Ramalinga's teaching, also supported this view by using the rays of the falling sun reflecting on the ocean as a metaphor for understanding the range of rays emanating from the absolute. The rays of the sun undoubtedly drive away the darkness, especially when the sun rises above the earth, hills, valleys and the sea. This metaphor only concerns the rising sun. We understand that when the sun's rays cover the sea with its light, the seawater is purified, the impurities are removed, and the water becomes purified and good to be consumed.

Does this not resemble to the body of light of Ramalinga? Once the body is deprived of all its impurities and made pure, it is fit for divine absorption. The sun's rays pierce into the sea water, which glitters and bestows a golden hue and radiates a mellowed glow of light. Does this not correspond to the transformed body of Ramalingam, radiating the mellowed light of divinity? It is this divine light which He hid from the gaze of the curious by always covering his entire body, including his head, except his face, with long piece of cloth wound around, leaving only his face visible.

Another major transformation concerning seawater occurs when the structure of the liquid itself is altered. From the liquid state the seawater passes into the gaseous state to ascend into the heavens in the form of vapor. The water is neither dead nor destroyed. It is raised to the sky in another form under the influence of the sun's rays. Would not this correspond to Ramalinga's body of bliss when he melted into all the bodies of creation, into the very heart of the divine womb?

These transformations are neither deductions nor speculations, but real facts. This is a metaphorical image to better understand the transformations that Ramalinga's body did undergo. This reality has been confirmed by other saints of the Siddha tradition, as well as by his disciples who witnessed his transformations.

Nackirar had described three kinds of rays of Divine Light as they were expressed by Ramalinga and confirmed by other saints of the Siddha tradition, as well as by his disciples who witnessed his transformations.

Nackirar had described three kinds of rays of Divine Light: Flashing Light, Demonstrating Light, and Shining Light.

We can say that this Eternal Light reveals Divine Grace to all humanity, of all ages and all times.

These philosophical thoughts are not found in the west nor in the east. It is a new approach to divinity that has been preserved in Tamil Nadu, representing the Tamil genius. We cannot find a better analogy to show the mystical heights of these high philosophical thoughts as well as the transformations engendered. This analogy of purifying transformations due to the influence of sunlight on seawater is much more than photosynthesis. The same activity applies to all the corporeal transformations obtained by the aspirant as reported by Ramalinga.

There have also been other saints in the Tamil Nadu who underwent these transformations whose bodies could not be photographed as they became translucent with the Divine Light of His Grace, but they never recorded these happenings. This remained secret until Ramalinga showed up and declared openly that these spiritual benefits were not intended for anyone in particular but for everyone. He did not keep it for himself but invited everyone, in his clear voice, to share his blessing.

To make it a secret was nothing short of utter selfishness and he made known these processes by which these transformations come over and in his clarion voice invited the whole humanity to come and share the bliss.

Ramalinga's great contribution to human thought is this opportunity offered to all to now be able to access this state of immortality. Not only did he preach this blessed path, but he also followed it himself and attained the most exalted state of Supreme Bliss.

IS IT POSSIBLE TO REACH IMMORTALITY?

This question has always been and will always be relevant. Science has not progressed in this way of being able to confirm or deny this state. The comparison of this state, established in the Thirumurukattruppadai, has been clearly stated by the analogy of the transformation of water into vapor rising in space. This metaphor shows the stages of the transformation of the physical body into a spiritual body merging into divinity without passing through death. These facts are recounted in the Tamil literature which testifies to a number of people who have reached this state of immortality. This secret has been preserved in the Tamil science of the Siddha tradition.

Burying a saint and calling him "Videhamukthi", a soul having reached the state of deliverance of bodily rebirth is a huge nonsense. When a saint dies and is buried or burned, we must call him samadhi and not otherwise, it is only an ordinary death. None of the four great saints of Tamil Nadu dropped their bodies on the earth nor was buried or burnt. Their body vanished into the Almighty Lord. Thirugnanasam bandar vanished into the divine light which shone forth at the time of his marriage at Thirumana Nallur Siva Temple, presently known as Achapuram, after the wedding, himself, his bride and the people present at the wedding went into Sivaloka Tyagar Temple of Siva. Here, Sambandar prayed to Lord Siva, seeking salvation, Siva appeared as a blazing flame and granted his wish. Then, Sambandar, his bride and all the wedding guests, including Tiruneelanakka Nayanar merged into the Light of Siva. Appar merged with his body with the Lord absolute at Pugalur. Sundarar merged with the Lord at Mount Kailash and Manickavasagar vanished into the ether of Siva Veli (space of Lord Siva) at Thillai.

This secret of attaining deathlessness was evidently kept as a secret and it was left to his Holiness Ramalinga to preach it openly to all, inviting the all of humanity to share the very same Bliss he has experienced.

Ramalinga Vallalar was the one who openly and clearly affirmed, in an unequivocal language, the immortality of his body which he himself had attained by the power of what he called "Arut Perun jyoti", the Supreme Grace Light of the Divine in which he recognized the True Light of Knowledge, "Satya Jnana Jyoti". Vallalar reiterated the immortality of the body as an essential part of the realization of the supreme bliss of the One,

God, possessing himself the divine knowledge and the science of the immortality of the body, having himself attained this state immortality. Vallalar was also a critic, a writer, a publisher and commentator who integrated the knowledge of occultism, alchemy, astrology and medicine with in particular the nutritional and medicinal values of plants and metals contributing to the transformation, the purification and the alchemical transformation of the body, from a rude and impure body into a golden body. He was also a musician with a refined and lively taste, especially for lyric songs. He has also composed words expressing, in a simple and popular style, his highest and sublime achievements of the divine, especially on the awareness of the Omnipresent Truth of God. In his compositions, Vallalar reveals the index of the transformation of the impure body into a body of gold. He says that the Lord of "Cit Sabha" (the supramental understanding or consciousness of truth) embraced him objectively in all his outer being on the plans of "Samarasa Sanmarga Sabhai" (tertiary session of the consciousness of truth called Suddha Siva Jagrata state) and through this embrace, the Lord has imprinted on his body the form of the immortal gold body.

Ramalinga declares that God is present in the totality of all universes for eternity. With His Benevolent Power, He goes on flourishing and expanding unceasingly, from the finest particle of the soul of man to his perfect realization of God himself. This shows us that God is truly Omnipresent, Omnipotent and Omniscient. Because of its divine attributes, the Almighty alone speaks through all the souls of people incarnating on earth or other planets in the unlimited universe.

The appearances of the human are innumerable, not being permanent, they change constantly; they disappear and reappear continuously. However, the one living deity in each soul performs his work at all times and in all places. Therefore, God the Eternal, alone is manifested in the form of each person for the time allotted to him, in conformity with the quality of his actions. In reality, the physical form of a person is the expression of God and of God only. Through the Gracious Knowledge of God, we come to the understanding that the entire universe space is fully filled with the Great Form of the Universal Body of God, and that every human form and living being is the extension of His Own Body whose external appearance is constantly changing. It is only for the realization of the divine, that God assumes this human life by swirling around His small form of soul as great as an atom. It is from this soul-atom, soul-consciousness, that God, through immeasurable Love and Mercy, comes to realize Himself fully through the experience of His omnipotent grace.

Ramalinga asserts that the soul and God are not two, but the same Divinity in the Universal and the individual spiritual atomic forms. This true knowledge of the Divine Soul is not understood by the vast majority until today. Therefore, we find that the knowledge of the soul has been misunderstood and had different misinterpretation and adaptations over time. Thanks to Ramalinga, it is now possible for everyone to rectify their own understanding of the soul, which is truly the first impulse of the Divine Light into the atom, as God Himself manifested in the human embryo at the very beginning of creation. Therefore, the soul is nothing but the atomic form of God Himself, capable of generating all the power of the knowledge and grace of life for the ultimate salvation. It is because the soul of man is God Himself, that it cannot do otherwise, to rise from sensory levels to the plane of the Gracious Soul of God. Ramalinga repeated that the purpose of life was to acquire quickly during this existence, the Supreme Grace and to obtain the blessing of the soul "Anmabalam".

This goal will lead the aspirant to the truth, to the realization of the Supreme God. He explained that the atoms of the human body composed of impurities, would thus, be washed of all impurities to be transformed into pure atoms. It will be a body of Light in a golden halo that will never perish. The Grace of God makes this transformation possible according to the philosophy of "Suddha Sanmarga" (the path of truth and purity leading to God).

According to Ramalinga, the foundation for living and realizing such realization is the devotion to God. He called the masses to the true form of worship to God, which consists in adopting a loving and compassionate attitude for all living creatures, who are the Manifestations of God and thus, developing the Love of the Divine. He explained that the Almighty God is the supreme form of truth called "**Arut Perun Jyoti**" - The Light of Supreme Grace.

Ramalinga gave specific instructions to his disciples, asking them not to waste their time and energies to continue searching through all the ancient social, spiritual and philosophical beliefs, but to follow the path of Suddha

Sanmarga, especially now that the coming of God is eminent, as it has been announced by the prophets and sages of all times. Vallalar gave the Mahamantra of the Light of Supreme Grace to all: "Arutpreunjyothi – Arutperunjyothi – Thanipperun Karunai - ArutperunJyothi, (Supreme Grace Light – Supreme Grace Light –Supreme Compassion – Supreme Grace Light), for the transformation of the body of humanity into a Universal Brotherhood. This Mahamantra was revealed to him by God in the assurance of His Manifestation and consequently marked an effective start to the path of Suddha Sanmargam.

Vallalar declared "Arut Perun Jyoti" as being the Supreme God. This Infinite God, whose throne is in the midst of every soul, at the center of the brain – the medulla oblongata, expresses himself. A deep study of this particular atom would reveal the truth about the soul. This mysterious atom dispenses the energy of life to the physical body, the feelings, the sense organs, the intellect and all the activities of the mind. Spiritual Knowledge is only and truly accessible from this particle, the atom of the Divine Soul from which the infinitude of the One Almighty God expresses Thyself and immortalizes the whole body and the environment of the soul by His All Gracious Alchemy.

"Arut Perun Jyoti" is the Universal Dancer, the Dancer of the Light. The purpose of His Cosmic Dance is to free the souls and to embrace them in His Grace. He performs His Dance in the hearts of those who without any reservation, consider all human creatures equal and believe that it is their responsibility to see them all living in the same happiness.

"My God, even among those who show the least compassion towards others but who, in the depth of their hearts, only want good and see Thee in them, O God, their pure and blessed knowledge are your dwelling, there, my God dances, and there my spirit always learns more from your admirable prophets. "

Thus, it exists in all living creatures, in the form of an Intimate Light, the love and compassion shown to them, and are recognized as the expression of the love of God. William Law said:

"I do not mean by love, any natural tenderness, which exists more or less in people according to their nature, but I mean a greater principle of the soul, founded on reason and piety, which makes us tender, kind and gentle to all our fellow creatures, as creatures of God, and out of respect for Him."

In showing His love for all living beings, there can be no discrimination of race, caste, color or ethnicity, country and sex.

Ramalinga condemned the Orthodox system which gives shelter to different caste communities. He condemned the false beliefs and superstitions that the people have been peddling for decades.

Ramalinga has always affirmed that all souls are identical, the manifestation of God in one's own soul and one's own mind being the same in all souls. Once we all understand that we are all equal, we will spontaneously begin to show love and affection to all and respect life everywhere. The result will be a universal and spiritual communion. Thanks to this unique and yet simple principle which Ramalinga envisioned through the integration of the entire human society. He wanted universal harmony. In other words, he advocated one God and one world in the universal communion of souls.

This comprehension of life has never been so crucial as it is today. It is obvious that we are at the heart of an era in which conflicts are perceptible everywhere, at all levels, both inside and outside the humans. There is a conflict between materialism and spiritualism; there is a conflict between doubt and faith. The remarkable achievements of men in the field of science and technology have only succeeded in providing temporary material comforts but have unfortunately failed to provide people with inner peace and happiness. The progress made by up to now, has led human beings to the loss of the faith in God which they have replaced by doubts, confusion and rational understanding. Without the realization that rationalism is not an end in the realm of knowledge, human beings are walking toward chaos and self-destruction.

This book opens the access to the knowledge of the truth "Suddha sanmargam" leading to God allowing human beings to progress together towards the creation of a Universal Brotherhood of the great family of nations, within which, beyond of all cleavages, will finally be able to live in peace, joy, creativity, love, respect, compassion, prosperity and immortality lived in the Supreme Bliss of God.

III – INTRODUCTION

**The last enemy, death will be defeated
we must be born again in a body of Light. This is the
challenge *facing all* humanity.
The questions we ask ourselves: do all forms come from a
common source?
Are we not indissolubly bound to God, the universal
substance of thought?
Are we not forming a big family?
Is every child, every man, every woman part of this big
family of humankind, regardless of *caste, colour or religion*?**

CAN WE AVOID DEATH?

I had to go to India to encounter the true teaching of the Siddhas, the teaching of those who have conquered death and attained deathlessness body. today I am sharing with you in its completeness, the teaching of Ramalinga, who has not only reached the highest pinnacle of spiritual achievement, the immortality of the body in a state of complete oneness with God, but also, has shown the way for everyone to attain this ultimate state of spiritual evolution.

Though historical evidences in the life of great saints which are ample proof, that they not only did not taste death but enjoyed eternal bliss in the union with God, there is no philosophy cogently setting forth the secret of immortality.

Modern science while proclaiming success in creating life, has also founded that "death is alien to the nature of man". According to Kuprevich from the Byelorussian Academy of science, aging is due to damage caused to D.N.A and R.N.A structures. He argues that "if aging is a disease of the genetic mechanism it must be cured and the cure, is an elixir of life readily available in nature".

This elixir of life has been referred to by Saint Manikkavasagar as replacing the marrow of bones. Saint Ramailinga Vallalar while describing the transformation of the human physiology, narrates that an elixir of life overflows and fills the human frame of the divine aspirant.

It appears that only the Grace of God through the action of supreme compassion towards all living beings, is making it possible to disentangle the skein of thoughts and memories (karmic links). Ramalinga's supreme science of deathlessness is actually imbedded in the divine song of Grâce, "Thiruarutpa" and "Agaval".
India, still today, is certainly the guardian of spiritual and philosophical traditions preserved through uninterrupted lines of great saints, rishis and siddhas from time immemorial until today

Through my encounter with the teaching of Ramalinga, popularly known as Vallalar, I received the answer to my deepest inquiries about the purpose of life and immortality thereby, my doubts melted away and my all life quest ended. Vallalar, the Great Munificent, is been regarded until today as the greatest of sages, saints and siddhas, given the heights, breadths and depths of his total realization with the divine that embraces all the deepest and innermost inner dimensions up to the outermost parts of his being.

Vallalar is the only one who has stated clearly and openly in an unequivocal language about the immortality of the body and has given the answers to all humankind by having opened the door of Supreme Grace Light and transformed his body into an immortal golden body of light. He has not only transformed himself into Supreme Grace Light body, but also, He has blessed humanity by giving the mantra to invoke Supreme Grace Light and has shown us the path and understanding for everyone to attain the ultimate state of spiritual realisation in this life.

To the question, can we avoid death? Ramalinga Vallalar explained that the human body is built from a perfect individual cell, the atom-soul-consciousness such as every form in the universe, be it a mineral, a plant, a tree, an animal, etc. This individual cell represents the microscopic unity of the body, carrying the torch of life everywhere. By means of the presence of the inner Light within that microscopic cell, the soul is Eternal and Immortal.

By passing through a repeated process of growth and subdivisions, the tiny nucleus of a single cell ends up becoming a complete human being composed of innumerable millions of cells. These specialize in different functions, while retaining some essential characteristics of the original cell. This original cell can be considered as the torchbearer of life everywhere. It transmits, from generation to generation, the latent Flame of God, the life, the vitality of every living creature, without which life cannot exist. The lineage of his ancestors is uninterrupted and goes back to the time of the appearance of life on our planet.

The original cell is endowed with eternal youth, having always existed, but what about cells grouped as bodies? Eternal youth, the latent flame of life, is one of the characteristics of the original cell. During their multiple divisions, the cells of the body have retained this characteristic. But the body functions as guardian of the individual cell only during the short space of temporal life as you are now conceiving it.

From time immemorial, educators, philosophers, sages and saints have transmitted knowledge and wisdom using metaphors, analogies and stories. We can easily imagine them haranguing their students under the banyan tree. In keeping them with this speech: look at this banyan tree, this giant tree. Within our brother the tree and in us, the stages of the vital process are identical. Look closely at the leaves and buds at the ends of the oldest banyan. Are they not as young as the seed from which this giant sprang?

Their vital reactions being identical to ours, it seems obvious that man can benefit from the same experience of the plant. Just as the leaves and buds of the banyan are as young as the original cell of the tree, the groups of cells forming the body of man are not called to die by a gradual loss of vitality. Like the original cell, the human body can remain young without ever fading. There is no real reason for the body not to remain as young and full of vitality as the vital seed from which it comes. The banyan tree, at any moment being taken to symbolize longevity, immortality, goes on extending ever more to infinity, thus symbolizing eternal life. He only dies accidentally. There is no natural law of decrepitude, no aging process likely to affect the vitality of the banyan cells. It is the same for the divine form of man. There is no law of decrepitude for man except the accident. No inevitable process of aging human cell groups is likely to gradually paralyse the individual. Death is therefore an avoidable accident.

The body is naturally indestructible. It is us who allow it to be destroyed. It is the thoughts and feelings we impose on our body which create age, sickness and disintegration. It is well known that every cell of our body is renewed every seven years. Therefore, we should have a human body completely renewed every seven years, but instead of creating a perfect body it is continuously duplicating our own mistakes and violations of natural Laws. We have testimonies through ancient writings related to the Siddha tradition of southern India, of great masters who have lived several hundreds and thousands of years. If someone can live many thousands of years, he can undoubtedly live forever. Ramalinga said that the soul cannot accomplish anything without the body, and therefore, it is only, when the body has been totally purified and has attained the deathless body state, that one will never have to go again through the cycle of birth and death. That's exactly what Jesus said, "the last enemy to defeat is death" and Ramalinga said: "the only test God gave to man was to conquer death".

Disease is above all the absence of health. Health is so called "Santi", meaning the sweet and joyful peace of mind. It is the quality of the thought we generate which reflects in the human body as health or disease. Men generally undergoes senile decrepitude, an expression of the ignorance of the causes, namely the pathological state of his thoughts and of his body. Proper mental attitude and actions helps to avoid even accidents. The siddhas said that we can preserve the vital energy of the body and acquire natural immunity against all contagious diseases, for example against leprosy or the flu. They say that it is possible to eat microbes without getting sick in the least.

It is good to remember that youthfulness is the seed penned by God in the divine form of man, the soul. In truth, youth is Divinity in man. Turning our attention to this eternal splendour is the spiritual life which alone is alive, magnificently loving and eternal, whereas old age is anti-spiritual, ugly, mortal and unreal. The thoughts of fear, of pain and sadness, engender ugliness called old age, whereas the thoughts of joy, love and compassion engender the beauty called youth. Aging is only a shell containing the diamond of truth, the jewels of youthfulness *contained* within the soul, which is seated in the centre of the brain, whose body is the Living Divine Temple.

The spirit of Eternal Youth is in the Temple, inside the soul as a Light spark within the Light.

Even before man knew the simplest arts of civilization, the siddhas went, here and there, teaching by word and example, the path of purity and truth leading to total union with God.

Hierarchical governors were born of this teaching. But the leaders quickly departed from the notion that God was the only force and intelligence that was expressed through them. They ended up believing that they themselves were the authors of their actions ... Losing sight of the spiritual dimension of life and forgetting that everything comes from a single source, God. They presented themselves in a personal and material aspect. The purely personal conceptions of these leaders provoked great schisms and an extreme diversity of thought which led us in such state of duality and ignorance in which we are now.

Throughout the ages, the Siddhas have kept the revelation of the true method by which God expresses Himself through all men and all His creations, remembering that God is all and manifests itself in everything.

THE SOUL AND ONENESS OF SOULS

The main aim of the Universal Path as taught by Ramalinga Vallalar, is to insist on one's becoming educated in the art of deathlessness. The ultimate ideal of human existence is to enjoy everlasting bliss of the Supreme Divine by equipping oneself in a body free from disease, aging, decay and death.

The soul or original cell is a spark of the divine which is not seated above the manifested being but comes down into the manifestation to support its evolution in the material world. As it is said in the Upanishad: *"when God creates, He enters into His creation"*. The Shvetashvara Upanishad explains that the primal cause of all existence or universal soul is living in every form of creation and expresses itself throughout all forms, every form in creation is a projection of that primal cause and that there is a Oneness, a unity of souls. It is at first an undifferentiated power of the

Divine Consciousness containing all possibilities which have not yet taken form but to which it is the function of evolution to give form. This spark of intelligence, this spark of Light is there in all living beings, from the lowest to the highest (i.e. from the worms, plants, animals to man).

Ramalinga Vallalar explains that God and soul are not two, but the same Divinity in the universal and the individual spiritual atomic form. This true divine soul knowledge is not yet understood by the public until this day. Therefore, the soul was interpreted wrongly and differently by many people at different times. Now by the gracious knowledge of God, one can come to correct his understanding about the soul as the truly primary Divine Light Atom of God Himself exposed at the very beginning of the creation of the human embryo.

SALVATION AND IMMORTALITY

Hence, soul is but an atomic form of God, giving out all power of knowledge about life and grace for the final salvation. Because the soul of man is God Himself, he should rise up from the sensuous bodily plane to the gracious soul plane. From there the life of Grace must began anew. In the course of time, the blossomed soul graciously fills up in the whole being of man to make him eternal and blissful being. This end is the real goal of man. That is the ultimate goal of human evolution to attain the Eternal Blissful Life of God Almighty in a complete Oneness with God.

TRUTH ABOUT GOD

Ramalinga has fully revealed that, this mysterious atom is giving out life energy to the physical body, to the sensuous feelings and sense organs, intellectual and mental thoughts to mind. The spiritual knowledge too, comes out from this original particle, and finally this is discovered to be the Divine atom of the soul from which the Infinite God expresses out completely and immortalizes the surrounding body by His Gracious transformation. We can say that God Himself has come through soul state in the human body and from this state He is making the physical body transformed into a form of His Gracious Light. Hence, the soul of man is but an atom possessing the full Almighty Power. This infinitesimal Soul atom is filled with the infinite God-Truth-Consciousness present in the whole of boundless space. This is the most Supreme Power of His infinite Grace. *We* cannot express God in the form of a person or a personal image. God is a universality that includes everything and interpenetrates all things. As soon as you personalize it, you idolize It. Thus, we have lost the ideal and what *remains* is the empty idol. God needs to be made alive and vital within ourselves by thinking, feeling and knowing we are existing in Thee and Thee in us. Thus, we cannot be other than Thee. This is the Divine science of Being. It allows the Supreme Grace Light, your only *saviour*, to come to life and be one with you. You are this Light, and He becomes the motive for all the acts of your life. Thus, you save yourself and you are one with God. By revering, loving with all your soul and worshiping this ideal within you and through all living beings, you incorporate it into yourself, you become that principle and God becomes alive and active within you.

THE GRACE LIGHT PATH

Being caught in the fetters of karma, experiencing birth and death, suffering, old age and disease, the soul might finally be aspiring to escape from it all and attain the sorrow less state. One will finally be longing to get freedom from all bondage and desire so that not even one iota of sorrow should ever afflict him. But he will be only getting rid of the mental and physical afflictions by external remedies temporarily and not obtain the ultimate state of sorrowlessness, the Eternal Bliss. He cannot even imagine where everlasting Bliss is available. So far, the old belief was, that it could only be attained by long time penance, meditation and prayer as the way to become worthy of God's Grace and Favour. In the Timeless tradition of the Siddhas from south India, as expressed by The greatest of the saints, Ramalinga, who has gained the deathless body state in the complete union with God, It is known that this Highest Pinnacle of knowledge lived in the Eternal State of Supreme Bliss, cannot be attained by mere practices of penance, yoga, meditation and prayer, without expressing compassion towards all living beings and practicing self-enquiry, meeting in truth with oneself "**Sat Visharam**". Connecting everything with God through which one will experience the end of suffering and pain.

UNIVERSAL BROTHERHOOD

The chief ideal of Ramalinga's Universal Path consists in the creation of a Universal Brother Wood. This doctrine implies not only Universal Love and the right of every soul to love and to be loved but also the equality of all individuals despite their social status, caste, religion, nation, etc...

COMPASSIONATE SERVICE TO ALL HUMAN BEINGS

The perception of One Supreme Reality, along with the knowledge that the tribes, castes, creed and different social strata are farce will remove all the barriers in the path of congenial human relationship all over the world, which should be developed through compassionate outlook and service. So next to the perception of the common reality, compassion is the other landmark of Ramalinga's Universal Path. In fact, this perception and unconditional compassion towards all fellow beings render his Path Universal. Ramalinga's defined compassion has the melting of souls.

"The melting of souls occurs when one sees, hears or comes to know about the suffering-ones due to hunger, thirst, disease, desire, poverty, fear and the suffering when being killed".

"The more the melting of the souls for each other, the easier will be the direct manifestation of God's Grace. It is human sympathy that leads to Divine Grace. Compassion is the key to unlock the free flow of Divine Love within everyone. Because the natural trait of the soul is compassion, if a soul realizes its ultimate sphere through compassionate service to fellow beings, it will surely experience the union with God".

COMPASSION IS THE WAY TO WORSHIP GOD

Ramalinaga explained that : *"the more the melting of the soul occurs in the life of living beings with regards to other suffering living beings, the more the Grace which is God's* *effulgence existing inside the soul will manifest and become effulgent to perfection; when that Holy Grace manifests, the God's Bliss is experienced to its completeness. The worship of God is the attainment of the perfection of that experience".*

WORSHIP OF THE LIGHT

The next significant aspect of the Universal Path is the worship of the Light. All the Siddhas and Ramalinga himself experienced the Lord as the Light. Jesus once said:

"If one asks you, from where you come from? You must answer: "I come from the light".

All Ramalinga's experiences in the higher realm of spirituality where chiefly related to the vision of a mount of Light. Thus, Ramalinga through his Universal Path brought the whole world under a common altar of Light worship.

THE ART OF DEATHLESSNESS

The main aim of the Universal Path is to emphasize the importance for everyone to be educated in the Art of deathlessness, the ultimate ideal of human existence being to enjoy everlasting bliss of the Supreme Divine, this by making one's own mind and body free from disease, aging, decay and death.

The various philosophies and religions of the world up to this day, have not succeeded to create world peace, perfect health and complete fulfilment among all the people of the world and create a universal brother wood.

In order to bring the all of mankind to that state of compassion and fulfilment, Ramalinga gave to the whole of mankind what he called the Mahamantra of Vast Grace-Light "Arutperumjyothi" as revealed to him by the Divine Himself in assurance of its manifestation and consequently to mark the beginning of "Suddha Sanmarga", the path of truth and purity.

This book was born to reveal the Light and Truth regarding the nature of the spiritual path by which to lead mankind once again to the ultimate state of peace, salvation and immortality.

In order to be more comprehensive concerning the very nature of the spiritual path, I will start by leading you through my own life experiences, reflexions and perceptions which brought me to surrender at the altar of the Supreme Grace Light.

It is not my intention to brag, but rather to unveil the Truth about the nature of God, the soul and the path to immortality "Suddha Sanmarga" to make it accessible to everyone.

This new teaching, which is as old as the world, is being made available today by the grace of Ramalinga in its purest form. This most precious and practical knowledge come at a time which has never been as urgent as now to make that shift of paradigm from an age of selfishness, crime, war, illusion and suffering and death to an age of love, peace, prosperity, perfect health, bliss and immortality through the creation of a Universal Spiritual Brotherhood.

IV - AN AUTO BIOGRAPHICAL JOURNEY - FROM DARKNESS TO LIGHT

THE POWER OF LOVE

As a child I was a shy, joyous but knitted with anguish who found the reverie as the only exit door to boredom. My happiness was there, on the edge of reverie, my only certainties were in the realm of the unreal. I drew strength from what could represent more certainty than the desiccating rationality of the world based on purely cerebral matter. And if the rational did not have grip on my imagination, it is doubtless for having discovered in the inner reality the surprising resources of the human soul, the power of love, the strength of feelings and the power of emotion. Every night, while my Mother put me to bed, hardly with eyes closed, an endless inner sky opened to me in which I found an indescribable peace and happiness. Spirituality originated here, in this call to feel and breathe the invisible, to dig heaven rather than the earth. My pain was not to find the words to talk about it, fearing of being misunderstood. At home, we were not talking about the mysteries of life and love, my father traced the road without expressing a word and without having a tender gesture, though I felt he loved me. Only Mother knew how to express her love and affection. I liked to stay in her aura to contemplate her sparkling green eyes filled with light, feeling her loving presence that enveloped me with strength and confidence. I remember, that outside of my Mom's presence, everything in the surrounding was frightening, leaving me alone in an imaginary world. School and college did not help me to know about myself and enliven my inner potential; instead the system was pushing me being involved in the mind and intellectual pursuit, letting aside any encouragement to move towards a broader perspective. All the power of my intellect was used to fulfil outward purpose, loosing gradually contact with the inner container of knowledge, myself. Therefore, I felt that education was serving a strategic issue alone to fit with the need of the outside world, the economical, religious and social believes of the time. As human being, we are equipped with an intellect and a consciousness than no other species possess, an intellect with infinite capabilities, but attention to it was not being paid and time was not been spent as much as it would have been needed, to use that powerful instrument. Thus, unfolding my inner potentialities and talents, rather than using it to fulfil the outside requirement.

I did not find a real relationship with the teacher that was not based on a hierarchical relationship. I found unfortunately, during my all schooling period, a student - teacher relationship representative of a worldly system based on authoritative ruled by the grading system, creating and maintaining division, comparison among the students. This, instead of cultivating a non – hierarchical student – teacher relationship based on a mutual inquiry, studying, sharing love and communicating together.

A system based on I know – you don't know giving information alone, is the representation of a hierarchical-structure, on which our society and our education system is still based today.

By pushing my mind and intellect outwardly through accumulation of information alone, without bringing about a quality of intelligence in me, that is much more than merely serving the activity of knowledge, a big emptiness started to open before me. I was losing all interest in studying, my relationship with my father deteriorated, my mother not taking position for me, I was lost without finding the courage to express it. A depression started. I was in the world but feeling that I was not part of it. This emptiness was the open door to my quest for truth.

RELIGION, MY ULTIMATE HOPE

Religion was my ultimate hope to get my questions answered about the reason of my being in this world, about who I am, the nature of the soul and the nature of God and how to reach God. I already figured out that I would never know anything about myself, about the origin and the purpose of life from the educational system. I was left with the unique perspective to get these questions answered from the religious books and religious representatives. I was still having hope, as a teenager to find a religious person who could guide and accompany me on my quest for truth, peace and purity. After having questioned the priests and the monks of different clergy, and having scrutinised all about it, I was left with the understanding that the Church could offer me nothing more than a "Moralistic Therapeutic Deism." In short, I was taught that there is a disinterested and unattainable Divine Power who wants to give me personal peace and prosperity, only to help me "be nice." The result is a faith that cannot withstand the scrutiny of trials or intellectual questions. Parents and mentors have given me an anaemic sketch of faith at best. A robust faith replaced by a code of conduct-we "do" these things (read our Bibles, pray, and go to church) and "don't" behave badly but replace them by establishing à relationship with Jesus Christ. The invitation was to follow religious concepts to continue being at the mercy of a hierarchical authority, created and maintained to keep everyone voluntarily blind to be more easily manipulated and controlled at their own will. I was left with the conclusion that religions have generated more confusion in my mind rather than clarity.

MAJI

Despite the despair and frustration, I experienced, I had the vision of a woman who would come to me and through whom I will receive full support on my path in search for truth. While I was studying interior architecture and art at Nancy Art College in France, I was invited to join a summer course among artists in Luxembourg, artists attending from all over Europe. After a sleepless night spent under a bridge, with no money to offer me lodging, I finally reached the place of the course to enrol and received my scholarship.

The enrolment finished, unwashed with uncombed long hair, dressed all in black, the mind unclear and unsecure, I turned back towards the exit door, the room still filled with people. A midst all the people standing in line, a woman of about fifty, appeared to me out of the blue, filled with determination and love and said: I propose to drive you to town after I finished my enrolment, so you can buy all the necessary art material you need for the course.

On the way to the city, she turned to me and said: Since the scholarship you received is far too little to survive until the end of the course, as I live alone in a big apartment, I propose you come to my flat, I will provide you with all what you need to successfully complete the course.

I was so overwhelmed by her kindness and generosity that I could only accept with a heartfelt gratitude and deep appreciation. Then she told me: "I was driven to you by a feeling telling me, you have something to say, I must help you prepare yourself to fulfil your task".

Every day passed like a miracle. I had found a unique and very special friend. She was like a mother to me. I did not have to wish or worry about anything; she was so much in tune with me that she fulfilled my wishes even before I could express them. I received everything I needed even before having to wish for them. It was only afterward, that I realized that she was giving me exactly all I needed. Our connexion became subtler and stronger day after day, month after month. She supported me throughout all my study. Despite the fact, I was reiving all I wished for, my inner being felt unsatisfied. I realised that the outside comfort and security could not fulfil my inner need to know who I am and the reason of my being in this human life. I had no interest in living the life I saw around me, which I knew was not the real life. I realised it was a mirage, but what was life then? I was crying, for truth and love. Yes, my heart was empty, and, it was painful to realise that nothing from the outside world could fill that emptiness, not even Maji's genuine love and compassion.

One day, during the time of the academy, I met Rodolpho Zanabria, an artist from Mexico residing in Paris. This happened at the time, I just completed my art history course, on the sacred art of the Native American Indian from Mexico, named the Huichol and Lacandon Indians.

By watching my paintings, Rodolpho felt I should come to Mexico to study the muralist and Native American Indian Sacred Art. He felt, in my artwork connexion with this timeless spiritual tradition. I must admit, I had always been attracted by the Native American Indians, and I was especially touched by the way they had been tortured and martyred by the first invaders who came to that magical land. I always imagined these natives through my childish imagination, as carrying within them the mysteries and secrets of humanity.

Realising that Rodolpho's invitation has such deep impact on me, Maji and Rodolpho did everything to make my trip come true.

MEXICO - PILGRIM IN THE DESERT

Once in Mexico, after visiting few universities and art colleges, I was faced with the reality that the traditional disciplines of Native American Indian art had simply been replaced by the American and European view of art, an art totally denuded of its original content and meaning. The frustration generated by not being able to study this traditional art, enlivened the call to go and meet with the Huichol Indians and learn from them directly. I thought they might be the right people able of revealing to me the secret of life and its purpose.

After weeks of preparation, among which, obtaining a certificate from the University of Guadalajara, allowing me to go to the Huichol's reservation and stay with the Indians, I was told that it was a very long journey to reach their first village, isolated and protected by long mountain ranges and deep canyons filled with jaguars, snakes and scorpions.

Despite the risky journey, I choose to face it. So, I left the civilization with very little stuffs flanked in a backpack including maps and compass, enabling me to move through animal tracks across an exceedingly, uncommonly arid land.

There was no road, no path, no trace of human existence and machinery whatsoever. It took uncountable days going deep down into the canyons and up to the high plateau above 2000 meters. I was sleeping in a hammock with a bursting fire close to me, all night, until the dawn, supposedly to protect me from predators. Very soon, I learned to stay alert during the all night to ward off any potential dangers. The Sierra was inhabited by a profound silence I had never experienced so far, the kind of silence you find in deserts, a silence so complete that speaking feels like a blasphemy. Sounds, movements, smells coming and going, within celestial light filling the immensity of the sky, made this silence even deeper and thicker. In those moments, I felt I was nothing and knew nothing; within the depth of that immensity I was facing the original fear of the unknown. I had almost no food with me, except nuts and tea, hoping to find fruits down in the canyons near the river, but apart from lime trees there was nothing. My biggest mistake was to leave with leather boots thinking they would protect me against snake and scorpion bites. In fact, the rubbing of my feet against the leather with the intense heat and sweating caused the flesh being torn and became infected. Continuing walking with the boots became so painful that I had to part with them and continue my path barefoot. I did so, until my feet became so infected due to the contact with the dusty ground, that I had to stop and seat down hopping for some help. My body started to feel weak and painful. After hours of feeling unsecure, being out of nowhere, not knowing at what distance the first Huichol's village was, and having seen no soul for days, the miracle finally happened, the first Huichols on mule passed by and took me along. I felt so grateful to the universe for this miracle to happen in the midst of nowhere. We exchanged few words in Spanish, just enough to expose them my situation. They immediately understood the urgency of it. They said you are really lucky, since once a week a doctor comes by plane from Guadalajara, to San Sebastian, our village. If he is there, we will bring you to him. After endless hours on the mule under extreme heat, we finally reached San Sebastien, one of the main Huichol communities. Another miracle happened; the doctor was there. After treating and healing my feet, a Chaman came, as if waiting for me, invited me to come to his house to get some food and rest.

WITHIN THE HUICHOL REALM

Once I entered the Huichol reservation, I went from community to community, my mind obsessed by the thoughts: what are you doing here, what do you really want, what is the purpose of your life?

I expected answers to come from everywhere. I felt my life was a non-sense, my mind filled with all kind of confusions, doubts and fears. I was chasing after the truth outside of me as if the source was outside. I went throughout the Sierra Huichols, running almost like a dog, thirsty and hungry of something I could not put in word. Nothing from the outside could substantiate this emptiness. What I saw outside, offered me a compensation for the unbearable, with some new concepts and ideologies which fed my own believes of the so-called reality. Nevertheless, I still believed that the Huichol way of living had something to teach me and help me to find my own self.

Looking at their social life structure, told me a lot about the understanding they had about the world and its connexion with the wholeness of life. Their living place, consisted of several single space structures arranged concentrically with a campfire in the middle, as it is in our galaxy, the sun giving us the heat and light, seated in the middle of the zodiac with the planets orbiting around it. As the alchemist used to say: "As is the macrocosm, so is the microcosm". This middle point, the seat of the sacred fire, was for the Huichols the sacred place around which they gather, with the father teaching his children the story about creation. Their houses were built from natural native materials as earth, stone, wood and thatch. Their construction techniques, passed on from generation to generation, was as an expression of their cosmogonic views and experiences of the universe and their relationship with it. Their communities were conceived as a part of nature in complete unity and symphony with it. I could see in it, an ideal society in which everyone had its own place while at the same time existing in a homogeneous unity in which everyone and everything was interconnected. This reality of existence reflected in me the feeling that the outside was a mirror of the inside and vice versa and that, evolution necessarily implies the integration of these two seemingly opposite values; the one melting into the other and becoming one undifferentiated wholeness.

LIFE IN ALLIANCE WITH NATURE

Living in accordance with the laws of nature, in one of the houses designed as the kitchen area, a woman kneeling down was preparing "tortillas" (wafer) on the ground. She soaked and grained the corn on a stone. Then, she prepared the dough and flattened the tortillas by hand, using a flatten piece of clay to cook them over the fire. All activities seemed to be done in a certain rhythm and patterns in alliance with the stars.

They were growing the crops and do single activity in alignment with the Lunar, star patterns and rhythms. The activities performed daily, done in the appropriate moment and the right way was generating an atmosphere of Sacredness, Peace and Beauty.

A woman being totally absorbed into silence, his body enveloped in a colourful wide piece of cloth, with so much dignity and introspection, walked towards me with so much dignity and silence holding in her hands blue tortillas on a plate. I still remember appreciating the first bite of that delicious blue tortilla, my first real food after weeks of starvation which was so satisfying and nourishing.

I started to recognise something outside which was part my consciousness, living together according to the rhythms and patterns of the universe.

The corn being their most basic food, it was from the beginning to the end, treated so delicately and sacredly, being blessed and prayed over every step of the way from seed to tortilla. Eating my first tepid blue tortilla, alive, rich, and so extremely tasty made my soul and body totally happy.

The Corn for the Huicholsis so priceless being their primary source of nutriment. So that, every spring the Huichols pray and dance for the blessing of the seeds and the coming of the crop to express their gratitude and love to the Gods. Then, the seeds are stored in a very special and respectful way in the community temple. Prayers are said for a good corn crop, and the men are honoured and blessed before the planting. The seeds are planted, and the crops are tended according to their old traditions. When the corn is ready to be harvested, the whole village gathers to pray and make ceremonies. The first corn is blessed and shared. When dried and ready, the crop is carefully picked up, without waste. It is the role of the women to preserve that tradition of soaking and grinding the corn, teaching their daughters the same traditional way. They make tortillas together, sharing them with love. Everyone participates and everyone gets fed. This is why the tortillas taste so deliciously divine. You can taste the love; you can taste the tradition and the history and taste the Laws of nature. From them I learned the power of food, the food for the soul, the nutrition, the nourishment, the love and the joy of the community and family. Shared together, these precious moments remained with me, the precious moments in honouring and blessing the food's journey from seed to belly and back to the earth.

All their life was orchestrated in tune with their beliefs, in which every action performed with love and gratitude to the source was bearing harmony, peace and fulfilment to everyone and the community at large.

BELIEFS AND PRACTICES

After months of living with the Huichols, sharing their life, going through their main communities, getting close to special families and shamans, I entered gradually into the secrets and mysteries of their practices and understanding about life and the universe.

Being an oral transmission, this teaching was mainly received during dream time and taught by the shaman to the student in the way of legends and stories. The Huichol religion is intricate and elaborate and difficult to separate from social and political practice. The core of the Huichol existence lies in the hands of the shamans, known as *"mara'akames"*, which is taught during five to ten years of rigorous training. These men and sometimes women, acquire the knowledge as healers, priests, and diviners. The dreams were the most common way they used to conduct the performance of the major ceremonial functions. They believe in a pantheon of 120 deities along with four principal deities: the trinity of corn, blue deer, peyote and the eagle, all descending from their Sun God. Disease was perceived and understood by the shamans to be caused by shadows and evil spirits, whose role is to intercede and restore the equilibrium of the patient. They do it by going into a mystical trance in which they leave their physical body and travel in the spirit to the realm of the supernatural beyond this world. In fact, the shamans received instructions from the spirit world through dreams, visions and trances. Certain drugs, such as peyote, a little cactus that grows in the desert of San Luis Potosis, was also used to achieve the desired results. They also used a wide variety of herbal remedies, using different magical accoutrements. Thus, they could use their power for good and bad.

I travelled during almost one year, through their main communities, to witness the same beliefs and practices that lead the shamans to experience what we may called altered states of consciousness. To encounter and interact with the spirit world and channel theses astral energies into this world, the shamans, as I noticed, was someone everybody feared, because of his power, not yet established in the field of Oneness, everyone knew he could use his power for good as well as for bad.

Despite a profound silence saturating nature and the absolute majesty of a raw landscape unmodified by man, I ran there and there, waiting for something which will change my life. I waited for a wise man to show me the right path, the true path. My goal became more and more confused. I never felt as lost as during those months of running through the Huichol's mountains. I asked for help, I asked for clarity. I was led to the evidence that they did not know the truth either.

THE HEART OF THE HUICHOLS BELIEFS

During all ceremonies, peyote is taken in large quantities to facilitate communication with the Gods. In my faded jeans and T-shirt, I felt entirely out of place there. Women in long bright skirts and head scarves were sweeping the dirt stoops of their houses or grinding corn to make tortillas. Men gathered around the fire in the square, all wearing embroidered white clothing and lavishly decorated sombreros. Musicians played handmade fiddles, while the shamans seated on a special bamboo stool sung shamanic incantations to their God "Tatewari", their God of Fire, who over sees all ceremonies sanctified with animal sacrifice.

The shamans were telling me that such a communication with the spirit world and the gods (subaltern gods) was impossible, without the sacrificing of animals. They belief that the sacrificial blood gives power to the Shaman's wands and other ritualistic object. Without blood – which contains the animals' life force – the objects are too weak to perform their spiritual tasks. Therefore, the prayer arrows and can't reach the gods and the message from the shaman remain unheard. They really belief that it is the blood from sacrificed animals that attracts the gods.

These scenes plunged me back into the village of my childhood, where the peasants were killing the screaming pigs in the village square. Now I witnessed in front of my eyes the same crimes committed in the name of certain gods and beliefs. If they were gods how come, they needed blood of living beings to get pleased and come to manifest their blessings to human?

At this moment, I could not see and feel anything but a frenetic sort of energy that's seems to be overtaking me. I found myself swept up into a crowd that headed towards the town main temple of San Andres. The group consisting of Huichols women and men, were walking in slow motion, following the rhythm pattern of the incantations of the shamans, songs, the violins and drums. The chanting shamans blessed everyone, holding over them his eagle feather wand, shots of distilled alcohol and corn beer. A shaman stool was placed at the centre of the crowd with dried deer skins heads tied to it. This to remind everyone about the blue deer god named "Kauyumari". From the presence of "Kauyumari's" presence and role, the shamans anointed tips of arrows with animal blood and touched the deer representation as an offering. In the main temple, the crowd was joyous, rowdy and drunk with beer. Several bulls laid on the dirt floor before me, legs firmly trussed, each one ready to be killed as an offering to different gods. The Huichols believed that if the shamans do not fulfil their secular and spiritual obligations, the gods will punish the entire population with alcoholism. The Huichol people live under the umbrella of the shamans who holds powers over all avenues of the Huichol's life. They are trapped in their beliefs, being dependant, having to rely completely on the shamans to keep their feelings alive in them.

REVEALING TRUTH

On that day, during the ceremony, while being sitting cross-legged on the floor, wondering what I was doing here, a member from the Huichol's government came towards me and told me: you do not worship the same God as us, therefore, you cannot stay here any longer. His words went straight into me like a spear through my heart to wake me up to the truth which as no room in plurality. Is there One God or many gods? Do the gods need the blood of killed animal to be pleased and do the shaman and his rituals tools need the blood of killed animals to gain power? why do the Shamans needs to use peyote "the magic cactus" to enter in connexion with the gods and the spirits. Were these realities true or mere creation in the mind like a dream? So many questions arose in my mind without receiving a true answer. In a spur of a moment, months of visions, experiences and beliefs birthed into thousand pieces. I remained in that nothingness for a while until one wise man from the Huichol tribe came to me. This old man seemed to understand truth and felt like sharing his vision of the reality with me to bring me back into peace:

"The earth is sick and dying. The lands of the Huichol Indians, hidden high in the remote Sierra Madre Occidental Mountain of north western Mexico, are dying. The forests are shrinking, water is becoming scarce and the animals are suffering and disappearing.

Mankind must be a steward of the Earth; Caretakers for all that dwells upon it; to be of one heart with all things.

Human beings must learn to share the tears of every living things, to feel the pain of the wounded animal, to feel each crushed blade of grass;

Mother Earth is our flesh; the rocks our bones; the rivers are the blood of our veins."

These profound words pierce my heart and made me remember about Black Elk, a wise man from the Dakota tribe, who experienced and saw clearly the Unity of all things. During his time, Black Elk was feeling sad because he did not know how to share his vision with his people who were not able to understand him. Obviously, his people as well as the Huichols Indians kept one aspect of their spirituality through rituals and stories which they maintained for many centuries back, but, unfortunately, they have lost the knowledge about the One Divine Source of all that exists in every bit of creation, and the way to connect with It, to live life in the state of supreme bliss. Black Elk said:

"And while I stood there, I saw more than I can tell and I understood more than I saw; for I was seeing in a sacred manner the shapes of all things in the Spirit, and the shape of all shapes as they must live together like one being. And I saw

that the sacred hoop of my people was one of many hoops that made one circle, wide as daylight and as starlight, and in the centre grew one mighty flowering tree to shelter all the children of one Mother and one Father. And I saw that it was Holy."

"We should understand that all things are the work of the Great Spirit. We should understand that He is within all things; the trees, the grasses, the rivers, the mountains, all the four-legged animals, all the winged people etc…and even more important we should understand that He is also above all these things and peoples."

These words echoed in my being as being true and have guided me ever since then.

MEETING WITH THE LACANDON INDIANS

After leaving the Sierra Huichols, a combination of circumstances led me to Hugo. Hugo was living in Mexico -city and was in close contact with the Lacandon Indians, the direct descendants of the Mayan. I had just met Hugo when he offered me to lead me to the old Mayan city of Palenque, in the midst of the tropical forest, to meet with the Lacandon Indians. After travelling all night by train, from Mexico-city we arrived early morning while it was still dark, at the nearest station from Palenque. From there, we had to walk for almost one hour to reach the glorious and majestic city situated in the middle of the jungle humming to a beat of clicking cicadas, buzzing insects and exotic birdcall; the air was warm, dense and humid. In the midst of the tropical rain forest, Palenque appeared as a mystical and a magical city, arguably the most spiritual of all the ancient Mayan cities in Mexico. As we got close to Palenque, I was overwhelmed by an indescribable power and a dimension of sacredness, mixed with an impression of déjà-vu. I became very eager to discover the inner secret of Palenque and to experience the mystery belonging to this place. I could intuitively fill that within the pyramid's appearance, a truth about human evolution was secretly kept. My experience of living with the Huichols for almost one year taught me that we had to rediscover the way to access to the source of existence and that it could only be experienced from within, not from without. I was hopping, that through the encounter with the Lacandons, could be gain the opportunity to penetrate into the mystery of creation, the mystery of myself.

Once, the Hopi Indians from Arizona, said about Palenque" *in the olden days there was a red city to the south inhabited by people with all the great knowledge. Perhaps that great city was Palenque; archaeologists reported that the city of Palenque was once painted red"*.

There are those who said that Palenque was a red city, built to hold all the great knowledge in the world and was meant to be the place of study and initiation, not inhabited by people. The more time I spend at Palenque, the more I believe that this city holds great knowledge, but the contemporary world does not know how to access it.

The Lacandon Indians are the most direct descendants of the classical Maya who fled in the rain forest at the time of the Spanish Conquest and remained linguistically and culturally pristine ever since. This assumption was made because as I saw it myself the Lacandons' physical appearance and dress is very similar to the ancient Maya. The Lacandon men have long hair with their bangs cut. They wear white tunics that extend to their knees. The women keep their hair long, generally braided with ribbons or bird feathers. The women wear colourful skirts underneath their tunic. They all look always happy and peaceful.

REVELATION

The first evening I had the surprise to realise they were going to dedicate me a ceremony. A ceremony during which, they gave me a name, a name in accordance with their calendar. That name was "Kan Chick Chan Ik". Having the same name in the "tonal" (physical world of existence) as well as in the "nahuatl" (the spiritual dimension of the soul), they told me that I was destined to follow a spiritual path and be a teacher of Truth. During the ceremony they gave me a special plant sweetened with honey which was to bitter. Almost immediately after having taken this plant in a sacred manner, I began gradually to feel that I was entering into a space filled with love, extreme delicacy and beauty. In that vast space-consciousness, I felt intimately connected with everything. Butterflies came flying and turning swiftly above my head, while making sounds, seeming like music of the cosmos.

This sounds acted as a scale bringing me to a higher level of sensibility and immense happiness. In these blessed moments, the sacred bird of the Maya, the quetzal, appeared in front of me with royal blue and turquoise feathers to lift me up to higher level of sensitivity and happiness. All my being was inhabited by an indescribable feeling of love for all. I felt bewitched by an ecstasy which enveloped me completely. Warm tears were flowing along my cheeks filled with compassion for all things, visible and invisible. In those moments one couldn't miss the powerful presence of a beneficent light connecting and enveloping everything.

Here I was, sitting on the top of one of the Palenque's temples, from where I witnessed the alchemical transformation of matter in subtler substance.

Then Hugo arrived and invited me to climb Palenque's hill, along which there were many temples, invaded by a dense tropical vegetation at the edge of which flowed a meandering river. During this journey, the elements spoke to me. I experienced this dialogue with the elements within me and realised that actually everything was existing me. At the same time the origin of Palenque was revealed to me. Long ago, Palenque was inhabited by immortal beings, by gods who had all powers and knowledge about earth and heaven. They could accomplish anything at will. They all left, taking with them their bodies, transmuted in Light, as it was written in the pyramids of Palenque. They did leave the earth long time before the arrival of the Spanish Conquerors invaded Mexico. So the remaining natives retired far into the tropical rain forest. Years passed, until they gradually forgot about the truth of reality and forgot that truth was existing and accessible inside themselves. The secret remained hidden for them of how to connect with the source of the fountainhead of life.

INSTRUCTION

Through this pilgrimage into consciousness, Hugo, the wise men, made it clear to me, that I had to return to Europe. He said, everything will be revealed to you about your path when you will have returned to France. He added that: you would be actively contributing to a collective endeavour for the creation of a new shift of switching paradigm from an age of illusion, hate, selfishness and suffering to an age of Light, peace and harmony among all people and all nations of the world through the creation of an universal brotherhood.

ENCOUNTER WITH THE SPIRITUAL MASTER

Once being in France, seeing that I could not reconnect anymore with the experience I had in Palenque, I found myself suddenly stripped of everything. I was left with an existential anguish that inhabited me, paralysing me.

This uncomfortable and unpleasant feeling made me search for an outside solution. I did not recognise that at the time I was looking for something to replace this uncomfortable feeling of fear and un-security. It came to my attention that this awful feeling hadal ways been inhabited me. My quest for happiness and enlightenment, although, an outside quest, found a response in Maharishi Mahesh Yogi's Transcendental Meditation, called "TM".

In November 1979, I was instructed into "TM", in the south of France. Surely, "TM" gave me an immediate Inner peace and contentment. I was so happy to have found Maharishi, the founder of the Transcendental Meditation Movement, who represented the image of an ideal father, the father I always wished to have. It is not easy to describe in word, what I felt in his presence. Maharishi was radiating so much wisdom and purity, so much kindness, love and an unbelievable light and beauty as I have never experience and seen before. I was certain to have finally found what I was looking for. Then, to surrender at Maharishi's feet, who I recognised as my spiritual master, was easy and natural. During the following 17 years I followed diligently all his instructions and guidance.

From that moment on, I followed precisely what my Master said, being persuaded that would lead me to the highest spiritual attainment. Having my attention caught up on the goal, I followed all his instructions, all the courses, the most advanced seminars and even went around the world as a soldier of peace as we were called, to bring coherence, harmony and peace everywhere where chaos prevailed.

In spite of these apparent seeming about the influence of TM, the quest for truth outside of me did not stop. I knew there was something more. I became more and more thirsty to know about myself and about God. Consciousness was still a very abstract word to me. I saw that a simple technic as TM was not enough to dissolve all my obstacles, resistance, past memories and old patterns habit in order to experience the true light of my-self. For years I was repeating sacred words, mantras and followed instructions without knowing and understanding their profound meanings and without having checked within me the validity of it. Moreover, everything became a routine work without feeling. Having been so far, inhabited by a dominant inferiority complex and fears, the time came to transcend the mind limitations and do something to unfold my inner creativity and intelligence. This led me to enrol at the Maharishi International University of Management, Iowa, USA. 5 years later I left the university with a B.A in Art and political science and a M.A in the science of Creative Intelligence crowned by the study of Indian philosophy/Vedic Science.

During my study, my great shyness and lack of self-confidence brought me to do something to get out of limitations, I learned to be more practical and trained myself in public speaking. I started to feel more comfortable with the outside world, to come out of that self-centred state.

Once my study ended, I had to choose between two opposites directions: either to continue my studies in another University in the US or to join a group which Maharishi had created. This group, called "Purusha", was a group of single men living together in a "ashram" (Indian monastery), situated at Vlodrop, Holland, near the German border. At that time, Maharishi was emphasizing the need for silence, harmony and love in this world filled with turbulences, ignorance, stress, chaos and violence.

Maharishi's recruiting campaign for Purusha succeeded to reveal in me, the image of the Samaritan, the one who was ready to sacrifice himself for others. Maharishi was using powerful words such as *"the outside world is trash"*, telling me, not to lose time in such a world. Maharishi's words enlivened the feeling that I might be more useful to serve the world from inside, by contributing in generating silence and harmony through the group practice of advanced meditation. I gathered that I should not waste my precious time in a world of trash. My spiritual master made me believe that in order to gain enlightenment, I had to renounce the world, a world condemned as nothingness and illusion, a world that was representing as the main obstacle to my full spiritual realisation.

During these years I was filled with the feeling of security and contentment being constantly within and around my Master presence. I never had to take a decision nor make a choice; Maharishi was orchestrating all our life. He did send me to different parts of the world teaching His Vedic Science and generating waves of coherence and harmony wherever there was problems and chaos. Life in the ashram was unfolding in a mechanic way, loosing track of the deep motivation which brought me here.

One day, Maharishi called me back from Crimea, where I was teaching TM for one year, to take the responsibility of the Luxembourg TM movement administration, to set up a Vedic university and an ayurvedic clinic. This news was quite shocking since I was not yet ready to assume responsibilities on such a scale. I did not feel like being in the front: I rather wanted to hide from the world and to escape from my own reality. That's why the life of the ashram was perfectly suiting my ego. Until Maharishi called me back into the world, I had nourished a false idea about the true meaning of renouncing the world. I just realised that renouncing, meant a deep involvement in life. Renouncing meaning not being implicated or identified with the body and everything appearing within the mind: thoughts, emotions, feelings and sensations. Being in the world was serving as a mirror to meet my own reality. The world is as you are, and you are as you see the world. I suddenly recognize that I was covering my soul with the pleasantness and the bliss I felt being around my spiritual master, not realising that what I felt was not part of me. By allowing it to continue, I could not experience subtler and subtler level of my own being.

Maharishi's call came to me like a boon; it was an opportunity to face my own limitations, my own functioning pattern habits and my own fears.

I remembered, once Maharishi said: "my role is not to kill the ego, my role is to make it bigger not to suppress it".

Maharishi created this situation, in order to see where I was standing with my attachments, desires and fears. I was still attached to a goal, to a past and future. Letting go of all this, was not easy, but certainly the most fundamental principle of all religiousness, religiousness meaning the return to the source. I knew it was an art of being totally immersed in God's presence. But how to proceed, how to put it into practice? I did not know yet the path of purification. Everything was still intellectual. I have been meditating for15 years, but I was using meditation to cover the unbearable, to search for more pleasantness, for deeper experiences, for silence and an ephemeral well-being. Meditation has been used to cover up something in me, something that was still separating, judging, comparing, evaluating.

At the time Maharishi decided to send me back to Luxembourg, the Laws there, did not permit the creation of a private university and the opening of an Ayurvedic clinic. While everything seemed blocked, I had the idea to organise a symposium with a topic of international interest: "The songs of the Veda in the human physiology".

I always believed that all the universe was fully alive in our brain and that every single cell of our human physiology was acting as primordial sounds, constantly pulsating and humming. I had that conviction that if we knew how to connect ourselves to the source of creation and function in perfect tuning with the rhythms and patterns of the universe, we would have the solution to prevent sickness, suffering, violence and death. Despite the fact that150 people attended the symposium, there was not much interest shown afterwards and no return gained. I realised that due to my total implication in this project, I was profoundly disappointed. Actually, I had organised this symposium to gain attention and recognition from my master and the people present. The objective being to gain their full support and contribution for the establishment of Maharishi's plans for Luxembourg.

Being left empty-handed after the symposium, I lost all enthusiasm to give myself thoroughly anymore in the TM movement activity.

Nevertheless, I did pursue the activities of the TM academy for a while until It became clear to me that the seminars and lectures I was giving did not seem to raise much interest. Moreover, I was not teaching the TM technic anymore, just because my feeling could not demand 1000 Euros per instruction into TM which the TM movement expected from me. How could I ask so much money, for something I felt should be available to everyone, without any discrimination. As a consequence, the Luxembourg TM academy could not afford the rent of the house anymore and the proper functioning of the academy be continued. In the end, we were forced to cancel the lease and dissolve the association.

The time had come to have a close look at my actual situation by reflecting-back on myself. I saw that this all process was just a mental affair, I was not living and sharing the knowledge from inside myself, nor living the teaching, but instead, I was merely imitating Maharishi like a parrot. A s a result, the teaching was meaningless out as empty words. Therefore, how could the people be touched by the teaching I was giving them; a teaching addressed to their intellect, not to their soul.

Once the academy was over, I felt desperate, not being able getting in touch with my spiritual master anymore. The result out of these activities left me with a deep feeling of failure and guilt, not having been able to fulfil my master's wishes, unable to satisfy the people attending the academy.15 years of deep bondage of love with my Master was ending.

Despite the fact, I had Maji, my spiritual mother, around me with her unconditional love to support me, I knew I had to face all these feelings, thoughts and limitations, no one could solve them for me.

Suddenly, something important flashback into my memory. It was about an important meeting I had with Maharishi before the symposium. I remembered asking him a very specific question about a deep concern I had during all these years. The question I asked my Master was reminiscent of my childhood. It was about the immortality of the body.

I wanted to know why, despite of all you told us about immortality and perfect health, so many of your very sincere and committed followers, are falling sick and died.

And what about, spiritual masters, Maharishi? They died from severe illness, although, they were apparently fully enlightened. Maharishi, you told us, that when one attains moksha or enlightenment, it is the final extrication of the soul or consciousness from samsara (the karma or past memories) and the ending of all suffering and the repeating cycle of death and rebirth.

Maharishi's response was that it was because of the karma of the body. Then I asked Maharishi, why you did not teach us the way of restoring the body to its original state of perfection, the deathless body. Maharishi responded that: you must search and ask for it.

Coming back to the world I had always fled, leaving behind what has led me here. It is with a heartfelt of gratitude and love towards my spiritual Master who has guided me in stretching out my limitation and broaden my awareness, giving me strength, faith and understanding, enabling me to step out into a new journey which marked the very beginning of my spiritual journey, in search of immortality.

THE BEGINNING OF MY SPIRITUAL PATH

My spiritual journey began when I jumped into the world, leaving behind all attachments linked with any outside spiritual security, for a total immersion in the world, while being aware of the big mess in my mind. By entering into this world, I first experienced the fear of being alone. It was terrifying. I became aware that meditation was not the true solution to complete freedom and full enlightenment. The only solution was a total involvement with myself in the world, though meditation might have been necessary at the beginning to get an initial push. Truly, I experienced some dimension of silence and bliss when I was with my master but the moment I stepped outside, I fell right back into the unusual turmoil along with a split of awareness between the inner and outer.

I was finding it difficult to transform the outer life and the body. I found that my actions did not correspond with the inner light; they were following the old, mistaken paths, still obeying the accustomed, imperfect influences. The truth within me continued to be separated by a painful gap from the ignorant mechanism of my external nature. It was as if I was living in another, a larger and subtler world and had no divine hold, perhaps little hold of any kind, upon the material and terrestrial experience. This observation led me to the necessity of a divine rehabilitation of matter and gave to my painful path its meaning and hope. I had denied the divinity in matter, confining it to ashrams and holy places, and now nature was taking its revenge. I was aware that as long as I accepted this imbalance, this division, there was no hope, but to continue to swing from one pole into the other. If I wanted to discover my true self, I had to leave the old one behind me. Everything now depended upon my determination in taking the first step. I found it hard to break the crust of the ego to follow the inner path. It was like entering the Amazon: you know when you go in, but you don't know when you will emerge. There were all kind of colors, noises, rhythms, shapes and animals. This is precisely what I was facing inside me. Alone, I felt deprived of resources. For the next seven years, I skimmed off the best I could find from the field of personal development. I barely had time to learn its name before I was already there; if someone had told me that I would become enlightened by eating cow-dung, I believe I would have swallowed it. At this point, I was in a race. To summarize this outside quest and make it as concise as possible: I did five years training in psychotherapy, during which I followed many seminars, retreats, all kind of workshops in rebirth, Gestalt therapy, hypnosis, psychic phenomena, mediumship, astrology, divination, reading Tarots and more. I wish it could have happened in a flash, but actually, it took 15 years.

These brought me to the realization that I was nothing, but a dark mass of mental, nervous and physical patterns held together by a few ruling ideas, desires and emotions associated with many self-repeated forces. I was truly encountering the fact that what I took to be myself was nothing but the past filtering itself through clusters of thoughts, feelings and sensations.

All past experiences had to be met with full awareness. They were all stored and glued inside as deposits covering all the cells of my soul, mind and body consciousness. These memories and behavioral patterns crystallized, wherever appearing and repeating themselves, layers after layers, which you peal like an onion until you reach the very core of it, the pearl.

What I needed, was to live a complete life; I needed to live the truth of my being every day, every moment, beyond isolation, meditation and yoga, or whatever other experiences were unable to achieve complete fulfillment. In order to achieve this, I had to incorporate the outside world, all living beings, to live the wholeness of life, but how to do it? Having been encased so long in my spiritual seclusion, I found it difficult to pour myself triumphantly out and apply this to my life for higher evolution. On the other hand, when I wanted to add the external kingdom to my inner conquests, I found myself too much accustomed to an activity purely subjective and ineffective on the material plane.

The only solution seemed to practice silencing the mind, just where it appeared to be most difficult: on the street, at work, in the midst of people, in the subway, everywhere.

Instead of doing things in a rush, I learned to walk with a slow motion - I called it walking in consciousness. Instead of living haphazardly, dispersed in a multitude of thoughts, which not only lacked any excitement but were also as exhausting as a broken record, I gathered the scattered threads of my consciousness and worked on myself relentlessly. Then life started to be surprisingly exciting, the least little circumstance becoming an opportunity for victory; I was focused; instead of going somewhere I was going nowhere, remaining as much as possible in the space consciousness, aware of itself. In this way, I found the inner work easier, positively rather than negatively oriented.

The beauty of this work could only be taken up by a Grace from above, to which I aspired. For I thought that these yogic experiences were all very nice and interesting, but that they were far beyond my ordinary human grasp; how could I, such as I am, ever get there? My mistake was judging on the basis of my present self-knowledge, which belonged to another self. By the simple fact of setting myself out on the path, the yoga automatically awakened in me a whole range of latent faculties, and invisible forces that far exceeded the capacities of my outer being and could achieve for me things that I was normally incapable of doing. I realized that I had to clear the passage between the outer mind and something in the inner being for they (the Yogic consciousness and its powers) were already there within me. The best way of "clearing" the passage was to silence the mind by gathering the mind. I did not know yet who I was, and even less about my total potential intelligence.

INITIATIONS

I realized that the soul could never aspire to reach salvation, unless it was able to have the support, cooperation and guidance of a spiritual master. I needed to know about the role of the human body and how to restore the human body to its full dignity.

This got me searching to transform the body so that it would be able to receive the Light and stabilize higher levels of consciousness. My search for immortality brought me into the "I AM" movement of Saint Germain in which I became fully involved for seven years. During these years I attended almost all the training sessions and classes in the "I AM" Temple of Chicago, at Mount Shasta USA, and in Geneva, Switzerland where I gave the violet and blue flame classes. I did it with full dedication and conviction until I recognized that there was a fundamental mistake that had crept into this teaching. In spite of what was claimed, it did not have the capacity to bring anyone to the so-called goal, the ascension of the soul with a transmuted body.

In search of the knowledge of immortality, the teaching of Siddha Thirumular came to me, as transmitted by Sivapremananda from Bangalore. He initiated me into all the levels of the Kriya yoga of Thirumular and Mother Tripura Sundari Sadhana (the transcendental Mother). After three years of practice, I joined a three-day Tripura Sundari seminar with my spiritual master, Sivapremananda. At the end of the seminar I met my Master individually. I told him about my experience, and he responded by saying that I could teach. I told him that I felt my experience was still incomplete, knowing there was something more. Then, I told him that I wanted to encounter Ramalinga's teaching. Sivapremananda's response was this: if you go to Ramalinga, you go beyond everything, you go to the source of the Divine itself.

THE POWER OF SILENCE AND ALTRUISTIC LOVE

I was not seeking holiness but immortality, an ever-progressing being; I was not seeking a lesser being but a better being and above all a vaster one. I made all kinds of discoveries which started when the mental stopped. At this moment, I realized that if the power to think is a remarkable gift, the power of not thinking is a far greater one. By going through the total silence of the mind, it made me see what this means! It made me realize that I lived in a surreptitious racket, an exhausting and ceaseless whirlwind exclusively filled with thoughts, feelings, impulses, reactions – bearing always me, as an oversized gnome, intruding into everything, obscuring everything, hearing and seeing only myself, knowing only myself. These unchanging expressions managed to give the illusion of novelty only through their alternation, revealing different faces we call culture or "our" self-will. I was in fact shut off in many mental patterns, which were like lead, without even a small opening, as "graceful" as a minaret. But whether in a granite skin or in a glass statue, I was nonetheless confined, forever buzzing and repetitive. My first task was to breathe freely, to shatter that mental screen, which allows only one type of vibration to get through. This in order to discover the multi-colored infinity of vibrations: that is, the world as we really are, and another "self" within ourselves, that is beyond any mental appreciation.

Being a monk and walking on the path of the earth in search of this union, I did not receive any answer. Whether I went to the past or reached the spiritual heights the result was the same; I remained just as an animal, in pain and small in my miserable human flesh.

The Truth within me continued to be separated by a painful gulf from the ignorant mechanism of my external nature. I could certainly gather the scattered threads of my consciousness and work on myself at every moment. Then life became surprisingly exciting, the smallest circumstance turning out to be an opportunity for victory.

In the end, it was Siva Premananda who led me onto the path to Victory by showing me the way to immortality as revealed by Saint Ramalinga Vallalar; Ramalinga who transformed his physical body into a golden body of pure Grace Light in the 1850s. His teachings revealed to me that love and compassion towards all living beings was the sole key to access immortality, the highest pinnacle of spiritual achievement.

COMING BACK HOME

It was in Thirunnamalai Ramalinga's Trust that I first saw and experienced that altruistic love and compassion was the true way. There, I could feel that all the atmosphere was completely saturated with sweetness, purity and love which was pouring out naturally from everyone, from every particle of air I was breathing and from everything I saw. It was an overwhelming experience. In this moment I knew, I had reached the end of my quest; I had come back home. Me who thought of reaching the highest realm of spiritual attainment through the intensive practice of yoga and meditation, while living in seclusion or in separation with the world, I finally understood that it could never be possible. I figured out that as long as I was not including the whole world in my practice, not realizing that all living beings were a part of God's natural truth and the manifestation of Grace, expressed in each and every one of them, there was no access to the attainment of the highest fulfillment.

GOD IS ONE AND WE ARE ALL ONE

I realized that we all come from the same Light source. During the process of creation through the five elements, the physical body is formed starting from a single and perfect cell-atom, the soul, containing a divine spark. Therefore, it should be possible for us to reverse this process and turn this physical body from impurity and ignorance into the original pure light of the soul, here and now in this plane.

There is only one God which is the Absolute Eternal Light, then why worship other forms of God? If we are all one, the concept of caste, colors, cultures, religions, is only pursuing the idea that we are all different. All religions, philosophies, and organizations are hiding the truth by propagating the notion of separation and difference. In fact, one should not believe in scripture but gain one's own understanding and knowledge through direct experience. All humans, being created by the All-powerful God, with the same characteristics, form an integral part of Natural Truth. Hence, it is the inherent right of every human being to feel that we are all brothers and sisters belonging to the same family, the family of humanity, the Universal Brotherhood. As Ramalinga and Jesus said: "One should treat all life as one would treat one's own life". When we express love, compassion and bliss we can feel that we are all connected. Ramalinga reveals that compassion generates an elixir in the brain which transforms the human physiology into a body of light.

THE BODY AS THE TEMPLE OF GOD

Compassion is the key for the Love of Mercy to gather all human beings under one single umbrella, the Universal Brotherhood.

I finally discovered that the body is the temple of the soul, and therefore, both body and soul are interconnected, the body being as important as the soul. Thirumular, who brought me to Ramalinga, said:

"Divorced from the body, the soul is naught. If the physical body perishes, it is a doom to the soul, and one would not attain the true knowledge firmly. So, by knowing the technique of tending and nourishing the body well, I will not tend and nourish the body alone, but the soul too."

IMMORTALITY

The body is like a glass: it must be handled with care. Even though the body appears as a fleshy tenement, the soul being only a tenant, it needs a tenement. The fact the tenement is made of flesh, there is no reason decrying it. On the contrary, as it is fleshy and therefore vulnerable, it needs great consideration. The human body is subject to a thousand ills and it is our duty to protect it from all sicknesses. Ramalinga, who has vanquished death, knew the fragility and delicateness of the mechanism with which he had to deal with the body. He therefore made a thorough study of the physical and other more subtle bodies. And it is only with the help of this that the soul can reach its goal. Before dealing with the soul itself, he had to deal with each of the soul's envelopes. Before dealing with the soul or the spiritual body, the physical, vital, mental and intellectual bodies had to be dealt with. I discovered that the quintessence of Ramalinga's teaching is that God, the Supreme Grace Light is to be realized not only in the spiritual plane through awakening, but also to be made manifest progressively in the other planes and corresponding bodies: intellectual, mental, vital and ultimately the physical body, wherein the body in the complete union with God, glows with the fire of immortality. Love and compassion towards all living beings are thus necessary for all true seekers of truth to achieve their goal; such love becomes both the means and the end of the path.

Thirumular said: "If by His Grace, one is surrendered in service to the Universal Lord and the substance of his physical body aspires for the Lord of the Golden World of Pure Knowledge, and becomes pure without a shadow of darkness, remaining equal without "ego-consciousness, in the duality of action. He is verily "swa", the Divine in human form and knowledge "Siva Vedam" becoming consecrated to His Service." - Thulasiram verse 1976.

One might ask oneself, "do I accept death and aging?". If one does not accept this, then one must do something about it and follow the Sanmarga path about which this book is written. It is the path of truth and purity which will surely lead one to the most sublime experience, the complete union with God, lived in the state of Supreme Bliss.

V - THE DIVINE LIFE OF RAMALINGA VALLALAR AND HIS MESSAGE

THE DIVINE CONCEPTION OF RAMALINGA

He who appears
As the source and origin of all,
As the light that gave the knowledge of the beginning and end of all
He who appears
As my love, my light, my guide and my blissful experience,
As the ultimate end of the path of Sudha sanmarga I have adopted,
As the embodiment of justice,
As the one who reigns supreme beyond all stages

As the one who ordains all that happen
As one who just not teaches but enlightens
Such a vast power that pervades all over
Such a brilliant power that radiates the light of knowledge
Such a power that gave me the knowledge of truth
I have realised such a power within me

Those were the rejuvenating words which Sinnamai heard distinctly. They sounded music to the ears. They were no mere words. They were powerful Mantras that would remove fears, instil confidence, give protection and shower Grace. She knew its value and rushed to the main door, leaving her household chores behind. What she saw outside the door amazed her. A saint was standing, clad in his characteristic saffron robes, his face serene and sublime, body smeared with white ashes of **"Vibhuti"** and tongue chanting the Sadakshara Mantra of Muruga. His delightful face radiated a light of divine spirit. There was something unique in his eyes.

Sinnamai greeted him and welcomed him. She offered to the wholly man a seat and paid obeisance to the distinguished visitor. He was treated courteously and fed with a good meal.

Having been pleased immensely with the courteous treatment given to him, at the time of His departure, the saint blessed Sinnamai with some sacred ash "Vibhuti" and uttered these graceful words:

"I see the divine presence of Lord Muruga here. You will be blessed with a son who will rise up to the great height of glory, who will deliver the art of deathlessness which will be a boon to the entire world".

Sinnamai was overwhelmed with joy and before she could gain composure, the saint had disappeared. Ramayya Pillai, her husband, turned up later and felt equally happy hearing the incident.

Ramayya Pillai and Sinnammai belonged to an average family in Marudhur, near Chidambaram in South Arcot District, Tamil Nadu, India. Ramayya Pillai was a teacher in a local school and an ardent devotee of Lord Shiva, the Almighty God. They were blessed with two sons, Sabapathi, Parasuraman and two daughters, Sundarammal and Unnamali.

Though it has been acknowledged by all as a remarkable event which need to be understood only from a higher plane.

The very moment the lady, Sinnamai, has heard the words of the saint that she would bring forth a child, she conceived.

This form of creation is termed as *"Sambupaksha Shrishti"*. The way to conceive a child has been classified into five division:

Of these, the world is only aware of these first two sections:

The most common way of conceiving a child happen through the combination of the male and female substances which create the condition for the creation of an embryo, which gradually grows into a child.

The second way to conceive a child, which is a very rare phenomenon in the world, the embryo comes into existence at the very moment the utterance comes from the mouth of a holy man.

RAMALINGA'S BIRTH

Days passed in and at the end of the gestation period, Sinnammai gave birth to a male child, the fifth child of the family, on the fifth day of October 1823. As the baby started crying, the tears of labour pain turned into tears of joy. The mother was unaware that the baby she just delivered was destined to change the world and was to be known as ArutPrakasa Vallalar, the sage of inexhaustible grace. They named the baby as Ramalingam. Even in the stage of a tender child, taking the first few steps, Ramalingam showed signs of wisdom and steadiness.

Blessed by Divine Grace, the beloved parents showered their love and affection to the darling child and brought him up with great care.

Ramalinga tells in "Peru Vinappam" that he was conscious of his birth not merely at the time of birth but even during all the processes that culminated in fertilisation, during which the emanation of his soul took active part in the formation of the sperm-cell of his formal father and the egg-cell of his formal mother with the divine inner light of protection for keeping up the divine qualities of his soul and a good physique.

RAMALINGA'S VISION AND REALISATION OF NATARAJA'S TRUTH

In India, as it is the tradition to take a new-born child to the temple and offers prayers before the deity to bequeath the child with His blessings, once Ramalinga was five months old, the parents took him to Chidambaram temple to offer their grateful prayers.

After having lit the camphor and offered it to the Lord at the Sanctum Sanctorum, a vision soon appeared before Ramalinga, the child laughed loudly and gazed for a few seconds before the deity of Nataraja during the formalities of worship, in front of the adjacent sanctorum called *"Chidambaram bara Rahasyam"* signifying according to popular notion the vacant sunya or space, the child sensed infinity, which is expressed by Ramalinga himself in one of his songs *"Arulvillakkaamaalai-Bk.11-36-44"*

People realised and felt by the atmosphere generated saturated with the presence of divinity, that the child has laughed due to its ecstasy.

His laugh was the expression of Ramalinga's vision and realisation of Nataraja, the dancing Shiva, as the effulgence of the inner Light of Grace "Arul Jyothi" as soon as the outer light came to his visibility.

This divinely and most sublime experience has been expressed in some of His poems:

"No sooner the light was perceived, happiness prevailed in me".
"The sweet nectar was tasted by me as soon as the Great Grand Light "Arutperunjyothi" became visible".

RAMALING'S CHILDHOOD

From the experience they had in the temple of Chidambaram, all the family members were jubilant as they felt they had a God's gift. Ramalingam turned out to be a prodigious child, just as the saint had predicted. But Ramayya Pillai, Ramalinga's Father, could not live longer, to see the blooming of his son into a divine personality. Soon, the responsibility of the family felt on the shoulder of Sabapathi, the elder son of the family. The family then moved over to Madras.

Being a teacher himself, Sabapathi, wanted to give the best education to Ramalingam but Ramalingam showed no inclination for studies. He preferred to spend his time in the precincts of Kanda Swamy temple, composing songs and worshipping Muruga.

Sabapathi then sent him to a learned Pundit named Sabapathi Mudaliar of Kancheepuram. He thought that Ramalinga would be receptive to an erudite scholar like Sabapathi Mudaliar. Having come to know the brilliant qualities of the child, Sabapathi Mudaliar said that there was nothing that he could teach to a person like Ramalinga who had the capacity to teach the whole world. Wishing him well, Mudaliar sent him back.

But Sabapathi was not aware of Ramalinga's extraordinary qualities. He thought that Ramalinga was squandering his time. He instructed his wife not to give Ramalinga food. Sensing his resentment, Ramalinga avoided meeting Sabapathi. Invariably, he used to sit in the precincts of the temple and return home at his own will. Ramalinga felt that Kandha Kottam Murugan was beckoning him.

Ramalinga derived immense inspiration and strength from the temple. Looking at the shrine of Muruga at Kandha Kottam, Ramalinga felt intense and most profound feelings from where all his devotion came out in the form of *"Deiva Mani Malai"*.

"Deiva Mani Malai" laid out criteria for good and noble life for all. He said that he needed no relation with those who speak something and does the opposite. He prayed for being blessed with noble qualities. He prayed for being endowed with the power of exercising mind-control. He prayed not only for wisdom and knowledge but also for Lord's Grace. What an ideal prayer! It seems that only one who received the grace of God could compose such eloquent and uplifting prayers.

It was Pappathi (Sabapathi's wife) who used to look for him, gave him food and attended to is needs like a mother does. One day, Pappathi performed the *"Sradha Thidhi"*, the ceremony to feed the departed souls and invited few Brahmins for the ritual and for a feast. Ramalinga who was away, came along after the event was over. Pappathi received him through the back door and served him food. She told Ramalinga:

"Being a member of the family, you should have been in the forefront at the time of ceremony. Why do you have to sneak in later and take the cold left-overs?"

On another occasion, after returning home, Ramalinga was taking the food served from Pappathi, when he casually lifted his head, he saw tears swelling in her eyes. So far, he had not seen tears in the eyes of anyone, except in Pappathi, who was serving him like a mother. Then, Ramalinga asked her why she was crying. She responded:

"How long would you avoid your brother and come home late. If your brother had rebuked you, it was only out of his concern for you. He is interested in your welfare. You are causing anxiety and tension to all by your "erratic ways". You should not wander like this and adopt the normally accepted way of life".

Pappathi poured out her deep concerns and emotions. Ramalinga who saw reason in her contention, responded that he did not wish to be the cause of tension to others and that he could confine himself in the house if that was their wish. He only requested for an exclusive room for himself, a lamp and a mirror on the table. From that moment, Ramalinga confined himself in the room. Sabapathi was satisfied with the new arrangement.

Sitting in the room, Ramalinga used to study scriptures like Thiruvachakam, Thevaramand works related to Saiva Sidhantam. He studied Periyapuranam containing the life of the 63 saints who hailed the Glory of Lord Siva. The doctrine of Saiva sidhantam had made a profound influence on him. He felt it was Lord Siva who was conducting and guiding him.

Sabapathi, though appeared to be rude, was very loving and affectionate towards Ramalinga. Being a teacher himself, he was just anxious that Ramalinga should not miss out his studies. Obviously, he was not aware of Ramalinga's divine qualities and masterly knowledge. He was unaware that Ramalinga who was an institution by himself, could impart education without having to receive it from outside of himself.

RAMALINGA'S FIRST DIVINE DISCOURSE

Soon, Sabapathi too realized the greatness of Ramalinga.

It was at the time in which Sabapathi was scheduled to perform a religious discourse at Madras, but for some reasons he was unable to do so. He deputed Ramalinga to convey the message of his inability to perform it. As the authorities could not make alternative arrangements, they insisted Ramalinga himself to perform the role of his brother. A reluctant Ramalinga took the stage. Then his brilliance came to the light and his exposition of Shaiva Sidhanta kept the audience spell bound. No ordinary person could perform a divine discourse as effortlessly and magnificently as Ramalinga, one from the audience remarked. Sabapathi felt ashamed that he had not been able to see the greatness of his own brother before, residing under the same roof.

Ramalinga was used to spent most of his time in his room. Sitting before a mirror, he used to meditate and compose poems. Once, during meditation, his individual self-disappeared and experienced God within himself; the Lord he had realized from within, revealed himself as a reflection on the mirror. Usually, devotees sought God outside, in the idol of a temple or a symbolic picture and then realize His presence within. Here, in sharp contrast, Vallalar was seeking the outside reflection of the God who was already being experienced within, being already illuminated within himself.

He composed songs invoking the Grace of Muruga, like Kandar Sarana Pathu, Shanmugar Kalaipattu and Deiva Mani Malai etc.
Visiting the Kanda Kottam Murugan temple became the daily routine of Ramalinga. Looking at the shrine of Muruga at Kanda Kottam, Ramalinga felt intensely emotional and poured out his devotion in the form of 'Deiva Mani Malai'.

"You are the embodiment of love, who has no equal, who is enlightened, who gives happiness to all. When would the rose petals of your Lotus Feet extend their gentle grace to my heart? When would you come, mounted on your beautiful transport of peacock to give me the treasure of your grace?"

So went the lines of Deiva Mani Malai which he composed at the age of nine.

His divinity came to be recognised by the devotees in the early age of eleven years when he began to visit the Siva shrine at Tiruvottiyur, a suburb of Madras, where he sang impromptu devotional hymns and songs in praise of the One Divine, the impersonal Person of formless-form, in the forms of Shiva and the goddess Uma.

Even in these early songs we meet and feel with his intense and fiery aspiration for the Grace-world of truth-Knowledge "ArulVeli" and for deathlessness of the body. These songs also touch on his inspiration for spiritual life, purification, consecration, devotion, surrender, compassion and reverence for all human beings and creatures and for the Oneness for the Divine. These poems of this period form three volumes of his Thiruarutpa.

Between the age of 15 and 30 years many disciples came to him seeking illumination. Notable came to see him. Among them was Veelaayuda Muladaliaar, a scholar in Tamil, Sanskrit and English. During this period the swami wrote commentaries and interpretations on some of the rare Tamil works like "**Olivil Odukkam**" which brought out the integrality of the Divine through a synthesis of both Vedanta and Siddhanta in an age thickly beset with the sectarian philosophical schools of Advaita, Visishtadvaita and dvaita.

RAMALINGA'S MARRIAGE

It was the time, as it is the Tradition in India, Ramalinga married much against his will, but in deference to the advice of a saintly soul and the insistence of his immediate relatives, but he remained wholly detached to the married life since the very beginning of it and sought to turn his newly wedded wife towards spiritual life.

RAMALINGA'S PILGRIMAGE TO CHIDAMBARAM

Later, Ramalinga undertook pilgrimage to Chidambaram along with some of his disciples and visited shrines on the way at Conjeevaram, Pondicherry, Cuddalor etc... After a tour of the south from Chennai, he settled in Chidambaram for some time and thereafter in Karunguli near Chidambaram since 1858 for 9 years. Here he had the opportunity to worship, often with songs to Nataraja of "Cit Sabha", the holy of holies in the Chidambaram temple, his favourite deity answering and satisfying at once his inner aspiration for the Grace-Light of Truth-knowledge or Truth-Consciousness and the outer needs, modes and forms of worship. Ramalinga glorifies the Lord of Dance as the Supreme Divine making the world-founding dance, that is, the dance of Universal Vibration, the flickering of the Omnipresent Space of Universal Light of Supreme Truth-Consciousness; Lord Nataraja being a metaphorical representation of the Light of Supreme Grace Light within the light.

Many miraculous events are attributed to Ramalinga during the time he was in Karungkuli. He had mastery over wind, water, rains, fire etc..., and over living beings and creatures like serpents, ghosts and spirits of this world and also on vital beings of the other worlds.

RAMALINGA AT KARUNGKULI

Here, at Karungkuli, he wrote much of his later works except the six volumes of Arutpa. One day when he was writing his poems, seated near a clay pot oil lamp at Karungkuli house, at midnight, it happened that Ramalinga poured water, in the oil lamp clay pot water believing it was oil. By the Divine Grace the oil-lamp kept on burning. Sometimes, it happened that Ramalinga has transmuted baser metal into gold and threw it away not to run after such things. He cured many diseases like leprosy, cancer, etc…, by giving them sacred ashes known as *"Vibhuti"*.

Vallalar despite the fact he was not against performing miracles, as they form the powers and plays of the Divine. However, he was not after miracle-mongering. His eventful life was interspersed with many divine miracles of various kinds. He promised in the last part of his life that the Divine Himself was soon to manifest on the earth to rule and play Siddhis of Grace, such as resurrection of the dead and transforming the aged into youths. Thus, Vallalar progressively grew into the Divine Nature, as he went on writing inspired poems and doing miracles since his early life. His miracles are continuing even now.

In 1867, Ramalinga settled at Vadalur, two miles away from Karungkuli, and about 40 miles from Pondicherry. It is there that he founded a home for feeding the poor *"Dharamsalai"*, a school for spiritual learning and literature *"Samarasa Veda PataSalai"* and the shrine of *"Satya Gyana Sabhai"*, The hall of wisdom.

RAMALINGA'S SECLUSION AT METTUKUPPAM

In 1972, Ramalinga withdrew himself in seclusion for about six months at Mettukuppam, three miles away from Vadalur and in the concentrated state of realisation of the World of Truth-Consciousness and the Beyond, he wrote his master-piece of *"Joti Agaval"*. This poem describes the self-determination of the Supreme Grace Light, the poises of the World of Truth-Knowledge, planes of ascent, involution and evolution, golden plane of the earth, purifying and transforming powers of the Light, transformation of his body, knowledge and science of deathlessness of body, general nature and characteristics of the World Truth-Knowledge, the worlds of *"Satchitananda"*, The bliss Truth-Consciousness and beyond etc.

Ramalinga continued to live at Mettukupam and by his divine inspiration poured out in verses and lyrics which form the last of the sixth volume of his writings. The disciples noted down his teachings in oral discourses and copied down his poems. He managed and guided his Institutions at Vadalur from his cottage-house at Mettukuppam village called *"Siddhi Vaalega Maaligai"*, the house of fulfilment and perfection. He considered In January 1872 the opening ceremony of the shrine of *"Satya Jnana Sabhai"* at Vadalur in abstentia, by sending a lamp lit and blessed by him to be installed there for worship.

He became so much one with the Divine Grace Shakti that one day, as directed by the Divine, He informed the disciples by a short notice and had all arrangements of decoration and formalities made for his marriage with the Divine Grace Shakti Herself. He married Her symbolically within an hour of the divine direction. From that unique and cosmic moment, Ramalinga expressed having invincible power in him for performing all the five-fold universal function: 1.Creation, 2.Maintenance, 3.Destruction for purification, 3. Control and renewal, 4. Involution, and 5. Evolution and also all the siddhis or miraculous deeds of divine perfection.

In the last part of his life beginning from 1871 he began to preach incessantly on the deathlessness of the human body as an essential part of the realisation of the Divine. He affirmed deathlessness of his own body and that he got triple indestructible of the physical, subtle and causal (*i.e., Suddha deha, Prana deha and Jnana deha*). He began to promise about the coming of the Suprime Divine as God of the Vast Grace-Light in the near future to rule on the earth directly; and that all religions God would go away and lose their influence; and end the sectarian religious and philosophical schools of discipline will fall away and be replaced by the

"Samarasa Suddha Sanmarga Satya Sangam", That is the fellowship for the integral and harmonising path of purity, truth, right and harmony. He made the forecast that the rule of Kali Purusha of Kali Yuga will end by 1899 and the rule of Jnana Siddha of the new era will begin.

ON RAMALINGA VALLALAR

Ramalinga, popularly known as vallalar, the Great Munificient, may be regarded as the foremost of the saints and sages of our time, considering the heights, widths, depths and intimacies of his integral realisation of the Divine in all the "inmost, inner, outer and the outmost parts of his being. Vallalar had a magnetic personality. A fascinating face, strangely haunting, eyes beaming with compassion and grace.

Uran Adigal wrote in Tamil, *"To those who have not been blessed to see Vallalar, it will be interesting to say, such was Vallalar, such his colour, such his presence".*

It is said that the blessed saint had a body which transcended photography. His human body could not be caught on the film by photographs. Ramalinga Vallalar did cast no shadow.

In personal appearance, Ramalinga was a moderately tall, spare man – so spare indeed as to virtually appear a skeleton – yet a strong man, erect in stature, and walking very rapidly; with a face of clear golden complexion, a straight thin nose, very large fiery eyes with a look of constant sorrow on his face. Towards the end he let his hair grow long; and what was rather unusual with yogis, he wore shoes. His garments consisted only of two pieces of white cloth. His habits were excessively abstemious. He was known to have hardly ever taken any rest. He was a strict vegetarian, he ate only once every two or three days, and was satisfied with a few mouthfuls of rice. But when fasting for a period of two or three months at a time, he literally ate nothing, living merely on hot water with a little raw sugar cane dissolved in it.

He was a yogi who put before the people deathlessness of body as an essential part of the realisation of the One blissful Divine, a saint whose very soul-stuff was made of infinite love and compassion, a sage of Truth-Consciousness who possessed the Divine Knowledge and the science of deathlessness of body and attained its deathless transformation along with the self-creative power of creating all substances of whatever kind including bodily substance. He was a born Tamil-poet of divine inspiration who could distinguish the various level of inspiration and who received in silence the

"Word of Truth and Grace from the Chit-shakti of Grace in the transcendence of Chit-Sabha, the transcendent and universal world of Truth-Consciousness".

Besides, he was a critic, writer and commentator and had knowledge in occultism, alchemy, astrology and medicine, particularly in the nutritional and medical values of herbs and leaves. He was a musician too, with a keen musical taste for lyrical songs and he composed lyrics to express, in an easier and popular style, his highest and sublime relations with the Divine.

Of the six volumes of *"Thiruarutpa"*, the poems of divine inspiration, the last volume is unparalleled in spiritual history as it gives expression to the realisation of the vast world of Truth-Knowledge and the Beyond and touches on subjects like transformation and deathlessness body. If any sort of comparison has to be made at all or even for its own proper understanding, it can be done only with reference to the proper understanding and with reference to the vast and infinitely detailed spiritual and yoga literature.

Ramalinga was the one who affirmed openly and clearly in an unmistakable language the deathlessness of his body which he attained by the power of what he called *"ArutPerum Jyoti"*, the Vast Supreme Grace Light of the Divine which he identified as the Truth-Light of Knowledge, *"SatyaJnana Joti"*.

RAMALINGA'S PHILOSOPHY

Vallalar gradually started realizing God as the supreme power manifesting throughout the universe. Vallalar was immensely moved by the divine power of the Lord of Chidambaram. Here, Lord Shiva appeared both in form and without form. One can experience that which has a form by seeing it and feeling it. One can visualise that which has no form by imagining it or contemplating it. Vallalar experienced both the characteristics of form and formlessness in Jyothi (Light), the divine light. It has a form because one can experience it and see it. It is also without form because one cannot feel it and it is likely to be extinguished.

Vallalar believed that the Eternal Truth remains unrevealed and it is the Jyothi, the Vast Grace of Light, that causes the revelation of truth; a subject is able to perceive an object only when the reflection of the light falls on the object. If a precious stone meant for public display, is kept in a dark corner, it never gets noticed. It needs the focus of a light to bring out its full value in sparkling brilliance.

The power of Jyothi is highlighted in all religions. It forms the foundation of all thoughts, all activities and systems. Jyothi is the eternal divine power that first originated in the universe. The cause of all actions, whether physical or chemical, is energy or heat. The source and origin of energy or heat is Jyothi. The Jyothi is invisible and merges with the energy. It is present everywhere; in sun, moon, light and fire. The universe operates within its own inherent energy. There is self-sustaining energy in every atom or human cell. It is this energy that causes all movements and all activities. Jyothi gives the sustaining-power and life to all, and there is Jyothi in every soul (Athma Jyothi). Rig Veda (the main Vedic text), says the significance of Jyothi is beyond human comprehension. Brihadaranyaka Upanishad says:

"Oh Lord, lead me from unreal to the real,
from darkness to the light,
from death to immortality,
May there be peace, peace and perfect peace."

As Jyothi gets manifested in different forms throughout the universe and within every human soul as Divine Power, Vallalar advocated the Jyothi form of worship. He said that the Supreme Lord had revealed to him the powerful Mantra of Divine Light.

"ArutPerum Jyothi – Arut Perun Jyothi
The Vast Supreme Grace Light – The Vast Supreme Grace Light
ThanipPerumKarunai, Arut Perun Jyothi
Supreme compassion, The Vast grace of Supreme light."

Another important aspect of Vallalar's philosophy is Jeeva Karunya Ozhukkam, which means having a compassionate outlook towards all lives. It refers to one's attitude towards all fellow beings and towards all other creatures like animals, birds etc. Vallalar could not bear to see the agony of people suffering from hunger. He stressed the quality of compassion for all. The privileged ones should help the less privileged and service to humanity is equal to service to God.

God created all living beings, within which Manhas been endowed with intelligence. He was supposed to respect and take care of nature as the whole, including the mineral, vegetal and animal kingdom. Unfortunately, he turned out to be the biggest threat for their survival. Man has silenced the feeble voice of his consciousness coming from his heart, surrendered to the dictates of his mind and fulfilled the nefarious demands of his body. According to Vallalar, he or she only is entitled to receive God's grace who lives in harmony with nature and shows compassion towards God's creations. He who takes non vegetarian food forfeits his privilege to seek entry into the temple of God.

Vallalar wanted the whole humanity to integrate into one single objective, the divine unity of souls, based on supreme compassion. The path of Sanmarga symbolizes truth, love and discipline which leads to the highest stage of divinity and immortality. Vallalar underlined certain principles which formed the foundation of Samarasa Sudha Sanmargam, the path of truth and purity.

SUDDHA SANMARGA

God is one. He is Arut Perum Jyothi, the Vast Supreme Grace Light.

All are children of one single God and there is no caste, religious or regional differences.

One should recognize the divinity in every soul, respect it and live in peace and prosperity, in a spirit of love and unity.
Compassion towards all fellow beings and compassion towards all living beings, should form the basis of all actions.

To reach God, tread the path of simplicity and humility and not through rituals or extravagant way of worship.

Vallalar established Samarasa Sudha Sanmarga Sabhai as the medium to translate his ideals into practice. The term Samarasa means equanimity, the concept that encompasses all religious thoughts and respects all faiths and religions. The term 'Sudham' implies purity and sublimity. Sanmargam means the right and truthful way. In short, it is a philosophy that transcends all existing spiritual thoughts and shows the perfect way of truth. It emphasizes the importance of discipline which Vallalar classified as discipline of senses, the disciplines of the mind related to the mental faculties, Attitude towards fellow human beings and acquiring the knowledge of the soul. Vallalar also stressed the importance of charity. He considered food offering "Annadhana" as the most sacred duty of all. Vallalar dreamt of the day when hunger and poverty would completely be eliminated. He established Dharma Salai as a humble effort towards this direction. The Salai continues to render its inestimable service to the society even now.

The philosophy of Sudha Sanmarga, meaning Pure Gathering, built on the concept of love and compassion, aims at purifying the body, enlivening the mind, enriching the intellect and enlightening the soul, the different steps that lead to immortality. This philosophy follows the path of simplicity and discipline; a path where there are no human distinctions. Usually, a seeker, bound by various attachments in the world, finds many obstacles in his spiritual journey. The family ties, the properties, passions, prejudices, attachments and affiliations are binding one, incapacitating one for any meaningful action.

Vallalar has anticipated the upcoming of many ills plaguing humankind. A humanity steeped in ignorance, in which, people are following certain outmoded customs, dogmas, beliefs and various practices. The need of the time is the transformation of the socio-religious-concepts or mis-concepts and change in way of life. Vallalar felt this need. He wished everyone living in the spirit of universal brotherhood, showing compassion towards all lives.

Vallalar perceived God not as an identifiable image, not necessarily in the form of an idol and not restricted to any religious, philosophical believe, concepts and dogmas. He perceived God as all-pervading divine power. He pointed out the lacuna in the prevailing practices and sought to dispel many ill-conceived notions. He sought to dispense with various practices like rituals. He sought to remove the artificial barriers and unite all aspirants under one common platform. He then took the role of a reformer, introduced the universal and uniform concept of Jyothi worship and Sudha Sanmarga.

Some expressed doubt whether these concepts tantamount to deviation from our established practices. Vallalar only wanted to rid the society of certain aberrations while retaining the basic values. He wanted Sanathana Dharma to flourish, took the role of a gentle reformer and brought about a renaissance. God himself manifested as Adi Sankara and Ramanuja to give the direction and guidance to humanity. Many great saints and reformers appeared in this land from time to time to give the correction as the changing conditions in consciousness necessary. Vallalar has rightly come into that lineage.

Hinduism is never a set of codes or dogmas. It is a way of life, ever vibrant, ever seeking the truth. It is all-tolerant, all-comprehensive, all-absorbing and always reforming itself in the process. The strength of Hinduism lies in its infinite capacity to adapt. "Let noble thoughts come to us from all sides" said Swami Vivekananda. In a changing world, every order has to change in accordance with the necessities of time. Hinduism has come a long way from how it was practiced some 500 years before. It has evolved, over a period of time, correcting itself and reforming itself according to the demands of the time.

Ramalinga believed in the dignity of man and emphasized that religions should respect this dignity. He was the embodiment of compassion. When he saw people suffering for want of food, it reminded him of falling young plants drying up for want of nourishment. He expressed this feeling in one of his songs thus:

"I felt sad seeing the falling ear of tender plants, withering for want of nourishment. I felt sad seeing frail people crestfallen for want of food." ("Vaadiya Payirinai Kanda Pothellam Vaadinen").

He led a life of virtue, abstinence and discipline, though he prayed for all people, accepting their vices as his own. He always wore spotless clean white cloth around his body that symbolized gentleness and peace. He looked serene and majestic, his sparkling eyes conveying the message of love. He spoke in a low gentle tone. Even while singing, he maintained a low pitch. Perhaps, one could hear his voice raised while speaking for vegetarianism. He performed many acts of miracles but never agreed that he consciously exercised such powers or even possessed them. He not only fulfilled the aspiration of the soul but also healed the body. He was a good physician who prescribed clean diet habits, exercise, Pranayamam and Yoga for good health.

Vallalar believed that just as the soul, body also undergoes a spiritual transformation by the grace of Jyothi. When the body functions independently of sense organs, it becomes pure. When the soul within is sublime and sacred, it implies that the body in which the soul lives is also pure. Just as the content is pure, the container also has to be the expression of purity and sanctity. As a result of spiritual transformation, the body assumes a stage of divine Golden Deathless Body. It continues to remain in this divine stage deriving its own inherent energy and then attains immortality.

UNFURLING OF THE RAMALINGA'S SANMARGA SANGHA FLAG

Ramalinga unfurled the flag of his sanmarga Sangha on October 22, 1873, making the day as its effective beginning and also gave the Mahamantra of the Vast Grace Light by Divine Authority, to the disciples on the same day since he was actively expected the coming of the God of light to the earth for his direct reign. About this period, he also expressed his will to enter into all physical bodies (i.e., on a universal level).

DEMATERIALISATION OF RAMALINGA'S DEATHLESS BODY

In line with his belief, Vallalar believed to have attained immortality. On 30th January 1874, Vallalar drew some of his close disciples near and said:

"I wish to confine myself in the room here. Do not search for me and if you do, you would not find. I believe, God has willed it that way and I hope it would happen that way".

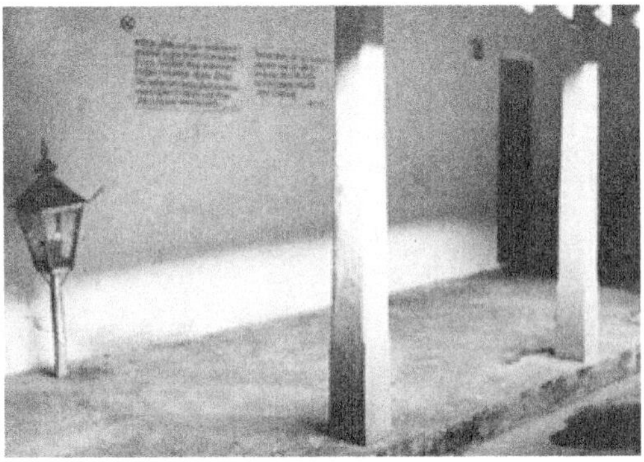

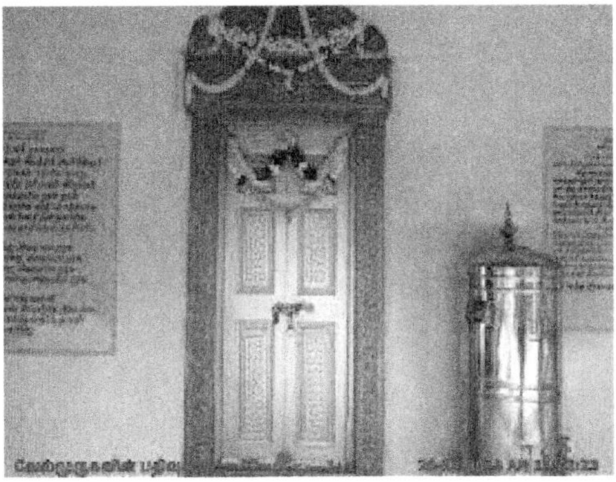

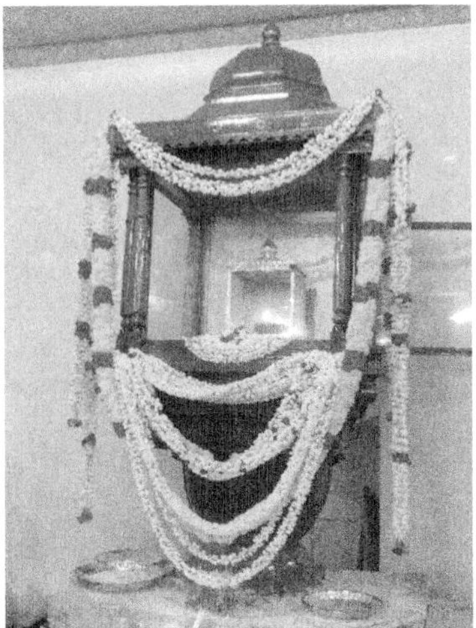

Then, he did withdraw in seclusion in a closed room in Mettukuppam, promising the disciples that the God of Light was imminently coming, and he would disappear from their sight for a period and would come back when the Divine Light become manifested. From his last song, message and spoken words, it is seen that his dematerialisation of his deathless body occurred in the divine presence and in the process of the stable manifestation of the Supreme God of the Vast Grace-Light on this earth. Thus, the dematerialisation of his body was a sacrifice and a consecration for a supreme purpose.

A RARE VISION OF THE DEMATERIALISATION OF RAMALINGA'S SUPRAMENTAL DEATHLESS BODY

As experienced by Sri Gangadharan

It was by a rare virtue "Punya" that on the first day of the Tamil month Thai (14-01-1978), I had a continuous Vision between 2 and 3 a.m. in my usual meditation in the night. The vision of dematerialisation of the physical body of Ramalinga into and as the Truth-Light of Supreme Grace which contains or possesses in itself Supreme Compassion and Bliss of Grace.

sometime in the Truth-World of Grace-Light wherefrom I could see the earth as part of the universe, the said vision came to me when my consciousness was on the earth itself, though aware of the Truth-World and the Beyond.

To begin with, I sensed an ineffable Silence and Peace (Para Shanta Mauna) prevailing everywhere and I heard continuously Para Nada. The mysterious divine sound in that Supreme Silence and Peace. Then the Vision broke out.

A small village in its simple and beautiful surroundings, though not endowed with a rich beauty of nature. There was the concrete Presence of the Supreme and Universal Divine with the beautiful Truth-Grace and Fragrance, which enriched the place and enraptured my heart with ever increasing aspiration for Grace. At the centre of the village was seen a small house standing in its purity and peace from where, sweet fragrance of Grace radiated everywhere.

Vallalar, the Great Munificent, was seen entering the house. His face was calm and peaceful. He was seen as the very embodiment of Compassion and his body was filled with the Fire of tapas of Truth-Consciousness as the Purity of the Supreme Divine (Suddha Deham). His whole body was radiating the Light of Grace. Besides, his body was silken or light-golden shining colour. He entered into the veranda and kindled the wick of a burning oil-lamp and it began to burn more brightly. Then he stepped into his room and closed the doors and bolted inside.

At that time there was the Concrete Presence and Universal Divine in the room. The presence could be sensed even physically and even by the born-blind. There was also, silence, peace, fragrance and the Light of Grace due to the Presence.

Vallalar sat on the white cloth spread on a low wooden plank and began to concentrate. In that poise he was seen as a Mountain of Truth-Knowledge with the Truth-Light of Grace and Peace along with the Fire of Tapas. He was verily a Supreme form of the Divine. Flood of Light was radiating from his pure and luminous body into all directions.

Supreme Grace, Supreme Compassion and the Light of Grace are expressive of the secret truth that hold the key for the transformation of the physical body into the deathless body of Grace in its state of eternal youthfulness. One has to live in the depth of the ocean of Blissful Grace Light for getting transformed into the divine nature and as a divinised body.

The intensity of the flood of Light that radiated from his whole body was very powerful and one shall have the strength and capacity to bear and receive it. My whole body vibrated with a joy and blissfulness because of the Vision of Light of Ramalinga's body.

After some time of concentration, he rose up and saw the physical sky. Full moon was shedding its blissful cool rays over the earth. A little distance away from the moon was seen a very bright and concentrated Splendour of Light. It appeared like a bright dazzling star of Light. Ramalinga poured his concentrated gaze at it for some time. His heart became enraptured with blissful joy, which radiated on his face. A little time thereafter, he again sat on the white seat on the plank and entered into deep concentration.

Though Ramalinga was inside the closed and bolted room, he could see clearly the whole universe "Vishwa Prapancha" with its tiers of many worlds of mind; life and the physical including the physical earth and sky with its moon, stars and clouds.

When he was thus absorbed in deep meditation, an effulgent Truth-Light of Grace broke out from his heart and with its unique heat began to burn his radiant physical body very slowly, as if at a snail's speed, and that in an upward direction, from the heart towards the head. The burning of the body may be somewhat likened to that of an incense-stick which however burns downwards by its inner heat of fire, forming ash-covering but without the falling down of the ash-form.

When the upper part of his radiant body was burnt completely from heart to head, there was lets in its place a form of pure white substance, which radiated its Light of Consciousness. The burnt part, however, showed all its features intact and clearly as well as the burnt hair of his head which was seen distinctly as luminous white hair. Then the Heat of the Pure Light of Grace descended to burn the lower part.

After the whole body was burnt, Ramalinga was seen as a bodily form of pure white substance from head to foot, radiating it's Light. Even the blood has changed into a white luminous substance. Ramalinga white body of light had kept intact all the different kinds of cells of his body including all the distinctive features and formations, interiorly as well as exteriorly. Ramalinga's bodily form did not shrink in size after the burning. I saw no visible flame nor sensed its heat during the burning of his living body, nor smoke, nor any bad smell as burnt tissues, nor heard any cracking noise as burnt bones. But instead there was a sweet fragrance since the time his body began to burn as it spread everywhere. I sensed in my heart an ineffable Calmness and Silence, which gave me in turn a state of bliss.

Then, a second stage of burning began with the unique heat of Grace-Light began to burn slowly Ramalinga Luminous Form of White Substance from head to foot downwards. When his White Substance-Form was full of its radiating Light, it was burn completely. The White-Substance became very fine sub-atomic consciousness particles which permeated and pervaded the conscious particles with its radiating light which also entered into and got distributed everywhere in the earth, even in matter and in the inconscient. After the universal pervasive distribution of the particles, they could be seen no more and disappeared from my sight. But now, there is a sweet, soft and fine fragrance of camphor pervading everywhere, which gave my body a blissful sensation and enraptured my heart as well.

Then I had the rare vision of Ramalinga's Universal golden Form. As a matter of fact, the immensity of his golden form contained in it the whole universe (Vishva Prapancha). This form too disappeared from my view and was replaced by another vision in which I saw the Golden Light of Truth-Knowledge and Grace entering into all directions more speedily than the lightning. It permeated and pervaded the whole universe and the further Pure Worlds of Consciousness. It entered into our earth and its cores of the physical forms of beings and objects, in the apparently insensible matter "jada" and even in the dark realm of the vast inconscient. All the forms that were permeated by the Golden Light of Truth changed into golden forms of beings and objects. The Golden Light entered into my whole adhara including the physical body. My body felt in all the cells vibrations of ease and pleasantness.

Then I heard some words of Grace, but they were indistinctly heard and could not be deciphered, as I was absorbed in a raptured of Bliss due to the sublime vision and experiences.

Thus, the vision lasted an hour of time and came to an end.

INSPECTION AND CONFIRMATION OF RAMALINGA'S DEMATERIALISATION

Ramalinga was never seen thereafter, and the place of his disappearance was soon inspected by the ten District Collector and Medical Officer who have reported, confirming his disappearance. One can very well feel today the spiritual and supramental forces of deathlessness in the pace of his las resort i.e., Siddhi Valaga Maligai at Metukuppam, in Vadalur where the shrine of Satya Jnana Sabhai stands as a symbol and monument in honour of the coming of the Supreme Divine to the Earth.

That marked the end of a great sage or the beginning of a new age. That marked the end of a glorious chapter of Vallalar that opened up a new chapter for man's eternal quest to know the truth. That marked the end of a period of darkness that heralded the advent of a new era of awakening, the era of light and Jyothi.

May the light of love, the light of grace he kindled radiate its brilliance all over. May the beacon light he lit brighten up the world. May the flame of grace he brought bring a sense of unity and peace all over the earth.

RAMALINGA'S AURA AND ESSENCE OF HIS TEACHING

When Vallalar was staying at "Siddhi Valagam", at Mettukuppam, he was used to remain absorbed in the Bliss of Supreme Grace Light for some days continuously, and then he would come out to give discourses to his disciples. Purushottama Reddiar, who served Vallalar as his personal attendant during Vallalar's stay at Karungkuli and Vadalur, continued to attend on him at Mettukuppam also. In the last periods of his life, Vallalar was used to drink a sugar-solution prepared in hot boiling water, that is to say, the water was boiled so as to be reduced to three-fifth of its quantity and then the sugar was added to it. The attendant would prepare and take it to Vallalar who drank it as such in its boiling state. The said attendant would sweep and clean the rooms and inner apartment where Vallalar used to remain absorbed in his blissful state, and feed in time the sacred lamp (originally lit by Vallalar) with oil and keep it trimmed and ever burning. One day he happened to enter Vallalar's room for his daily routine. It was just the time, after a blissful absorption, Vallalar had just opened his eyes of Grace when he met incidentally (or rather by an act of Grace) the eyes of his attendant. At once, his attendant was transported into a trance of higher consciousness, and he remained absorbed in it. Other devotees were surprised to know about the incident and asked Vallalar what was to be done with the said Purushottama Reddiar. Vallalar replied "Do not disturb him. After four or five days of unmoved and absorbed trance, he got up to move out, but yet he remained still in a state of silence continuously for months without speaking to anyone. It was this attendant who once, had asked Vallalar to show him Grace, by giving him a Sadhana, i.e., a way of practice for his spiritual development. Vallalar said:

"You are as humble as I am. If you do sadhana (i.e., practice of yoga discipline such as meditation) you may receive some light within and the power to do some siddhis (i.e. lower siddhis of an occult nature) and you would grow proud of them to boast of and you would get ruined. So, you do not need any sadhana. You may just follow the practice of seeing all beings as your own self (i.e., cultivate the vision of equality with all beings) and get it as your habitual nature. One who gets in his nature this habit of seeing all beings alike, is certainly the omnipotent Divine".

Then by Vallalar's blessings Purushottama Reddiar took up the work of receiving all the visitors and devotees coming to Vadalur, with warmth and tenderness of love, and served them with food and drinks at the Dharmashalai, after making kind and due enquiries, as to their needs in that respect. Thus, with his attitude of equality, tenderness of love and dedicated and humble service to one and all alike he carried out many and varied functions, notably as secretary of the Dharmashalai and Satya Gnana Sabhai for many years in the later part of his life. It is not surprising that Vallalar poured on him his eyes of Grace and uplifted him to a state of higher consciousness, as happened in the foregoing incident at "Siddhi Valagamaliga".

In Karunguzhi, Ramalinga had his house by the side of the road, and He was a friend to every man. People flocked to him for advice and relief. Reference to this may be found in some of his verses quoted earlier. People from distant places left their homes to be near him. They invited him to function and musical recitals in their houses. Such invitations to him are extant. They considered it a blessing to be of service to him. Spending days and nights in meditation and composing poems, he gave discourses in the house or in the Sabhai at night, and they flocked to listen to him. In

Venkata Reddiar's house in Karunguzhi, the mistress of the house, Muthiyalammal herself used to light the lamp in his room and keep near it a mud pot of oil, with which to refill the lamp. One day, the mouth of the pot broke, so Muthiyalammal wanted to change it. She bought a new pot, filled it with water and let it stand beside the lamp, in order to season it before use. Then she left the house for the next village. Writing his poems through the night, as he often did, Vallalar mechanically kept refilling the lamp with water, from the new pot instead of oil from the old. When Muthiyalammal returned the next morning, she found Vallalar absorbed in writing, and the lamp burning. She discovered his mistake which, without any conscious mess on his part, had resulted in this miracle. That's was the says, Vallalar who used to keep a record of his experiences and refers to this in a poem, attributing this kind office to God, and not to his own powers. Thozhuvur Velayuda Mudaliar and Madurai Chidambara Vallalargal also refer to this in their tributes to their master. One could fill pages with miracles that the legend attributes to him, but it would be wearisome. Appasami Chettiar, one of Vallalar's admirers, used to come to Karunguzhi from Cuddalore (then called Gudalur) to see his master. Having had his brother cured of an indolent sore on the tongue by the grace of Vallalar, he put his hospitality at Vallalar's service. Vallalar stayed with him for some months in Cuddalore in 1866, to widen his Mission. It appeared that towards the end of his Karunguzhi years, with the founding of the Sanmarga Sangam, Vallalar felt that he had sufficiently prepared himself for his mission in life. He spoke like any inspired prophet, with a sense of his mission derived from God and from his living in God:

"The Lord sent me to this world to help men that abuse the earth, Blotches of black within and white without, to restore them and set them on the path of the high quest, so that they may attain the fulfilment of the soul on the earth here and now. For this He blessed me with His Grace."

He gave his call in no uncertain terms:

"Men of the world, you have missed the truth, your body was fed on rot, your mind remain only at a surface level, your learning goes down, your joy is deception, your ears listen only to the tribal, your sight only look at the past. Hear the truth of the common final path. Seek the Grace so you may gain a life of rejoice and an undying body. And again: I say only what the Lord tells me, no words plus or minus Indeed, by myself, what wisdom do I have but what the Lord gives me?"

After founding the Sanmarga Sangam in 1865, he stayed in Karunguzhi for two years, visiting now and again the places in the vicinity. During one of his visits to Cuddalore, he mentioned to the fellows of the Sangam his intention to build a free feeding house which would be opened to all, irrespective of caste, creed, country and habits. They suggested various places for its location. Finally, Vallalar himself chose an open plain, north of Vadalur, a village also called Parvathipuram, about thirty kilometres from Chidambaram. The open space was at the meeting of two highways, one from Madras to Kumbakonam, and the other from Manjakuppam to

Vridhachalam. On getting to know this, the people owning the land (amounting to eighty kanis or one hundred and eight acres) at this site, made him a gift, in a deed dated 2 February 1867, bearing the signatures of forty owners. A temporary building of mud, thatched with reed grass, was erected. The feeding of the people in the temporary hutment, the construction of permanent structures, the digging of a well, pond and tank for the Hall were started on the same day with a ceremonial opening. A thousand printed invitations were issued to the public. Invitations, written by Vallalar by hand, were sent to sadhus or ascetics. It is stated that one thousand and six hundred people were fed daily for the first three years. The feeding of the hungry and whoever calls there continues to-day. At the opening of the Eating House on 23 May 1867, Chidambaram Venkatasubba Dikshitar read out extracts from Vallalar's tract Jivakarunya Ozhukkam (The Discipline of Compassion). The foremost Vallalar's message was compassion for life. This, he said, leads one to God. There were two aspects concerning compassion, he said. One is non-killing, including rejection of animal food, the other is relieving hunger. His tract on compassion has reached noble heights of poignancy. He named the Free Eating House Samarasa Veda Dharma Salai (Free House of the Good Fellowship).

The word which connotes a free feeding house in Tamil is chattiram. Avoiding this with its associations, he chose the word salai which means `path'. He changed later the name as Samarasa Suddha Sanmarga Satya Dharma Salai, or Satya Dharma Salai (Path to Charity). The same year he founded a school, Sanmarga Bhodini (School for the Fellowship). The unique features of the school were that it was opened to all, irrespective of age, boys as well as old people, and that three languages were taught - Tamil, Sanskrit and English, specified in that order. Thozhuvur Velayuda Mudaliar, a reputed scholar in Tamil as well as in Sanskrit, and proficient in English, was in charge of it. The school however did not run for long. During this time Vallalar also planned to bring out a monthly magazine called Sanmarga VivekaVriddi. A prospectus was issued, signed by forty-nine people, including one Muslim, named Kadar Sahib, who undertook to contribute monthly towards bringing out the journal. But the journal was never published.

VI - THE SUPREME AND ULTIMATE SPIRITUAL PATH

SUDDHA SANMARGA – THE TRUE AND PURE PATH LEADING TO SALVATION AND DEATHLESS BODY

The main objective of the "*Samarasa Suddha Sanmarga Sathya Sangam*" is to provide all the tools to everyone to be educated in the Art of immortality. Immortality represents the highest ideal of human existence that is to be blessed with Eternal Beatitudes of the Supreme God. This giving rise to a body free from disease, aging and death. Ramalinga said:

"Despite the different religions that have spread over the face of the earth for decades for the welfare of humanity until today, people have continued to die and to be buried in the ignorance of reality. I am asking you to understand the importance of my request to spread the common path of "Suddha Sanmarga".

It is with the objective of establishing this common path, beyond any cleavage, that Ramalinga founded in 1865 an association of devotees and people with common interests, called "*Samarasa Suddha Sanmarga Sathya Sangam*".

Before going further, let's see the meaning of the words that makes up the name of this society open to all without exception, whatever their race, colour, caste, religion, belief, nationality or language. Ramalinga wanted to establish on earth a philosophy, namely a way of life ignorant castes or sects, God of second order and expiatory sacrifices as well as superstitious cults. It is to this effect that Ramalinga created the "*Samarasasuddha SanmargaSathya Sangam*" the pure universal path of truth.

Ramalinga wanted the all of mankind to be integrated into a communion directed towards one single objective, the divine unity of souls, based on

"Jeeva Karunya Ozhukkam", Supreme Compassion. It is possible for one who follows the path of truth to attain the ultimate stage of realisation. The word truth has a wide range of ramifications. God is truth, the Absolute Reality. Truth alone would triumph and one who adheres to truth reaches God ultimately. According to Vedanta philosophy, *"Sathya"* meaning truth is what is not subject to change, which is eternal, infinite, beyond time, space and knowledge and shines on its own. God is truth, the Absolute Reality. Truth alone would triumph and one who adheres to truth reaches God ultimately.

The path or "**Marga**" refers to the means one adopts for attaining the truth.

The word *"Samarasa"* means universal, open to all.
The word *"suddha"* means pure, ideal. The word *"San-margam"* symbolises the path of truth, love, compassion and discipline leading the devotee to the highest stage of divinity and immortality.

Ramalinga has defined 4 Margam or pathway to attain immortality:

1- *"Dhaasamaargam"* Becoming the servant of all living creatures.
2- *"Satputhra-Maargam"* Becoming the son of all living creatures.
3- *"Saha-Maargam"* Considering all living creatures as their friends and reciprocally.
4- *"San-Maarga"* Considering the life of all living creatures as one's own life.

When Born, we have only one identity, the "Self" or the "Atman", but as we grow, we get different stamps of identity, based on religion, country or region, caste and creed bringing unintended and unnatural division. People belonging to each faith believe that their religion is supreme. As each religion started asserting its superiority, religion and not God, took the centre stage. Instead of bringing the all world family under one umbrella, Unity, religion has only contributed dividing people. Gandhi himself said God has no religion, because He is the primal cause of life in the entire universe. He infuses life to all races and species. He bestows his compassion to all lives and graces them all to flourish and prosper, irrespective of which religion they belong to. Religions are different mode of expressions of the one and same God. Despite its inherent sanctity and despite being an effective vehicle of life, religion only limits people to a particular faith or belief.

Adi Shankara had said that human race has made three "wrongs" for which he craved pardon of God.

1. We have given form to the God who is formless.
2. We have described, by our own imaginations through songs and hymns, the God who is indescribable.
3. We have confined within the four walls of a temple, God who is Omnipresent and all pervading.

God is one Supreme Being, one without a second, a single universal, infinite and eternal power.

Ramalinga viewed God as a universal power, not confined to any human boundaries or divisions; the God whose grace extended beyond time, space and beyond human comprehension. He visualised a universal God, beyond country, region and religion, and called for a uniform, universal mode of worship. He saw God manifesting as *"ArutPerum Jyothi"*, The Vast Supreme Grace Light who is all compassion, *"Thanip Perum Karunai"*.

Ramalinga adopted the truthful path, to attain the end of truth, the means and the end being the same. In order to fulfil a noble objective, one has to follow the noble path as well. The Sanmarga which symbolises truth, love, compassion and discipline leads the devotee to the highest stage of divinity and immortality.

SUDDHA SANMARGA'S ATTAINMENTS "PURUSHARTHAMS"

By pursuing the right and truthful spiritual path of Sudha Sanmargam as preached and practised by Ramalinga Vallalar, the following four attainments could be obtained:

1. Transformation of the physical body into a golden body by means of changes effected on the body by the Effulgence Grace (**Eama Sithi Seithal**).

2. Acquiring the knowledge of changing the mortal physical body to a deathless one **(Saaha Kalvi Kattral)**.
3. Controlling the activities of all the mental faculties and not to be distracted by the false views/illusions created by the mind, etc..., **(Thathuva Nikraham Seithal)**.
4. On realizing the nature of God, attainment of the state of "oneness with Thee" **(Kadavul Nilai Arinthu Ammayamathal)**

THE UNIVERSAL CREDO OF THE SANMARGA PATH

1. There is only one God, *"ARUT PERUM JYOTHI"*, the Vast Supreme Grace Light, who is present in everything and in all living beings.
2. We love and cherish God in the form of Light with pure love.
3. The gods of second order are not worshiped.
4. No sacrifice of living beings is practiced.
5. No flesh coming from living creatures is consumed.
6. There is no difference between castes, religions, sects, etc...
7. All life is considered as one's own life, based on the principle that all live has the same value in the eyes of God. Contrary to certain societies that have emerged in India and abroad, The Universal Brotherhood of Suddha Sanmarga's principle considers all living beings, from animals, plants to human beings as equal.
8. Giving food to the hungry opens the door of the kingdom of heaven.
9. The dead is buried and not cremated.
10. All beliefs, habits and superstitious practices are denied.

"The Samarasa Suddha Sanmarga Sathya Sangam" was proclaimed by Ramalinga as the society of people who follow the 4 Maargams, which are the very essence of the teaching of "Thiruarutpa", The Universal Wisdom scriptures destined to the followers of all religions.

This human life is a precious gift of God to humanity. It is meant to be lived in peace, happiness and harmony. Unfortunately, the life today is generally not directed towards the way it was intended but through a different path, resulting in unnecessary anxiety, fear and tension.

DESIRE - THE ROOT CAUSE OF ALL PROBLEMS

The root cause of all disease is desire. Even from childhood, the mind starts generating desire. As one desire is fulfilled, another one crops up till disappointment sets in. While fulfilling desire for basic necessities of Life is legitimate, desire to acquire wealth or power beyond certain limit leads to various problems.

Desires satisfy the false sense of "I", more commonly known as ego. The realisations of desire such as wealth and power, provides the ego with an imaginary sense of pleasure. The ego, the creation of the mind, projects a false notion of pride and in the course of projecting this false notion, the individual loses all sense of morality, ethics and decency. It is said that, he who frees himself from desires realises the Glory of Atman, the Self. In Thiru Arutpa, Ramalinga expressed all his gratitude and love to God for having been blessed with a steady mind free from such impurities.

The mind acts as a recipient or storehouse of all pasts memories which get expressed through the thinking process. The mind never rests for a while and hovers around various objects of illusion. It clouds our thinking process and detracts our attention. It generates evil thoughts like lust, passion, anger, avarice etc… whatever knowledge gained and whatever achievements made are all nullified by the mind.

Saint Thayumanavar said:

"You may control a mad elephant;
You may shut the mouth of a bear or tiger;
Ride over a lion and play with a cobra;
By alchemy you may earn your livelihood;
You may wander through the universe incognito;
make vassals of the Gods; be ever youthful;
You may walk on water and live in fire;
But control of the mind is more difficult."

HOW TO BE FREE FROM THE MIND

Through the practice of "Sat-Vichaaram" as explain below, and the way of meditation that is a constant pouring out of love and compassion towards all living beings, for all true seeker of God; such love becomes both the means and the end.

"The ignorant prate that Love and Siva are two,
But none do know that Love alone is Siva.
When men but know that Love and Siva are the same, Love as
Siva, they ever remain."
-Thirumandiram verse 270

"To him who renounces, no kith or kin has he;
To him condemned to beg, no true delights has he;
To him who charity less is, the Lord denies His Presence;
By the measure of thy charity done,
The Lord is known to thee."
-Thirumandiram verse 256

SELF-INQUIRY / SAT-VICHAARAM

In his great sermon, Ramalinga advised everyone to not waste time in vain since time is pressing. For those who want to evolve faster on their way to freedom and Supreme Bliss, Ramalinga has emphasised the necessity to be continuously involved in self-inquiry, the inquiry about God and the soul, about the divine life in order to free ourselves from the veils of illusions. This practice is called Sat-Vichaaram which means the removal or destruction of misery and sorrow. Self-enquiry (Vicharam) is enquiring about, what is our human situation, what is the nature of the powers that lie beyond us and move us? What is the nature of self-existing Almighty God who is mastering and ruling us, being seated above all of us?

Accordingly, everyone should do Sat-Vicharam; either individually solitary or collectively, along with amicable friends who are harmonious, fit to your intelligence, knowledge and discipline. Through the regular practice of self-inquiry, the foremost three veils black, blue and green colour, which obstructs strongly our soul-knowledge and prevent enlightenment will get removed and vanish. If those first veils vanish, all other veils will vanish more quickly and automatically. We should appeal to the Almighty Grace-Light, Arut Perum Jothi with continuous thinking and singing with prayer for the removal of the so-called thick veil and also realizing our short-coming and faults combined with needs, even when we are sitting and relaxing by lying down on bed or other; and also we should make efforts with devotion and Divine Love so that the real truth will be revealed to us. This Sat-Vichaaram is of two kinds:

1) Param, the self-inquiry related to the Supremely higher One, Arut Perum Jothi.
2) Aparam, the self-inquiry related to the lower World of the Divine, the manifestation of worldly activities upon earth.

Between the two, the one related to this world is not correct. Because if anyone is involved in Vicharam: it should be not considerate as standard. Vicharam is revealed only if we refer to para loka-Vicharam, that is the inquiry about the Divine world and the Divine life. Just as we remove the fungus above the stagnant water of the pond, it is not easy to remove the thick dark green veil of the likes and dislikes which obstructs the vision of our soul knowledge. Without the transcendental heat of Divine self-inquiry, this kind of Divine causal heat can't be realized by the spiritual experience of the adept Yogi. Only for creating this heat the Yogi go and live in forests, mountains and caves, for hundreds and thousands of years, the Yogis have gone tremendous penances, severe tapas, strict observances and self-control. This Divine heat is not known to be created or kindled by this type of human efforts. Even more than that, through Vicharam exceedingly great heat can be created by doing melting prayer, praying with devotional song combining together with meditation and thinking about the Divine nature, about the Truth and Glory of the Lord. By practicing Vicharam as it has been described, it is possible to create thousands time more inner heat than the Yogis have been doing. How can we produce the heat coming from Vicharam? If we can seat three or four hours continuously involved in the practice of Vicharam, we can attain and achieve whatever we have to attain.

In this world, worldly people would refer to Vicharam as misery and sorrow without knowing or understanding the real truth and meaning of Vicharam, in Tamil the meaning of Vicharam, at the first level is, vi: remove and charam: sorrow.

Moreover, somebody may ask: Oh! This is the best occasion or proper time for the advent of the Almighty Arut Perum Jothi.

Why is it necessary to do efforts at the time of the manifestation of God? Can't we attain and achieve whatever we have to achieve when the Supreme Grace Light will manifest on earth?

Yes, it is good asking this question. it is really true that the Almighty is to be manifested and that the veil and the dark screen is going to be removed by Him. It is also true that you will achieve or obtain whatever you have to obtain.
But the already mentioned dark green veil or screen which is connected with the dislikes and likes, is existing at two levels. The green veil is the door between AsuddhaMaya (impure Maya) and Suddha Maya (pure Maya).
1) The AsuddhaMaya veil: which is related to the impure kind of Maya or illusion, is base at the lower portion, the dark-green veils which includes the black and blue veils. They represent the aim and tendencies of

searching the joy and pleasure in the outside world, having forgotten that the source of lasting happiness and peace is within oneself.

2) The Suddha Maya veil: which is related to the pure kind of Maya, is based at the upper portion. Suddha Maya is related to achievement and perfect realization or Paraloka, the Divine world and life.

When the Almighty will manifest, He will grant favour by His Omni Grace. He will remove only the Asudha Maya veil at the lower part of ordinary human beings who had produce no effort in practicing the True Self enquiry, Sat Vicharam. When the lower veils are removed it is possible to be blessed with purity so we can be purified, but we can't achieve any wish and goal of perfection. We can't obtain the Divine favour of performing the five divine functions of creation, production, purification, involution and evolution by the blessing of Grace, along with other siddhis or supra-natural powers of perfection.

Only if we live with a continuous effort practicing Sat Vicharam the veils of AsuddhaMaya and the upper veils of Suddha Maya can be removed. At this point the following veils will be removed quickly. Therefore, if one generates enough good and sincere efforts, it is possible to gain proper and sufficient benefits and profits.

By looking at the philosophical art's and mythological stories such as the Vedas, Ahamas, Puranas, Ithihasa… because they are like imaginary arts of symbolic and hidden Truths, they did not reveal the real fact, the authors of those books had veiled and obscured the truth, as though somebody is covering with soil and dust over a death body. Even without revealing with a little atomic measure, they had symbolically represented the micro-cosmic "Pinda" superimposed upon the macro-cosmic "Adan". For example authors had named and represented the Almighty as Kailasapathi, Vaikuntapathi and Sathyayokaayhipathi, and also imaginarily constructed the proper shrine which have become the vehicle, the inner mould, the external form…made exactly like a human being which had forgetting the Truth, they had expressed their imagination itself as Truth. If anybody enquires about it: does the Divine God possesses hands and legs similar to a human being? They hesitate and get wildered without knowing what to reply. The later followers, calling or naming themselves as great men, had puff led and bluffed nonsense things by closing their eyes of Truth vision. But the ancient one who had covered and hidden the Supreme Truth where a great adept of genius and powerful person. Till now, nobody had discovered and found out what he had veiled and hidden, what he had locked or covered, no one had struck and broken the lock that he had sealed.

In the false religions, some occult power or Siddhi had been imaginatively promised. If we try perseveringly for ten to eight years for every siddhi, it is impossible even to attain little siddhis. If we put our goal or aim for these siddhis, will get deviated away from the goal towards the Almighty God. If the aim of God realization goes, at last the great profit or benefit will go in vain. otherwise, if anyone tries for a long time, and attains a little siddhi, the great gain or soul benefit will go away. Therefore, let no one aims at the little siddhi but at the Almighty God only. It is possible to attain super-human powers and to work miracles. But do not aim at these. The smaller gains are not worth-while: they rob you of the bigger, true gains, the knowledge of the soul-consciousness.

Therefore, un-distracted by desires, let your mind dwell wholly on God... Likewise do not pin your faith in religions. They do not give you the spiritual experience born of true knowledge... Ramalinga told us that the faith he had in Siddhantha Philosophy was hardly possible to exaggerate. His poems and prayers in his books are standing testimony to this. Ramalinga once told: "The reason why I had such deep faith then was my lack of true knowledge. Now God has raised me to a pinnacle. This is because I gave it all up. You may likewise gain divine life if you likewise abandoned everything, all attachment. If you do not surrender entirely to the Almighty, you will not gain any profit.... If anyone think that the attachment and aim on the religion had lifted me up, it is a mistake. What have lifted me is Dhayavu, the supreme compassion. In my early prose writing, I viewed all Gods and Devas as the shadow or similitude of ArutPerum Jothi, up to when I realize, that the only truth is the one of ArutPerum Jothi. Only Dhayavu the supreme compassion and Orumai the oneness or the unity feeling of the soul is necessary. Only when this unity of the soul is realized the compassion will emerge or manifest, from there we can go to the greatest heights. From this Oneness of the soul, my knowledge had transcended so many millions of universes (Adams). If anyone who is obstinate and does not come along with my path or does not heed to my words, or obey my advices and instructions, in whatever manner, but behave rudely, I will try my best to bring them to the path using skilful stratagem by:

1) Saying good or friendly words.
2) Teaching good thoughts to them, even by using a threat voice to awaken them.
3) Falling at their feet, surrendering with obedience, so they become more receptive to my words.
4) Giving money and other desirable objects and gift, so they can become under my favourable cooperation.
5) At least, I will try my earnest prayer. Likewise, I will bring anybody to come to the path of virtue and goodness of compassion and Grace.

Let all of you also try and pursue, like me in the same method and manner. Even during the previous night, I had been appealing and soliciting with prayers to the Almighty "Arut Perun Jothi", that without my active presence, even for a second, the people here would feel at home and live satisfactorily. That is not meant only for the people living here but for the ones living all over the planet, because all are my brothers and sisters, all souls are melted into One. If anyone does not come to the path of discipline and perfection, I will try my best as there is little short time before the manifestation of the descent of Grace Light upon the earth, the collective evolution is coming soon...

Many people come to me putting their power in my hands, considering me as the Divine embodiment or Godhead. O pity, they do not understand. The reason why they think like this, is that they did not experience the Divine directly. For this reason, may you be involved in doing Sat-Vicharam, the true self inquiry. The enquiry is as follow:

What is the real position and status of the sun, the moon and the stars in the macrocosmic universe (Adam)? –

Who is in this physical body, the microcosmic form (Pidam)?

What is the reason there is overgrowth of hair on the eyes-brows, arms-pit...?

What is the factor and reason for the hair, not growing upon the parts of the body, like the forehead?

What is the reason for the emanation of germination and their further growth of the nails on the fingers of the foot and hands?

What is the inner form, outer form and self-existent Nature of them?

Likewise, one should enquire about the microcosmic phenomenon (Pindam). This should be done uninterruptedly and continuously. If we do self-enquiry and create carelessness or no desire for the worldly enjoyments, the state without desire would be attained.
And hence the fifteenth state of yogam in gnanam will be attained (see what are the four margam), which is among the four kind of steps of divine practice, like:

1) Saryai, the Divine discipline and observance.
2) Kiriya, the Divine action or divinely deeds of devotion…
3) Yogam, the Divine union.
4) Gnanam, the Divine wisdom. Then the third step of Yogam in Gnanam, whereas:

1) **Gnana- Sariyai, the 13th level of consciousness. In the 13th State of Consciousness:**

"The Lord and I have become one mold and He has separated from me, giving his body of bliss."

"In embracing the purpose of the Divine, I reached a body without death by receiving pure Light."

2) **Gnana-Kiriyai the 14th level of consciousness:**

In the ascension, "the soul that has been realized as the center or soul-form and soul-movement of the divine, One,

Transcendent and Universal, joins him in the 14th state of consciousness.

3) **Gnana-Yogam the 15th levels of consciousness**
"It was in a state of supreme bliss that I joined him, melted in Him and became Himself in the (15th state). "I became Himself" I realized myself as the soul centre of the Divine and became myself enjoying the state of Oneness with Him, a state of I-He in Him. O Lord of the Game of the Knowledge of the Vast-Light-Golden that I have become"

4) **Gnana- Gnanam the 16th level or state of consciousness.**

"O Supreme Divine! The high-seated level of experience is that of the complete and perfect existence of bliss. "
"I became one with him in the state of Suddha Siva Turya."
"It became the space of the vastness of heaven (16th space). He plays in the excellent Heaven of Knowledge. He became the King, the Lord, abiding and sorting in me, in a play of loving relationship."

If you involve yourself fully in this sadhana, the Almighty will reveal to you limitedly for the conditioned knowledge… At this moment, the Almighty "ArutPerum Jothi" had removed or abolished everything untruthful. Everything is been revealed to me in order to attain the supreme, soul bliss, with the favourable help and guide of the primary sadhana, for the ultimate experience or enjoyment of the Divine Bliss of eternal blissful life…

The Divine commandment of our Almighty "ArutPerum Jothi" is as follow:

As our first and foremost sadhana or spiritual practice is Karunai, the discipline of soulful compassion, the Almighty had taken explicitly this Divine formula as the foremost practice or primary sadhana, as:

"Arut Perun Jothi, (Vast Supreme Grace Light)
Arut Perun Jothi, (Vast Supreme Grace Light)
Thanip Perung Karunai, (Vast Unique Compassion),
Arut Perum Jothi, (Vast Supreme Grace Light),

Dhayavu – Supreme-Compassion, the Omni-grace of Arul will reveal itself at the end; the soul-knowledge with supreme compassion itself which is the fully perfect Bliss.

The meaning of this Secret Formula is the Supreme knowledge with Supreme Compassion.

If you surrender yourself to this sadhana there is no reason to find any obstacles on the path to the ultimate realisation, the complete joy of Divine Bliss…

Whatever Veda or truth knowledge, you take as the word of belief or faith, you can only realise…In accordance with the path I have been telling you to follow. Then, you will have a life based on truth, knowledge and bliss.
Till now, there have been no prevalence of Suddha Sanmargam, the absolutely true path of compassion and eternal blissful life. Moreover, even the dead would have got resurrected back to new spiritual life.

Only now, is the period for Suddha Sanmargam; to witness this truth the flag has been unfurled, it is the external symbol representation that there is a system of plexus, starting from the navel and terminating at the eyebrow centre. At the fore end of the forehead, there is a membrane hanging within. The base or bottom of that membrane is of white colour, whereas the upper part is of yellow gold colour. Bellow this membrane there is a nerve moving up and down in simple harmonic motion. This kind of flag could be realized in our soul experience. Only to refer to this experience, symbolic colours had been unfurled. Furthermore, better experiences will be revealed for all in our soul knowledge. Even when I started to reveal the truth, as I had been ordained to do so, there is none, to understand and realize this fully. The Samargam flag is unfurled externally so that everyone can realize the truth. Those who had come earlier with this mission of messengers to reveal the truth had not only hidden the truth but also obscured it as though throwing mud and soil upon the truth… If you persist in this enquiry, God will come to you and reveal to you what is fitting. When you develop further, He will let you know more. For a while, after me, none will be forthcoming to counsel you. For that reason, do not continue on the path of indifference. This is my last word to you. This is true, true, true, and true as this is the Divine commandment or the ordained decree of the Almighty. "Arut Perum Jothi – Arut Perum Jothi Thannip Perung Karunai –Arut Perum Jothi.

To be able to have good success with the practice of Divine self-enquiry, it is necessary to have some foundation.

To understand how the mind functions and what is the nature of the mind? Have some knowledge about meditation and prayer and some experience of contemplation.

The practice of Divine self-enquiry is a combination of prayer, meditation and silence or contemplation. I would try to explain what I mean by this.

1) The Divine enquiry is like a prayer, you are not enquiring to yourself but to the Divine "ArutPerum Jothi", because you are addressing yourself to Him, it is a prayer. You must put yourself in a situation, where you are begging the higher force to give you an answer, you are becoming vulnerable and your heart is opening.

2) You must stay in your Divine manifestation, maintaining a high vibration; this is possible if you remain concentrated in the present moment, by keeping your attention onto the eyebrows, the access door to the divine spark within your soul, so you can become receptive. This is meditation.

 3) As you get deeper into the practice your inner heat and vibration will grow to such an extent, that there is no more effort of concentration. You are immerging with Divine Grace Light. In this moment, the presence of the enquiry and the silence for the answers come by themselves. This is Divine contemplation with Divine self -enquiry.

RAMALINGA'S JYOTHI MEDITATION

Ramalinga was highly recommending to meditate on a form not on the formless. He said, Later, when the form dissolves naturally into the formless state, from "Dhwaidam" one is taken into "Adhwaitam", in that state the Observer is annihilated, this is Adhwaidham or Advaita. The observer's object melts in the natural state of Advaita, pure silent-space-consciousness.

Yoga and meditation on the formless will tend to feed the spiritual ego in us, which itself will trigger the sympathetic nervous system and act accordingly to release cortisone hormone instead of triggering the parasympathetic nervous system to release Gaba neuro transmitter, "Amritham" (concentrated glucose to sustain body with less calorie intake) in the physical body.

Doing that for our own ego self, will not be able to give the full benefit in attaining salvation. It takes time to quit meditation as it has been understood so far since we have been enjoying it for decade.
The Supreme Divine has now chosen this Maha Mantra of Vast Supreme Grace Light, "ArutPerum Jyothi", so as to openly express and manifest the Truth of His being, so that all may attain the great life of bliss by the help of this mantra sadhana.

Ramalinga has revealed to all the mantra in the same way as he has received from the Divine Himself, so that all of you may realise, without any doubt, the integral Bliss of "Sat Chit Ananda" which Ramalinga enjoy in the Truth-Consciousness of His Being.

Ramalinga explained that there is a universal concept that the Divine Light is existing everywhere in its full-fledged form. But its exposure is realisable only in the perfect soul of the compassionate man.

THE WAY TO MEDITATE

As you concentrate on the flame, (the flame representing the Supreme Grace Light) with your eyes open, the attention turned on the midpoint between the eyebrows, you sing the Mahamantra "Arut Perun Jyothi -

Arut Perun Jyothi - Thanip Perun Karunai – Arut Perun Jyothi" with a heartfelt devotion and love.

Once the mind is calm, you remain in awareness, feeling the Mahamantra, chanting quietly in the mind, while allowing yourself to go within this space of silence opening up before you.

When thoughts are coming back, it can be any kind of movement crossing the mind, we come back to the initial practice, you contemplate the flame, (the flame representing the Vast Supreme Grace Light), with your eyes open, the attention turned on the midpoint between the eyebrows, you sing the Mahamantra "Arut Perun Jyothi - Arut Perun Jyothi - Thanip Perun Karunai – Arut Perun Jyothi" with heartfelt devotion and love.

From the calm and soothing state of the mind, you will experiment different states of intrinsic awareness as void spaces filled with bliss.

SURRENDER TO THE LIGHT

When one stands praying before the Light, deprived of his ego sense, in a completely surrendered form, its non-dualistic attribute begins to fill up his entire body, and his entire life get nourished with that. In due course, the entire body gets transformed into that mystic Light form. This body attains deathlessness.

This Light Divine body becomes the emancipated form of Man and this is termed as "DAEIOU" here. This word represents both God and the Eternal Man in a singular form. This "DAEIOU" Man alone will be living Eternally in Blissful life.

FAITH

Ramalinga said that Faith is a gift from God which can be accessed through Divine Grace. One way to get in touch with Divine Grace is to use the Jyothi Mantra "Arut Perum Jyoti", to invoke Grace, Light and Compassion. For that reason, Ramalinga suggested to seat before the oil lamp placed in front of a mirror which radiates its eternal Light of Grace, as the representation of the Supreme Grace Light, while having the attention between the eyebrows, *"Ajna Chakra"*, middle point of the forehead, being the direct access door to our soul located in the midst of our brain, the medulla oblongata, and sing the Mahamantra with upper devotion, love and gratitude to the Vast Supreme Grace Light, to get the experience of the Grace Light.

Ramalinga gave us the Mahamantra that He received directly from God's source:

Arutperunjothi – Arutperunjothi
Vast Supreme Grace Light, Vast Supreme Grace Light
Thanip Perun Karunai – Arutperun Jothi
Compassion Supreme or Supreme Mercy of the Lord- Vast Supreme Grace Light

This meditation is done with an attitude of love and gratitude towards God, a state of awareness, which we may practice at every moment during the day.

It is "ArutPerum Jyoti" that enlightens the intellect with eternal knowledge; knowledge that cannot be sought anywhere in scriptures or taught by anyone, the knowledge that forms the foundation of eternal light and wisdom (Odhatu…23-24)

As Ramalinga received this Mahamantra, he realised that this Jyoti Mantra would illuminate the heart of all, illuminate the world, remove darkness from the face of the earth and bring Divine Knowledge, Truth and Bliss. Having received this Mantra of Divine Effulgent Light and enlightened within, Ramalinga said:

"The Vast Supreme Grace Light is eternally burning in my heart, shining on its Divine Law of Truth and deriving its Infinite Power through which I became immortal."

Having received this Mantra, Ramalinga passed it on to his disciples for the benefit of all. Ramalinga has revealed to all the mantra in the same way as he has received from the Divine Himself, so that all of you may realise, without any doubt, modification and obscurity of consciousness, the integral Bliss of "Sat Chit Ananda" which Ramalinga enjoy in the Truth-Consciousness of His Being.

By the meditative chant of this universally appealing direct mantra of the divine as Supreme Light of Grace (Gangatharam) one can have the most powerful and integral experience in which the Vast Supreme Grace Light of Supreme Grace linked the truth – world of Super-Mind with the whole universal manifestation (Visva Darshana) and vast – nether Realm of the inconscient darkness.

It is readily seen that if an integral mantra at the best can give supramental transformation of the body "Arut Perun Jyoti" Mahamantra is all the more necessary for transformation of the body into its deathless state, because the Light of Grace invades and illumines the inconscient darkness which is the strong fortress of the dark power or god of death. This mantra received directly from the Divine by saint Ramalingam and soon given by him to the disciples and devotees in his last days, when he had already attained the deathless transformation of his body – that is, before its dematerialisation in 1874, for the universal manifestation of the Divine Grace – Light directly on the earth has an immense significance and value for the humanity which is seeking for an individual as well as a collectively evolution of its earthly life of ignorance into a Divine life of Bliss and Knowledge, and for the unity of the world and mankind.

The following stanzas from Ramalinga's Jyoti Agaval highlight the infinite quality of Jyoti.

It is Arut Perun Jyoti that pervades throughout
The vast space and bestows grace to those following

The path of Sudha Sanmarga.
(Sudha Sanmarga 29-30)

It is ArutPerum Jyoti that elevates the devotees
To the highest stage of realisation; Truth-
consciousness-Bliss.
(Sachidhananda 49-50)

It is ArutPerum Jyoti that forms the foundation
Of all Vedic Scriptures,
Of all spiritual doctrines and of all knowledge
(Vedakamangalin 57-58)

It is ArutPerum Jyoti, emanating its eternal flame of light
From Sathya Jnana Sabhai
That remains as the ultimate center of knowledge and power
(Sekaramam 79-80)

It is ArutPerum Jyoti, that does the Dance of Bliss
As its stage of vast space
And radiates the light of happiness throughout the universe.
(Vaduthal 101-102)

It is ArutPerum Jyoti that transcends all boundaries
Of religion, region and caste and has no beginning or end.
(Sadiyum 115-116)

It is ArutPerum Jyoti that transcends all identifications,
Bodily, mental and intellectual identifications
And reveals the true experience.
(Dhanukara 117-118)

The Power of Jyoti refers not merely to a flame or Light, it is the very foundation of life, the very basis of this universe and signifies the fundamental concept of truth. In Agaval, Ramalinga describes the four manifestations of Jyoti, Suyam Jyoti as being the Self, Param Jyoti as denoting the Vast Grace Light prevalent throughout the universe, Arul Jyoti which pertains to the Divine Light that is inherent in the entire space and expressed by way of Grace. The Transcendental Power of Truth symbolised by Lord Siva which is indescribable is expressed in the form of Siva Jyoti.

INVOCATION TO THE LIGHT

ARUT PERUM JOTHI, ARUT PERUM JOTHI,
THANIP PERUNG KARUNAI ARUT PERUM JOTHI
JOTHI JOTHIJOTHI SUYAM, JOTHI JOTHIJOTHI PARAM
JOTHI JOTHIJOTHI ARUL, JOTHI JOTHIJOTHI SIVAM
VAMA JOTHI, SOMA JOTHI, VANA JOTHI, GNANA JOTHI
MAGA JOTHI, YOGA JOTHI, VADHA JOTHI, NADHA JOTHI
EAMA JOTHI, VIYOMA JOTHI, EARU JOTHI, VEERU JOTHI
EAGA JOTHI, EAGA JOTHI, EAGA JOTHI, EAGA JOTHI
AATHI NEEDHI VEDHANE
AADAL NEEDU PAATHANE
VAADHI GNANA BADHANE
VAZHGA VAZHGA NADHANE

ARUT PERUN JOTHI : Vast Supreme Grace Light.
ARUT PERUN JOTHI : Vast Supreme Grace Light.
THANIP PERUMG KARUNAI : Supreme compassion.
ARUT PERUN JOTHI : Vast Supreme Grace Light.

MEANING OF THE WORDS

Jothi which is the root of all forms is Suyam that is "one which is not been produced but formed by itself."
The same Jothi is in the state of "param" that is the root and the cause for everything in the universe".
Jothi is "Arul", one which is in the form of absolute compassion".
Jothi is also "Sivam", one which is inside every atom, inseparable".
"VamaJothi", Jothi as in the form of the sun.

"Soma Jothi", Jothi as in the form of the moon.
"VanaJothi", Jothi as in the form of immeasurable ether or space.
"Gnana Jothi", Jothi as in the form of knowledge of space.
"Maga Jothi", Jothi as in the potential atom of the soul.
"Yoga Jothi", Jothi as in the manifestation of the soul.
"VadhaJothi", Jothi as in the action, the driving force of the soul.
"NadhaJothi", Jothi as in the bliss (Omkara Nadham) of the soul.
"EamaJothi", Jothi as in the everlasting immortal effulgence.
"ViyomaJothi", Jothi which is omnipotent without a smallest interval of space in the universe.
"EaruJothi", Jothi which is not interrupted by any forces.
"VeeruJothi", Jothi which is orchestring all actions at all levels in the universe and beyond.
"EagaJothi", nevertheless Jothi remaining to be one and oneness with all the above attributes.
"Aadhai Needhi Vedhane": one which is the truthful king of all living beings right from the days of beginning.
"Aadal Needu Padhane": the holy feet of one who is activating all atoms through His uninterrupted movement.
"Vadhi Gnana Bothane": it is the one who is the true Guru for the beings who are contemplating on how the above actions are taking place.
"Vazhga Vazgha Nadhane": hail the glorious Lord, the glorious Lord.
« Vallal Malaradi Valga Valga Ella Uyirgalum Inputru Valga ».
Let prosperity, prosper at the lotus feet of the one who gives freely.
Let all beings live in absolute felicity.

THE OMNI-GRACIOUS INFINITE LIGHT

The Omni-gracious Infinite Light is the Supreme attribute of God, expressing out from the innermost and spreading out to form into all material, physical, vital, mental, intellectual, spiritual and gracious stages in the universe. This functioning is the outcome of that Divine Infinite Light. This Light of Eternal Self-Existence is not to be sensed by the ordinary knowledge of man; but it can be realised and practically experienced by the perfect gracious knowledge of a soul, who will realise that he is that Divine Grace itself, and acknowledge its Light as his life and body. Thus, One Supreme Grace-Light alone, is eternally expressing itself in the universe, for the purpose of bringing out the never-ending Blissful life in the form of perfect man.

At present, man is in the penultimate stage in which he is undergoing all kinds of pleasant and painful experiences in the passing world In his Divine Life stage, Man tastes the existence of All Powerful Soul-God, and from there, he gets bestowed with a good amount of Divine Gracious Power to enjoy and live the Blessed life for an appointed time; and finally he vanishes from the worldly stage. This was thought to be Moksha, enlightenment or merging in God. No other end was contemplated or realised by any person on this earth till now. Nor was there any exception for anyone to live here eternally. But now, by His Omni-gracious ordainment, that Eternal Divinity itself has come out to live in the form of Ramalinga.

Saint Ramalinga – the Real Man, has found himself nothing but the inner Divine Light itself, and lives from that higher plan extending that Light throughout his whole being. Thus, that Divine Gracious Light of God has come to occupy in the whole being of Saint Ramalinga, to finally make him Arut Prakasa Vallalar (meaning the All-Giver of Gracious Light Being). This highest Omnigracious achievement is new to the whole humanity. Now the end or the goal of man's spiritual evolution is found in endless life, as that of God Almighty.

This comes to indicate and confirm, that it is only the Omnigracious Light of God Almighty which is taking step by step possession of human being, transformed or metamorphosed into the Eternal Divine Being.

THE SEAT OF THE VAST SUPREME GRACE LIGHT FOR ALL MANKIND

SATHYA GNANA SABAI – TRUE TEMPLE OF WISDOM

To attain the deathless blissful life, the whole humanity is directed towards the Omnigracious Divine Light, set up in the True Temple of Wisdom,

Vadalur *"Sathya Gnana Sabhai"*. It functions like a beacon light radiating the spirit of love and compassion to all corners of the world. In his song named *"Chidambara Malai"*, Ramalinga said that those who worship the Jyoti at Sathya Jnana Sabhai with a heart full of compassion and a mind without any difference, elevate themselves to the world of supreme consciousness and bliss. One should qualify himself for worshipping here by observing certain discipline in his life which Ramalinga classified as discipline of the body, of the mind, of the senses and of the soul.

The Sabhai is not a temple in the traditional sense. In keeping with the concept of Jyoti worship, an oil lamp is placed in front of a mirror which radiate its Eternal Light of Grace. It is place in the centre of a lotus formation, pointing out the Grace of Light in human soul. Ramalinga established the Sathya Gnana Sabhai, the Hall of Wisdom, to mark the advent of the Universal God as a Vast Supreme Grace Light. It has taken shape as a Temple that would transmit his message of Divine Grace Light to the universe. It is a unique Temple in which the Eternal Flame of Light "Jothi" is shining in its full glory at the centre. A devotee can reach here only by removing the 7 layers of curtains, symbolizing the different layers of ignorance covering his soul. He announced that powerful mantra which God Himself revealed to him, *"ArutPerum Jyoti – ArutPerum Jyothi – ThanipPerumKarunai – ArutPerum Jyoti"*. He exhorted the people to follow this Mantra that would get them Divine Grace and elevate them to a new world of Truth-Bliss-Consciousness and Pure knowledge. He requested the people to receive this spiritual power and get the Vast Supreme Grace Light. A seeker, pursuing his spiritual journey, is not able to move forward because he is bound by several chains: the family ties, the properties, passions, prejudices, attachments and affiliations all binding him, imprisoning him or her from any meaningful pursuit. The 52-iron links that are symbolically forming a chain which surround the Gnana Sabhai, tell us that one who is determined and dedicated can overcome these chains one by one, liberate himself and realise **"Arut Perum Jyoti"**

DHARMA SALAI

Ramalinga believed that hunger and poverty are the evils of society. He advocated that feeding the poor as the highest form of worship. Dharma Salai was created by Vallalar, as the very core of His **"Samarasa Suddha**

Sanmarga Sathya Sangam" at Vadalur, for feeding the poor. On the inaugural day in 1867, Ramalinga lit the fire of the stone stove with the declaration that the fire continue burning and the needy be fed forever. As per the declaration, Dharma Salai provides food to everyone irrespective of caste and creed throughout the year.

Ramalinga had the Divine Vision that compassion is the "**Master Key to spirituality**". He has shown his compassion and mercy not only for human being but also on plants, insects, birds and animals. This Ramalinga called "**Jeeva Karuyam**", (Mercy to all life). That is why he said, Vaadiya Payirai Kandapodhellam Vaadinaen. He opposed the superstitious beliefs and rituals. He emphasized on "**being a vegetarian**". He did forbid the killing of animals for the sake of food.

The primary teaching of Vallalar is "Service to mankind is the path to Moksha" (the ultimate path to enlightenment and deathless body). The path of compassion and mercy are the only way to God said Ramalinga.

"SUDDHA SANMARGA" DISCIPLINES
BEGINNING OF THE DAY

1- Waking up early in the morning before Sunrise (around 4 am), meditate on God in sukasana sitting posture for a while with spine straight.

2- **Chew** Bettle nut + $CaCO_3$ – optional for celibates, **discharge** the fecal-urine waste. Have a complete ablution with warm water. Then, brush your teeth.

3- Apply Karisalanganni paste on upper palate, moves slowly to uvula, stimulate vomiting sensation and wipe bile and white fluid.

THE 4 DISCIPLINES

1. Discipline of the senses (Indiriya Ozhukkam)
2. Disciplining the mind and related mental faculties (Karana Ozhukkam)
3. Attitude towards fellow human beings (Jeeva Ozhukkam)

4. Acquiring the knowledge of the Soul (Aanma Ozhukkam).

1 – DISCIPLINE OF THE SENSES (INDRIYA OZHUKKAM)

This discipline has been classified into two parts:
A – The senses of knowledge "Jnanendriya"
B – The senses of action "Karmendriya"
It is advised to listen to devotional song and spiritual teaching and avoid disharmonious and crude sounds.
To have a gentle touch rather than an impure one.
To have a kind look rather than unkind and cruel.
To not search for special, pleasant and outstanding taste and smell.
To speak only soothing and pleasant words.
To not lie.
To avoid and stop, by all means, any types of violence inflicted on all beings.
To meet with holy people
To visit holy places where people in search of God are living in order to render service to them, and also to other places where service is required.
To have positive and compassionate action to all the people in needs.
To take moderate amount of food.
To have moderate sex.
To have a normal condition of urine and faeces, without allowing them to be excessive or deficient.
To preserve the seminal fluid in order to have a healthy and long life.
To not practise sexual indulgence on the body and mind.
To always cover the genital organs continuously.
To cover the head and chest like parts continuously.
To wear foot wears while walking.
To always wear clean dresses

2 – DISCIPLINING OF THE MIND AND RELATED MENTAL FACULTIES (KARANA OZHUKKAM)

Do get poised keeping the attention on the centre between the eyes-brows Ajna".

Do not allow the mind to dwell on bad and evil thoughts.

Do not think or dwell on other's mistakes and ill-conduct.

Do not cultivate feeling of self-importance and too much dwelling on ourselves.

To become a true sattvic (pure) nature with the clarity and joy of consciousness by transforming anger, irritation, jealousy, pride, vanity etc…

To not express anger onto others;

Do control the movement of "tatvas" (the lower nature of the mind) from their excesses or outrageous behaviour.

3 – ATTITUDE TOWARDS FELLOW HUMAN BEINGS (JEEVA OZHUKKAM)

This is the virtue of considering all human beings, both men and women as equals without differentiating them on the basis of their caste, creed, race, religion, philosophy and social status and to treat all of them as one and the same as we are.

4 – ACQUIRING THE KNOWLEDGE OF THE SOUL (AANMA OZHUKKAM)

The soul that is present within the bodies of all living beings ranging from small creatures like the ant to the big ones like the elephant is *"Thiru Sabai" (Sacred Place)* and the *ever-shining Grace-Light* within the soul is God. It is, therefore, necessary to realise thy Presence everywhere and in everything and remain with the sense of Oneness without duality.

Anma Olukkam is further development of Jiva Olukkam. Here the soul looks upon all living beings alike (not only human but also sub-human beings also). Here, the soul feels great compassion for all the beings; It considers "Anma" as the "Sabhai" and the "Inner Light" as God.

Saint Ramalingam clearly said that "Jeeva Olukkam and "Anma Olukkam" are possible only with the help of Divine Grace.

To attain Divine Grace, one must follow the "Indriya Olukkam" and Karma Olukkam". Ramalingam explained to his disciples that in order to attain the supreme goal of spiritual development of Samarasa Suddha

Sanmargam, the deathless life, one may follow and apply these disciplines. Then, one will certainly attain the Karma Siddhi, Yoga Siddhi and Jnana Siddhi and the body will change into Swarna Deha, Pranava Deha and Jnana Deha. Thus, the disciplines of saint Ramalingam aims at the deathless life. Ramalingam emphasized discipline as a fundamental requirement. He clearly gave warning notices to the people who behaved in an undisciplined way. He said: "undisciplined life is not a life at all."
Samarasa Suddha Sanmarga is not mere theories and beliefs, it is a practical path, a path of Truth and Purity, based on disciplines, to guide everyone, to live a fulfilling life, leading to the highest pinnacle of spiritual evolution.

If the above mentioned four virtues/principles are sincerely and faithfully practised by the followers of Suththa Sanmarkam, the four Purusharthams (Attainments) mentioned in the opening paragraph could be achieved.

SUPREME COMPASSION

THE KEY FOR ENTERING THE KINGDOM OF GOD

To reach God, one requires the key to open the doors of then trance to His fort. The Key to it is Grace. This can only be obtained through love and not by any other way; the love towards God and the love towards all living beings. One cannot express love towards all living beings unless one is feeling and expressing compassion to all. Without compassion there cannot be love, and love results in compassion.
According to Ramalinga, Compassion is the only way to redemption. The enlightenment gained through compassion is the only enlightenment by which one can have the vision of God, and the bliss one enjoys through that, is only God's Bliss, and only those who have experienced this in full are those who have understood God properly, achieved Him and become God.

He says that the Yoga Jnana (true wisdom), tapas (penance), Vratham (vow), Japa (repetition of God's name continuously), Dyana (mental prayer – meditation) performed, cannot make one get the Grace of the Almighty. These different practices done without compassion are all nothing but jugglery.

Compassion may be defined as an expression of love, kindness and concern towards another being, an eagerness to share the sorrows and sufferings of others and a willingness to help and serve others by all possible ways. Ramalingam Vallalar calls it "Jeeva Karunyam Ozhukkam" (a compassionate way of life), a virtue that is the essential condition for receiving the Grace of God. Compassion does not mean a mere expression of sympathy or love. It is not an act of generosity that one does after all his own needs are fulfilled. It is also not an act of help or service rendered at an opportune moment. Compassion means going out of the way of comfort, being pro-active and seeking those who are suffering, identify their needs, helping them not only in coming out of their crisis but also guiding them into the way of God realization. He whose heart pours out in sympathy and compassion towards the sufferings of others and renders instant help merits the grace of God. Where there is no compassion, there is no knowledge, no order and no discipline, it will be wilderness.

No other spiritual doctrine emphasizes the importance of compassion as vehemently as saint Ramalingam's Jeeva Karunyam Ozhukkam. The prominence given to the question of compassion in Vallalar's philosophy has even evoked some criticism. They argued that while pursuing a spiritual goal, one should concern himself not with the plight of others which is the result of many factors like karma, planetary in fluencies etc....One should rather concentrate on himself, look inward and aspire to reach the highest end of self-realization. When the seeker needs to mobilize all energies, the act of being compassionate towards others might change his priority and hamper his ultimate objective. Besides, "Self" is supreme, and self-realization is God-realization, compassion is an aspect that relates to Jeeva. Jeeva is only a limited self, the expression of life in an individual which is conditioned by body and mind influence. Does it not mean that one is shifting his priority from the Supreme Self of Sat Chit Ananda to the physical and mental needs of the limited self?

Compassion is not a diversion from the main path towards God, it is a path by itself. According to Vallalar, one can acquire the Power of Grace only by walking on the path of compassion. Every soul is the manifestation of the Divine Power. While some undergo sufferings and hardship, others live in affluence and prosperity. As every soul is divine, the privileged people are the fortunate one, who can mitigate the sufferings of the less privileged, and share their happiness with the less fortunate. The Natural Laws are naturally based on compassion and concern for all living beings. The Natural Laws demand that all human beings live in a spirit of goodwill and harmony. "All human beings are part of Natural Truth of God and they have the same characteristics. Since all the human beings have been brought into existence in a human body made up of all the five elements (earth, water, fire, air, akasha) and the 96 tattvas (constituents or principles of existence) by God's Power of Grace, they are of the same kind and all of them do have one and the same right. Therefore, we can say that we are all brothers and sisters, part of the same family, the family of humankind. Thus, when one brother sees, hears or knows that one of his brothers or sisters is grieved due to a danger, he or she, naturally considers the body of the other as the body of his own brother and due to the right he has for the body, his soul gets melted for him or her. In the same way, when a human being is grieved due to a danger, his soul gets melted because he considers that living being as the being made up of the same soul as he is. He should, therefore, be aware that it is the right of the soul.

COMPASSION TOWARDS A LIVING BEING IS THE HIGHEST FORM OF LOVING GOD

The soul being divine, compassion "Karunyam" is the natural manifestation of the soul and it is expresses itself whenever anyone is suffering. The soul being the manifestation of God, doing service to others is doing service to God. Every human soul being divine, being compassionate towards all souls is the way to move closer to God. As compassion forms the basis of all human actions, by being compassionate, one gets the Divine Grace Power which takes one to the ultimate stage of realization.

Some people might consider that compassion is a human element, relating to body and mind and that it has no place in spiritual pursuit. When someone is suffering, it relates to his body or mind. Similarly, it evokes a reaction in the mind of others. It should be noted that the body and the mind are mere instruments of action "antakaranas" and not real. In other words, spiritualism is concerned with realization of the "Self" where mental or sensory perceptions have not role to play. This view of demarcating the function of the "Self" on one side and the body and the mind on the other side is untenable. The body is the house where the soul resides. When something happens unexpectedly in a house, it is not the house but the resident of the house that feels concerned about it. Similarly, when a person wearing a spectacle witnesses a tragic event, it is the eyes that shed tears and not the glasses. So, when a mind or body is wounded, it is as much the concern of the soul. The mind and body would experience the happiness or sorrow, but it does create an impact on the soul as well. In short, only in a condition where the body and mind are healthy and functioning in harmony, the soul can move forward smoothly towards its ultimate goal.

THE REASON OF SUFFERING AND SORROW

Why should there be sorrow at all in a world created by God? Why there is so much acrimony, ill-will and suspicion? How come there is poverty and hunger in a world endowed with enough resources? According to Ramalingam Vallalar, having violated the principles of compassion in their previous birth, some are destined to take their next life either in the form of an animal or as a suffering human being. It is a reaction or a consequence of their past actions. In spite of the apparent difference, between the body in which one lived in his previous birth and the body in which he lives in the next birth, the soul is same. Those who denied the basic needs of others in their previous birth have themselves reached the stage of needing them in this birth. However, it is the duty of everyone to show mercy to these living beings to find fulfillment in life.

WHAT ABOUT REINCARNATION?

How can a life that lived in one body in the previous birth, take another body in the next birth? A human being consists of two components; a physical and non-physical component. The non-physical component is variously referred as Jeeva (the life sustaining power). When death occurs, it is the physical body that perishes, and the non-physical body survives. The life within or the soul does not die and continues to live. It seeks the life of another body. Even though, in between two lifetimes, it forgets the previous experiences of previous life, it carries over the "Karmas" results of their past actions, and "Vasanas" behavioral patterns of previous life, including the inherent strength and weaknesses.

Ramalingam Vallalar explains this phenomenon by citing the example of a man who has shifted to a new residence. It is implied that he would have definitely stayed somewhere before. For some reasons, he found it necessary to shift to a new house. Even if the new house does not suit him, he might move from there too. Similarly, a life that lived in one body in the previous birth would need another body to live in the next birth. Because a life needs a body to live, just as a person needs a house to reside. So, for whatever sins committed in their previous births, they will have to face the consequence of their acts in the next birth. One is forced to leave the body of the previous birth and take a new form in the next birth in order to keep the life alive. It is like the man, vacated by the house owner for his misconduct, being forced to seek whatever shelter available.

Whatever act that one does, it must be done objectively and not subjectively. Whenever an action takes place, thoughts get manifested through words and the words through actions. The notion of "I", the doer or "mine" should not be attached to them. When an act is done while being non-identified with the sense of "I", the individual would not be affected by it. When the individual identifies himself with the action and thinks that "I" am the doer, he becomes responsible for it and suffers the consequence of it. Only one who does action without personal attachments or non-identification, becomes free from Karma.

According to Adi Shankara, when the past actions are in conformity with the Eternal prescribed Principles or Natural Laws "Sanathana Dharma", the soul attains immortality. If the past actions were more or less balanced in the previous birth, the soul may get another human form facing the sorrows and miseries again, with an opportunity for spiritual upliftment and ultimate union with God. When the past actions were motivated by self-interest, guided by sense objects and not in conformity with Jeeva Karunya Ozhukkam, the life may take the form of an animal. In fact, one himself chooses the form and nature of his next life by the way one lives in his previous life.

IS IT HELPING SOMEONE DESTINED TO SUFFER GOING AGAINST GOD'S WILL?

A person is destined to suffer in his next birth as a consequence of his own sins done in previous births. It is part of the Laws of Nature that every action has a reaction, a positive action produces a positive reaction and a negative action produces a negative reaction; one gets god or bad coming into oneself according to one's own actions in the past. This is called "Karma". The believe is that, if a person suffers as a consequence of his own deeds, there is no question to go against the wishes of God, on the other hand, the benevolent and merciful God helps to resurrect such a persons by providing a healing touch to their agony through some of his compassionate devotees. Let us rise up as these compassionate devotees provide all the needed human touch to these tormenting souls and qualify ourselves to the Grace of God.

Just as God created humans, He created animals, birds and other species too. It is God's wish that all earthly creations should co-exist in harmony and peace without having one trying to overpower the other. Just as God is present in the soul of every human beings, God is present in the soul of every living creatures.

It is said that human beings have a Sixth sense. It is the reasoning power given to man, intended to be used with compassion, not only towards all fellow beings, but also, towards all living beings. Every life is precious to Him. The humans should live in perfect harmony with all the living beings. Unfortunately, man claims his supremacy over all living creatures, instead of assuming his birthright as a guardian and protector to all earthy creatures. We have the duty, as human beings, to treat all God's creations with respect and love.

Today, we are witnessing, man driving away all wild animals to forests extinction and retains all mild animals in the land for his own consumption. Compared to the sixth sense of humans, the animals seem to have a better sense, because they give us love, company, milk, wool etc...., and serve us in many ways and sacrifice themselves for the nefarious taste of humans.

The practice of using birds and animals as food is not recent. It is old as the origin of man itself and was prevalent even in stone age. Man has come a long way since, but his food habit still remains the same. While everything about him changed for the better, the urge for eating flesh continues. If food habit is taken as criteria of his progress, he has not moved forward an inch from his stone age level.

Ramalinga says:

"When I see men feeding themselves on the coarse and vicious food of meet, it is recurring extreme grief to me."

Our scriptures say: *"**Ahimsa Paramo Dharma**"*, which means non-violence is the greatest virtue. By taking non-vegetarian food, one is not only causing violence to animals but goes against the Dharma one is supposed to uphold. By taking the non-vegetarian food, one is unaware that he wounds the feelings of the same God he worships. He whose body is nourished by non-vegetarian food forfeits his right to enter the kingdom of heaven, because by causing wounds of God's creation, he is wounding the feelings of God.

The birds and animals have come into being in this world as a result of their past actions. The very fact of living here, seeking food and shelter and facing many hardships and danger is a punishment for them. It is wrong punishing them more, by slaughtering them. By doing so, one is exposing himself to the same sin and fate.

It is time; humans realize the cruelty that animals encounter at different levels. It is happening at butcher's house. It is happening in the field in the name of crop management. It is happening in silk manufacturing business, at labs and at many other paces. It defies logic why compassion should be restricted only to endangered species, cats and dogs. Why not the same compassion is shown to other creatures? It is disheartening to see cattle being bred, forced to pull carts and ultimately killed mercilessly. The method of transporting them and killing them is, to say the least, merciless. If the cattle would have been given the power of speech, they would certainly say:

"Oh! Man, how inhuman you are"!

To be a vegetarian is not enough. Most of the vegetarians are silent vegetarians. It is time for a spirited movement for vegetarianism and against cruelty towards animals. Religious leaders, doctors, scientists, S.P.C.A activists should come out more openly for vegetarianism and highlight the evils of non-vegetarian food. Vallalar said that those causing violence to cattle by taking non-vegetarian food should be isolated from society.

THE CONCEPT OF GRACE IN THE PHILOSOPHY OF SAINT RAMALINGAM

In the theistic systems of religions, the doctrine of grace is an important concept. The souls must get divine grace to attain the goal of life. The atheistic systems like Buddhism and Jainism also gave importance to this concept. Grace is the unbounded love towards every living being. When love transcends its limitations, it becomes grace. Love is the stem in which grace flowers. So, all the religions emphasize the need for love and love becomes grace at the later level.

Human beings suffer from innumerable problems because they forget to cultivate the humanistic way of life. Human beings are ignorant about their nature which is love and they are suffering from alienation. In the process of love, one's ego melts away and the real nature of one's own being appears in the individual. When one realizes his own nature, he identifies himself with the world and he faces his own self in all the living beings. But, going away from illusion and putting the ego aside are not such simple tasks. One needs a life-time's constant labour and sometimes we need more lives' energy than one has, to perfect the process of weaning oneself away from the strong bond of ignorance and egoism. Due to this tremendous task, theistic systems emphasized the need for God. The atheistic system strongly believe that man can attain salvation and live a blissful life by his own moral and spiritual strength.

In Saivism God's grace is compared to Sunlight. In the presence of Sunlight not all the lotuses flower bloom. A few mature buds of the lotus alone bloom. Like this, only mature souls realize and enjoy the presence of God's grace. The souls must work for the eradication of the ego. Only in the egoless individual, God's grace will be reflected. The spiritual perfection of the soul is known as "Malaparibaka". An individual who lives a life of love, a man who follows the principle of, non-killing realizes the worth of life and, that state of mind is known as "Malaparibaka". The traditional religions are guiding people towards the scriptures and gurus for the attainment of this state. Even though Saint Ramalingam was born out of strongly religious parents and lived in the midst of religious surroundings, he never recommends any human guru or any individual text. As a spiritual humanist and a transcendentalist, he accepts only experience as the guiding principle.

He emphatically declares that only love can save the world. Neither, the scriptures nor the religion can save the world. According to Saint Ramalingam, all the religions and philosophies are imperfects and perfection comes to mankind only through their own realization and experience. His own experience showed him that love can remove the sufferings of mankind and lift to a higher state of life.

The path of Saint Ramalingam aims at the state of grace in which an individual identifies himself with all the living beings. In the state of Grace, one has a duty to help other suffering human-beings. In that ultimate state, the souls enjoy real bliss. Saint Ramalingam sang that only a heart which is full of grace can be the seat in which the divine dancer dances. In Arutperum Jothi Agaval, he explains that the nature of reality is grace. All the songs of Saint Ramalingam are known as the Psalms of Grace. This is the central theme in the philosophy of Saint Ramalingam. According to him, the nature of God is Grace. A life which is full of grace is the only real life. He believes that all human problems can be solved only by a life which is based upon love. He is not a theoretician. For each and every statement he gives, there is evidence from his own life and experience. If one attains a state of grace it will lead him to higher states of being. From his own experience, he explains that the material body-the physical body will change into a body of grace. Then the graceful body will change into a golden body and the golden body will change into light which is pure and indestructible. In short, if a man wants to conquer death, the only way is through love and grace. He emphasized these through non-killing and appeasing the hunger of poor people. In one of his prose books, Jeeava Karunya Olukkam, he very clearly says that love is the only master key to spirituality. Jeeva Karunya Olukkam is a short speech delivered by the Saint at the Opening Ceremony of the Satya Dharm a Salai. When all other philosophies show so many difficult paths, texts, temples, etc., Ramalingam showed the simple act of love.

RELIGION

By showing this simple, straight forward way, Ramalingam removed all ups and downs of religions. By emphasizing love Ramalingam removed the need for any professional gurus. Any man and woman, irrespective of caste, creed, religion, language, nationality, etc., can practice Supreme Compassion to all beings. In his speech at Satya Dharma Salai, he requested his followers to practice this act of non-killing and appeasing the hunger of the poor people, even though the whole world stood against it. He said that the practice of love will give all the benefits of all religious practices.

Therefore, one must do it without any delay. Human life is a rare chance. Therefore, one must gain all the benefits within this birth itself. We don't know what will happen next minute or where we will go in the next birth. He condemns all the religious practices and texts like Vedas, Agamas and Puranas because they do not teach love in a straight forwards way. God's nature is love. Therefore, only through love human beings can realize the nature of Reality. Ramalingam recorded all his experiences in the form of beautiful poems. At the repeated request of those who surrounded him, he allowed the publication of the songs. When they published it, they named the songs as Thiru Arutpa which means songs sung through the grace of God. The followers of Ramalingam named him Thiru Arutprakasa vallalar because his very life is based upon love and grace. The sixth canto of Thiru Arutpa is the most important part, this because it is only here, that he explains Transcendental philosophy in terms of love and humanism. The earlier songs also indicate that he enjoyed spiritual experience at the very early age of five months. In the sixth canto of Thiru Arutpa, he sang that his very life is grace. If one separates love from his own being, he says that he will immediately die. He sang that he suffered a lot because he wished to remove the sufferings of the world. He sang that his life mission is to transform people through love and truth. The biography of saint Ramalingam also shows that he was a born mystic. He appeared in this world not for his own sake but for the benefit of the all world. In one of his songs he very clearly sang that all the living beings must enjoy perfect happiness like his own self.

In Mahaperupadesam, Ramalingam advised his followers not to follow any closed religion or philosophy. He advised them to meditate, concentrate and carefully observe life, because philosophies and religions never save mankind from suffering. Experience, understanding and love only can save the human beings from their sorrows. So, he warned the followers not to waste their time in enquiring into philosophical problems and indulging in religious debates. He insisted on a constant enquiry into one's own self. He also advised those who are not able to do constant enquiry to do it collectively.

Ramalingam was inspired by the life affirming philosophy of Thirukkural. With his deep knowledge in the various philosophical systems of India, he evolved his own philosophy which is Samarasa Suddha Sanmargam which is similar to Saivism in the sense that both of them are theistic, pluralistic and realistic. The main difference between Saivism and Samarasam is Saivism centres in God and Samarasam centres in man. The realistic, pluralistic base of Saivism generates a good social philosophy. Samarasam evolved from the experience of Ramalingam. His experience showed him that man is the centre of the universe and his problems are important for philosophy and religion. In the name of spiritualism and transcendentalism, he never ran away from his responsibilities to fellow beings. He repeatedly advised his followers to run away from philosophies and religions which misguide human beings. Due to so many philosophical and religious conflicts, human beings are making their life miserable.

Ramalingam was an activist who established a few social institutions. He strongly believed that the social and spiritual life of man are inter-connected. When a man is pure and honest in his social relationship, spirituality will come to him automatically. He considered religion as an important method. He uses the word religion in the sense that which promotes brotherhood among human beings and that which makes man as a matured being. He established the association of Sanmargis, Satya Gnana Sabai, Satya Dharma Salai and Chitti Valaham. He planned to establish some new social institutions like medical centre and meditation centre.

MARRIAGE LIFE

Family in the company of the beloved, human beings enjoy their real nature. Love is a basic need in the human life because it helps them to break the hard cover of the ego. The institution of family begins with marriage and ends when a man realizes the whole world as his house and all the living beings as his relatives. The institution of family is not an end in itself. It is a means to the next stage of life which is "Sanyasa", celibacy. Indian philosophic schools like Buddhism and Jainism hold that a man can go to Sanyasa directly without going through the institution, family. But this view is not popular in south India, as Saivism and Vaishnavism speak the glory of family life and the responsibilities of the family man. Thirukkural, the ethical code of the Tamils, says that the world functions because of the family. It says that the responsibility of the family member is such that he must look after the welfare of his own family members and also the welfare of the members belonging to the other three groups – students, the mendicants and the people who live in the forest. The third part of Thirukkural beautifully speaks about the love between man and woman. Tamil grammarian Tholkkappiar not merely speaks about the grammar of language but he gave the grammar of a good life also. Life without love is incomplete. A man without family is not a full man. This is the philosophy of the Tamils in respect of family. Therefore, nobody is exempt from this rule. The great preceptors of Saivism and Vaishnavism led a family life. Most of the saints of the Periapuranam are married men. Spiritual life and worldly life are not opposed to each other. Family life is a stepping-stone to spiritual life of mankind. Following this philosophy in his life, Ramalingam married his sister's daughter, Dhanamma. He was twenty-seven at the time of his marriage. His songs clearly show that he agreed to the marriage because of the compulsion of the elders. His songs also indicate that he never lived with the lady. But he was not against the institution of marriage or family, as such. His biography shows that he participated in the marriage of his friends. When some of his friends asked for advice, he advised them that marriage is not a sin, if one concentrates his inner self upon God.

VII - THE SEVEN VEILS OF THE SOUL THE 7 MAYA SHAKTI

The awareness kept on the third eye along with the practice of Sat-Vichaaram and the constant chanting of the Mahamantra "Arut Perun Jyothi", with a heartfelt love and devotion, generate all the necessary heat and vibration to dissolve the seven veils hindering the vision of our inner light, our true nature.

1 – THE FIRST VEIL CALLED "MAYA SHAKTI" IS BLACK IN COLOR.

It represents the veiling of the reign of the Spirit within our soul, by the infinite and indissoluble black screen, the inconscient mass of darkness, Asat, the great obscuring power of Maya, the lower nature. It has been validated by all the great sages of humanity, that God is omnipresent, omnipotent, omniscient. It is the ignorance of this reality that acts as a screen impairing the vision of our soul-consciousness. Therefore, the soul is in full darkness, being completely identified with the world and the senses. The soul cannot even believe in God, being totally engrossed in the world of appearance.

2 - THE SECOND VEIL CALLED "KRIYA SHAKTI" IS BLUE IN COLOR.

It is the veiling of the evolving soul or psychic being, by the blue screen, the mind, that makes the "I" consciousness identified with any external form, keeping one in the illusion that any outside manifestation is an expression of the ultimate reality. For instance, when you look at a tree, the blue veil works in such way, that it makes you believe that the trunk, the branches, the leaves, the buds, the flowers and the fruits are the ultimate reality of the tree; the second veil is hiding the fact that the tree is nothing but the expression of a common source to all aspects of the tree, the soul-atom within the seed.

3 - THE THIRD VEIL IS CALLED "PARA SHAKTI". IT IS GREEN IN COLOR.

This veil is present on two levels:

1-At the lower level, "Asuththa Maya" as it is called, represents the impure illusion. It is black green in color. It is the veiling of Para Veli (the planes or range of spiritual mind) by the frightening green screen (i.e. the vital or life principle of desires, like and dislikes as referred in Upadesha, p.131). This veil is making human beings running incessantly after desire, guiding by this dualistic believe in likes and dislikes, thus creating frustration, un-satisfaction, hate, fear, jealousy, greed, attachment, sickness, suffering, destruction and death.

2-The upper level, "Suthta Maya." Is green gold. This veil represents the pure illusion. It indicates the efforts that the aspirant must do to attain the truth by leading a life of discipline, ethics and compassion towards all living beings, if he wishes to reach the highest spiritual heights leading to the realization of God and immortality.

4 - THE FORTH VEIL IS CALLED "ICHCHA SHAKTI". IT IS RED IN COLOR.

It represents the veiling of the space or plane into which the principle of Conscious-Force descends for manifestation, by the sorrowful or woeful or red screen (i.e., the physical matter). It is the veil of envy, of the concupiscence and lust. Instead of directing one's own attention to the source of all life, Arutperujyoti, the sense organs, fuelled by the belief in emotional deprivation and the need for recognition and existence, are found to be propelled compulsively, to grab by all means what one wants and experience as a momentary fulfilment. This veil hides the true knowledge of God who is all love and who alone can satisfy us and bring us true and lasting fulfilment.

5 - THE FIFTH VEIL IS CALLED "JNANA SHAKTI". IT IS GOLD IN COLOR.

It is veiling the space or plane into which the principle of substance descends for manifestation, Porul Uru Veli, i.e., the Sat over-mind. Egoistic ignorance due to the nature of darkness of the ego, as explained under the first screen is there sought to be progressively removed in the stage of the golden screen of Jnana.

Shakti, the power of the knowledge that separates or detaches the soul from animality and obscurity of egoistic nature and leads to the opening of psychic Consciousness and to the soul's direct knowledge of all beings and things, and all-around knowledge through the souls movements of consciousness and to the various kinds of knowledge by the dealing of soul with the nature and qualities of things.

6 - THE SIXTH VEIL IS CALLED "AATHI SHAKTI". IT IS WHITE IN COLOR.

This veil is covering the Truth-World or Truth-Home of the Divine by the closely proximate white screen (i.e., Sat over-mind, at the very border of the Truth-World or Super-Mind. The sixth veil is the veil of cosmic ignorance which, due to its ignorance of the timeless and space less Self, takes the mutable or variable cosmic being as the whole truth of existence.

7 - THE SEVENTH VEIL WHICH IS MULTICOLOR IS CALLED "CHIT SHAKTI".

It represents the veil of practical ignorance which is the result of all the seignorances and is the cause of life's confusions and discords and leads, in its extreme, to wrong-doing and suffering, which will in the end yields its place to the right will of self-knowledge, right consciousness, right action and right being, when our self-knowledge is made complete in all its essentials. The pragmatic or practical ignorance corresponds to the seven screen, Chit Shakti which help shedding off one's ego-sense and universalized its being and lead into its spiritual existence at once, transcending the cosmic and the individuality, to finally merge in the integral expression of the will of its soul, knowledge and action, and make it possible for the free soul to perform the eightfold siddhis (divine powers). The eightfold siddhis referred here, includes the transformation of body and the power of resurrecting the dead.

Before the soul attains its full and complete free status, it has to remain dependent on the tattvas for its knowledge, and thereby, suffer the life's confusions and discords, this inspite of a partial spiritual realizations and so long as the integration of its powers referred above is not attained.

The seven veils are comparable to seven steps to access to the Father. This path takes the aspirant from the first step representing the "maya shakti", the veil of illusion and ignorance, to the second step, "kriya shakti", the veiling of the evolving soul, to the third step, "para shakti ", the veil of Supreme Energy, Paraveli, to the fourth step," ichcha shakti ", the veiling of the Divine desire, ChithuruVeli, onto the fifth step," gnagna shakti", the veil of power of wisdom, Poruluru Veli, onto the sixth step, "aadhi shakti," the veil of the higher self which is nothing but the light of our own individuality, our soul, Meipathi Veli, onto the seventh step, "chit shakti," the Supramental Knowledge, Karudhu Anupavam.

Beyond these 7 veils are veils of the faculties of the body, life, mind and so diverse experiences leading ultimately to the experience of the self-sustaining Grace-Light.

VIII - DIET PROTOCOL OF SUDDHA SANMARGA

FIRST LEVEL DIET

"FOOD AS A MEDICINE FOR THE BODY, MIND AND SOUL"

Hippocrates, advocated in the 5th century BC, that "food be the first medicine. This Greek doctor, already knew, at his time, that in order to enjoy good health and allow your body to function properly, it was essential to have a healthy and balanced diet".

AYURVEDA'S DEFINITION OF HEALTH

> "Sama dosha sama agnischa sama dhatu mala kriyaaha |
> Prasanna atma indriya manaha swastha iti abhidhiyate"
> **– Sushruta Samhita**

One is in perfect health when the Three doshas (vata, pitta and Kapha) Digestive fire (digestion, assimilation and metabolism) all the body tissues & components (Dhatus) (the entire physical body) all the excretory functions (the physiological functions of urination and defecation) are in perfect order with a pleasantly disposed and contented mind, senses and spirit.

Siddha medicine teaches you to respect your body and how to listen to the signs and signals it is trying to communicate with you. It teaches you the tools and awareness to maintain or restore balance according to your unique mind-body type known as Dosha classification known as "vatam (air and ether element) – kapham (earth and water elements) – pittam (fire element)". Siddha medicine is about teaching you the tools to empower you to transform your health, wellbeing and vitality. At the very core of this healing science is the mind-body-spirit connection and digestion. The experiences and food we metabolized create who we are, and gives us the freedom, energy and mobility to live the lives we desire.

What is more empowering than understanding what sustains and gives life?

Through nutrition, lifestyle, daily self -care practices, discipline, movement and thoughts we can restore harmony, balance and vitality into our busy modern lives- in a time when now, more than ever before, we need guidance the most. Ramalinga's way of living in accordance with Natural Law is a complete way of life that not only improves one's own health, but also one's own well-being, behaviour leading one to higher states of consciousness.

With just a few small changes to a person's daily life, it is possible to live the suddhasanmarga way with the knowledge and timeless wisdom of deathlessness as taught by Ramalinga.

THE DIET'S FUNDAMENTAL PRINCIPLES:

1. Eating vegetarian food that is "**Sattvic**" pure
2. Eating when one is hungry
3. Eating a little quantity at each meal; fill no more than half of the stomach at lunch and 1/3 of the stomach at diner.
4. It is highly recommended to drink only hot water, cold water being a poison.

BENEDICTION BEFORE MEALS

ARUT PERUN JOTHI : VAST SUPREME GRACE LIGHT
ARUT PERUN JOTHI : VAST SUPREME GRACE LIGHT.
THANIP PERUMG KARUNAI : SUPREME COMPASSION.
ARUT PERUN JOTHI : VAST SUPREME GRACE LIGHT.
FATHER, MOTHER CREATOR OF ALL THAT IS,

VAST GRACE LIGHT;
THANK YOU FOR ALL YOUR BLESSINGS AND TEACHINGS
LET THIS FOOD BE PURIFIED AND MULTIPLIED AT THE
INFINITE SO ALL BEINGS CAN ENJOY THIS MEAL
LET THIS FOOD BE AN AMRITA OF LOVE AND LIGHT FOR
EACH ONE
OF MY CELLS.
THANK YOU, THANK YOU, THANK YOU.
VALLAL MALARADI VALGA VALGEA
ELAM UYIR KALUM ENPUTRU VALGEA.
LET PROSPERITY, PROSPER AT THE LOTUS FEET OF THE ONE
WHO GIVES FREELY.
LET ALL BEING LIVE IN ABSOLUTE FELICITY

ABOUT WATER

It is best drinking spring water, dew on banana leaves/herbal leaves and rainwater. If difficult to get, heat distilled water (reduce 5 cups of water to 2 cups), thereby you obtain pure water like elixir. It is not recommended at all to drink bottle plastic water since it is dead water and tap water being highly contaminated by all sorts of chemicals, heavy metals, hormones and all kinds of disrespectful actions humans inflicts to the 5 elements.

Drink only hot water beforehand boiled with cumin seed and black pepper. You can drink it all day around, little sip at a time, according to one's own need. Drinking cold water is a poison. There is no need of drinking water during meals since it curtails the digestive fire in the stomach "Jathar-Agni". In case one feels the need of drinking during meal, one may take a sip of hot water.

ABOUT VEGETABLES

Vallalar recommends a diet that is pure, which means that we eat food which will not deteriorate once in the body. Are favoured all vegetables whose life has not been taken with, which is the case of the root vegetables.

It is good to understand, that this path, is part of the suddhasanmarga, as such, it is designed exclusively for those, who realise and feel in their heart and being, the necessity to follow this path.

EATING HABITS

While eating avoid excessive carelessness and hurry. Early food includes cumin shaped rice (organic seeraga samba or ponni rice), or any type of white-brownish rice available. When cooked, the rice must not be too adhesive/pasty or too hard. Consume fairly cooked rice, not excessively or to less and to the right amount according to the appetite. Consume preferably steamed food or raw food at room temperature.

About twenty minutes after meals, you may drink hot water; not too much. Sour curd can be served. Among lentils, toor dhal or mung dhal can be prepared with cumin, fenugreek and black pepper powder as liquid dressing, as solid downy or tick paste, or as gravy with other vegetables; and can be served with ghee/clarified cow butter in seasoning the food. Sesame oil, gingili oil can also be used in small amount. It is best avoiding onion and garlic since they both are tamasic and rajasic (impure food) they bring the energy down instead of bringing the energy up. If not possible to stop, take only a little in food and not in every meal. All other types of lentils are not essential. If given, they can be consumed occasionally.

Drink dried ginger-water, when feeling thirsty. Preparation: First, fry the dried ginger, coated with calcium carbonate (Sunnampu). Next, prepare the ginger powder, after peeling the outer dust off the fried ginger, preserve it in an air-tight bottle. Then, add little of this power in a pure drinking water. With a pinch of cumin seeds and boil this mixture for a sufficient length of time, until it becomes 2/5th of its original volume in order to get the right quality of water for drinking. If the ginger-cumin water is not accessible, then, at least, drink very well boiled/hot water; but never drink cold water. After day-time food, without having a lie-down, never do anything. However, never lie down until the slumber puts you in sleep. Never ever go to sleep during the day. After seven hours of the day-time food, you can eat one or two payen banana, rasthali banana or bungalow banana, if possible, with little unrefined brown raw cane sugar. If feeling hungry in the morning, one can drink herbal milk along with little of these bananas with ghee and unrefined brown raw cane sugar. Never have day-time sexual-intercourse. After eating day-time food, meditate on God for a while. Then go on doing work almost without strains. In the late afternoon, go for an outdoor walk for a while so that the evening sunlight falls on the body. Avoid going outside when the outside wind blows heavily. Very hot sunlight, snow and rain should not fall on physical body.

RECOMMENDED VEGETABLES BY VALLALAR

EGGPLANT, BAINGAN IN HINDI, KATHIRIKKAI IN TAMIL

According to the medical News Today's article, eggplantor aubergine, provides fiber and a range of nutrients.

Many of us are most familiar with eggplants that are large and dark purple, but the shape, size, and color can vary from small and oblong to long and thin and from shades of purple to white or green.

This article will focus on the nutritional benefits of the traditional purple eggplant.

BENEFITS

Eggplants are rich in fiber and antioxidants. A serving of eggplant can provide at least 5% of a person's daily requirement of fiber, copper, manganese, B-6, and thiamine. It also contains other vitamins and minerals.

In addition, eggplants are a source of phenolic compounds that act as antioxidants.

Antioxidants are molecules that help the body eliminate free radicals — unstable molecules that can damage cells if they accumulate in large amounts. Foods that contain antioxidants may help prevent a range of diseases.

Among the antioxidants in eggplants are anthocyanins, including nasunin, lutein, and zeaxanthin.

HEART HEALTH

The fiber, potassium, vitamin C, vitamin B-6, and antioxidants in eggplants all support heart health.

A review Trusted Source published in 2019 suggested that eating foods containing certain flavonoids, including anthocyanins, helps reduce inflammatory markers that increase the risk of heart disease.

A 2013 study found that middle-aged women who consumed more than 3 servings a week of blueberries and strawberries — good sources of anthocyanins — had a 32% lower associated risk of heart disease than those who consumed fewer of these fruits.

In another investigation, researchers concluded that women with a high intake of anthocyanins appeared to have significantly lower blood pressure and less stiffening of the arteries than those who ate fewer of these compounds.

BLOOD CHOLESTEROL

Eggplant contains fiber, and this may benefit cholesterol levels. A cup of cooked eggplant cubes, weighing 96 grams (g), contains around 2.4 g of fiber.

Results of a 2014 study in rodents indicated that chlorogenic acid, a primary antioxidant in eggplants, may decrease levels of low density lipoprotein, or "bad," cholesterol and reduce the risk of nonalcoholic fatty liver disease.

CANCER
The polyphenols in eggplant may help protect the body from cancer. Anthocyanins and chlorogenic acid protect cells from damage caused by free radicals. In the long term, this may help prevent tumor growth and the spread of cancer cells.

Anthocyanins may help achieve Trusted Source this by preventing new blood vessels from forming in the tumor, reducing inflammation, and blocking the enzymes that help cancer cells spread.

COGNITIVE FUNCTION
Findings of animal studies suggest that nasunin, an anthocyanin in eggplant skin, may help protect brain cell membranes from damage caused by free radicals. Nasunin also helps transport nutrients into cells and move waste out.

Anthocyanins also help prevent neuro inflammation and facilitate blood flow to the brain. This could help prevent memory loss and other aspects of age-related mental decline.

Lab experiments have indicated that nasunin may reduce the breakdown of fats in the brain, a process that can cause cell damage.

WEIGHT MANAGEMENT
Dietary fiber can help people manage their weight. A person who follows a high-fiber diet is less likely to overeat, as fiber can help a person feel fuller for longer.

Eggplants contain fiber and are low in calories — they can contribute to a healthful, low-calorie diet.

However, eggplant can absorb a lot of oil during frying. Anyone looking to lose weight should prepare it a different way, such as by steaming.

EYE HEALTH

Eggplant also contains the antioxidants lutein and zeaxanthin.

Lutein appears to play a role Trusted Source in eye health, and it may help prevent age-related macular degeneration, which can lead to vision loss in older people.

PEERKANGAI IN TAMIL, LUFFA OR RIDGE GOURD

Ridge Gourd contains insulin peptides that lower and balance blood sugar. And these powerful peptides reduce the amount of sugar excreted in the urine. It prevents the sugar from exceeding what we consider normal levels and falling too low. Therefore, Ridge Gourd is very important for those who suffer from diabetes and hypoglycaemia.

Ridge Gourd is also a good anti-inflammatory agent, preventing cardiovascular disease, stroke and cancer. And because inflammation is the first step toward creating a disease, Ridge Gourd helps prevent diseases in general. In addition, the gourd ridge has antibiotic qualities that help prevent and cure bacterial infections.
Ridge Gourd juice is important for the cure of jaundice and liver disease, and the seeds and flesh of the gourd can also be ingested for extra

cleansing of the liver. A cup of fresh gourd ridge juice with a little sweetener taken twice a day is important for healing liver disease and jaundice. This amazing gourd is also a good detoxifying agent for the liver, the blood and other body tissues. And when toxins are eliminated from the body, our immune system is functioning properly.

Ridge Gourd contains a lot of fibre, which is important to provide a good environment for the growth of probiotic bacteria and boost our immune system.

Ridge gourd and its juice are both very alkalizing and thus preventing acidity, thus preventing disease.

Ridge Gourd works well for those who are hot all the time, it is an excellent internal cooling.

Ridge Gourd contains a lot of beta-carotene, a powerful antioxidant.
Ridge Gourd is also an average sources of B-complex vitamins such as thiamine, niacin (vitamin B-3), pantothenic acid (vitamin-B-5), pyridoxine (vitamin B-6) and minerals such as calcium, iron, zinc, potassium, manganese and magnesium. It has more vitamin A than many other gourd vegetables. The vitamin A is essential for the mucosal integrity, the health of the skin, the hair and vision. It also works as an anti-cancer, anti-aging at cellular level. The Ridge Gourd roots boiled in water are ideal for healing swollen lymph nodes, dissolving kidney stones and detoxifying the spleen. In addition, the leaves of the plant used for tea are ideal for relieving from diarrhoea.

CLUSTER BEANS, KOTHAVARANGAI IN TAMIL

They are native to India and grow in arid and dry regions. They are rich in nutrients, namely vitamin K, vitamin C, vitamin A, folate and abundant in carbohydrates and contain minerals, including phosphorus, calcium and iron.

Cluster Beans help resolving anaemia and control blood sugar. It is beneficial to the health of the cardiovascular system and strengthens the strength of the bone. The presence of iron increases the haemoglobin content in the red blood cells and improves the oxygen consumption capacity of the blood, thus improving the blood circulation. It is recommended to eat Cluster Seeds during pregnancy as it contains folic acid, iron and calcium. It helps manage blood pressure, stimulate intestinal transit and calm the brain. It's good for the foetus in the womb of the mother.

BROAD BEANS, AVARAIKAI IN TAMIL

Broad beans are rich in vitamins A and C; Vitamin A is necessary for good vision, skin, growth and bone development.

Broad beans are a source of dietary fibre. These fibres can help improve your blood sugar and cholesterol levels. Soluble fibre is particularly effective at lowering low density lipoprotein (LDL) cholesterol levels, commonly known as "bad" cholesterol.

Broad beans are rich in fibre, which the body needs to move food through the digestive system.

Broad beans contain high concentrations of an amino acid called L-dopa (dopamine), which acts as a neurotransmitter in the brain. The right amount of potassium in broad beans-Chikkudukaya-Fava, helps the body maintain blood pressure and regulate heart function. They are a very good source of phosphorus that is necessary for the formation of healthy bones and teeth. In addition, it also helps the body to use vitamins.

It is rich in thiamine, essential for maintaining normal nerve function.

ASH GOURD, KALYANA PUSANI IN TAMIL

Ash gourd helps treat acid reflux syndrome with the help of its active ingredients such as terpenes, flavonoids C, glycosides and sterols.

Because of its alkaline property, the ash gourd is used as a urinary purifier. Ash gourd treats bleeding disorders and helps improve body weight and is ideal for diabetic patients.

It helps fight against general debility and treats mental disorders by stabilizing nerve cells.

It often has a bronchodilator effect on patients, thanks to antihistamine activity (H1 receptor antagonism).It also acts as an anti-diarrheal agent and relieves constipation

SPINACH, PASALAI KEERAI IN TAMIL

The ash gourd pulp is a rich source of vitamin B and C and is also an excellent remedy for tapeworms. With the help of the ash gourd, one can also get relief from the withdrawal symptoms of morphine. In case of burning, the topical application of ash gourd pulp is also very beneficial.

Spinach is well known for its nutritional qualities and has always been considered a plant with remarkable abilities to restore energy, increase vitality and improve blood quality, mainly, because it is rich in iron. Iron plays an important role in the function of red blood cells, which help transport oxygen in the body, in energy production and DNA synthesis.

Spinach is also a very good source of vitamin K, vitamin A, vitamin C and folate. In addition to be a good source of manganese, magnesium, iron, vitamin B2, they contain vitamin K which is important for maintaining bone health.

The dark green colour of the spinach leaves indicates that they contain a high level of chlorophyll and health promoting carotenoid, (beta-carotene, leucine and zeaxanthin). These phyto-chemicals have anti-inflammatory and anti-cancer properties and are particularly important for vision. They help prevent macular degeneration and cataracts.

MORINGA DRUMSICK AND LEAVES, MURUNGAI IN TAMIL

Moringa has always been used to treat more than 300 diseases. In 2008, the National Institute of Health (USA) named Drumstick (Moringa oleifera) "Plant of the Year". It is known to possess 90

powerful nutrients. Drumstick is a powerful antioxidant; It contains antioxidants such as quercetin, which helps reduce blood pressure, flavonoids and polyphenols. Therefore, prevents damage and degradation caused by free radicals such as oxidative stress, cell damage, inflammation, etc. Moringa leaf powder works wonders for diabetic patients. It reduces lipid and glucose levels and regulates oxidative stress. It protects your heart against plaque formation in the arteries and reduces cholesterol.

SUNDAKAI IN TAMIL, TURKEY BERRY

Turkey berry scientifically known as solanum torvum is also known as plate brush, devils fig, pea eggplant, bhankatiya, pea aubergine, wild eggplant, gully bean, tekokak, susumber, and many other names is native to Central and South America and currently found in India, Africa, China, Thailand, The Caribbean, South America, Indonesia, Florida, Alabama, Brazil, Mexico, Ghana, Jamaica, Papua New Guinea, Puerto Rico (In the high mountains of Puerto Rico they grow thousands of pounds of Turkey Berries), and other places in US and the world. It grows in a wide range of habitats throughout the tropics and subtropics. It grows best in warm moist fertile conditions, but once established it can withstand drought by shedding its leaves. This plant is seen on vacant lands, roadsides, pastures, riverbanks, and other such areas.

PLANT

Turkey berry is an erect, branched, slender perennial shrub, 2–3 m tall and 2 cm in diameter and is sparingly armed, densely pubescent overall with many- greyish stellate hairs. It is normally found growing in locations with full sunlight and does well in light shade or shade for part of the day, but it cannot survive under a closed forest canopy and is quite drought tolerant and is adaptable on a wide range of soils. Root system consists of a deep and strong, woody taproot with numerous woody laterals. Flowering and fruiting start after the plant reaches a height of 1.5 m. Turkey berry reaches a height of 1.5 m during the year and dies after 2 years. Plant reproduces solely by seed.

STEM
One to several soft-wooded stems is branched above and is densely covered with fine stellate hairs and is distributed with broad-based, hooked prickles, 3 to 7 mm long. The stems are initially green becoming brown as they mature.

LEAVES
Leaves occur singly along the stems and are broadly ovate and 5-20 cm long, usually with seven broad, blunt lobes. Both surfaces are covered with very fine stellate hairs and have dispersed prickles along the main veins. The upper surface of the leaf is darker than the lower. They have finely hairy petioles, 1 to 5 cm long, and vary significantly in shape and size depending on genetic origin and plant vigor.

FLOWER
Inflorescence is a dense, compact, branched head consisting of 50-100 flowers at the ends of branches. These occur laterally (between two leaves) as the stems elongate. Each flower has five slender finely hairy sepals 2 to 3 mm long, five white to cream star-shaped petals each about 1 cm long, five elongate yellow stamens and a central stigma.

FRUIT
Fruits are small, smooth, globular berries 1-1.5 cm across and borne on 1–2 cm, pedicel thickened upwards. The turkey berry fruits are normally green and scurfy while young that turns into yellowish-green when mature and contain few to numerous flat, round, discoid, woody, often reddish seeds, 1.5 to 2 mm in diameter. Turkey berry normally have spicy flavour and are slightly bitter in taste. Because of its unique taste it is found used in several food items since ancient times till now.

HISTORY
The plant is said to have originated from Central and South America, where it is found from Mexico to Brazil and Peru, and it is widespread in the Caribbean. Although it originated in the America, it has been spread as

a useful plant and thus as a weed throughout the tropics and subtropics. It is now a common tropical weed but cultivated as a small-scale vegetable in southern and eastern Asia, and it is particularly popular in India, Thailand and Indonesia.

HEALTH BENEFITS OF TURKEY BERRY
Traditionally, the turkey berries are used in household meals, giving it a somewhat bitter taste. Apart from that, the turkey berries have some amazing healing benefits that are highlighted below

PROTECTION FROM CANCER
Dr. Paul Haider says; turkey Berries are antibacterial, anti-fungal, and help to stop the excessive cell growth making it significant for cancer. Research show that extract of Turkey Berry can help to protect against lung cancer. So, including turkey berry in your regular diet, help remain safe from all the life-threatening diseases.

TREATMENT OF DIABETES
Diabetes is one of the lifelong conditions that cause a person's blood sugar level to become too high. Including dried powdered leaves of the Turkey Berry plant to cooked berries help to control diabetes. They are used to lower blood sugar. Therefore, regular use of the turkey berry certainly helps to lower the diabetes level.

TREATMENT OF INDIGESTION AND DIARRHOEA
Regular consumption of turkey Berry is considered good for digestion and helps to treat indigestion, stomach-aches, diarrhoea, as well as other digestion related problems. These berries are capable of neutralizing acid in the stomach making them significant for healing gastric ulcers.

PREVENTION OF CARDIOVASCULAR DISEASES AND STROKES
Turkey berries consist of saponins, flavonoids, torvosides, alkaloids, glycosides, tannins, cholorogenome, etc. which are powerful antioxidants that help to prevent cardiovascular disease, strokes and cancer. The dried berries made into a powder helps to lower blood pressure and prevent heart attacks. Therefore, including fresh or dried turkey berry is extremely beneficial for dealing with cardiovascular diseases and strokes problems.

PREVENTION OF PAINS, REDNESS AND GOUT

The berries help to flush out uric acid, therefore, helping to prevent or reduce pain, redness and symptoms of gout. Apart from that, turkey Berry Leaf consists of a powerful anti-inflammatory agent and natural steroids called soasoline which is great for arthritis, lower back pain and swelling, and pain in general. Turkey Berries are very important for health since inflammation is the first step towards all diseases.

PREVENTION AND HEALING OF COLDS AND FLU

Apart from its health promoting benefits, turkey berries also help in preventing and healing colds and flu. Using the berries to make soup and consume frequently helps to overcome cold and flu symptoms.

TREATMENT OF PHLEGM AND MUCUS

Including turkey berries in your regular diet help to get rid of phlegm and mucus. Dry the berries and make into powder, this will dry up the mucus, helps with asthma, coughing, lung inflammation etc.

PREVENTION AND TREATMENT OF KIDNEY DISEASE

According to Dr. Haider, research shows that the berries can also help to prevent and treat kidney disease and even reverse tubular necrosis and glomerular congestion, thus making it important for treating kidney disease

REGULATE MENSTRUATION

Frequent consumption of turkey Berries help to regulate menstruation and so help with regular menstrual periods. Therefore, anyone with menstrual problems can include turkey berry in their regular diet to solve all the associated problems.

TREATMENT OF ANAEMIA

Turkey berries contain lots of iron which is extremely beneficial for treating anaemia. They encourage production of red blood cells. Apart from that berries can also be used in soups and consumed on a regular basis to increase red blood cell production.

PREVENTS INTESTINAL WORMS

Regular intakes of the berries help to prevent the development of worms within the intestine. Dried and powdered berries can also be added to gravies and eaten for better result.

ABOUT ROOT VEGETABLES

Among all the root vegetables, only the elephant foot yam is tolerated in the Suddha Sanmarga diet protocol. All the other roots like carrots, beet roots, potatoes, etc…which grow under the ground, by taking it, we take the life of the plant. This is the reason why the siddhas say that they have impure properties. The food recommended by Ramalinga is the food that generates less waste product, which possesses the purity, the good fire and ambrosia necessary to ensure the transmutation of the body from gross into light.

ELEPHANT FOOT YAM, KARUNAI KIZHANGU IN TAMIL

This root is also called Amorphopallus Paeoniifolius and Suran in Hindi. It grows in Africa and Asia. It has many health benefits. The big tuber looks like an elephant foot and is called "Elephant Foot Yam". It contains a large amount of protein and a large amount of carbohydrates that are important for vital energy and food, such as potatoes.

Elephant Foot Yam reduces bad cholesterol or LDL cholesterol and helps prevent cardiovascular disease, stroke and cancer. In Ayurvedic medicine, this yam is well known for its action against asthma and bronchitis.
Eating this yam for 90 days reduces blood sugar levels and reduces the amount of insulin. It helps prevent muscle spasms.

Elephant Foot Yam contains many great fibres that create a wonderful home for probiotic bacteria, helping to boost the immune system and prevent colon cancer. In addition, it contains diosgenin that is being researched for the treatment and prevention of cancer. It cools the body. It gives a good hormonal balance.

Elephant Foot Yam, if boiled with buttermilk and tamarind, is an excellent treatment for enlarged prostate. It is an anticoagulant thus preventing heart attack.

It contains zinc to boost the immune system, phosphorus and calcium for strong bones, potassium to regulate water, vitamin B6 for SPM, copper and iron for anaemia and many more minerals and vitamin A is a good anti-inflammatory.

It helps to reduce blood pressure. It is a powerful antioxidant that helps slow the aging process and prevent cardiovascular disease, stroke and cancer. It is a detoxifier of the liver, an analgesic, antibacterial.

Elephant Foot Yam contains a lot of omega-3 oils, important for preventing cardiovascular disease and cancer. It has a low glycaemic index, which makes it ideal for diabetics and weight loss. It has a relaxing and soothing effect, similar to that of diazepam on the nervous system

PLANTAIN BANANA OR GREEN BANANA, VAZAIKAI IN TAMIL

Plantains or green bananas look like bananas, but they are vegetables rather than fruits and must be cooked to eat them. You can eat green bananas only after they are processed, boiled or fried. There are tasty and delicious recipes of green bananas. Fried bananas have extra calories, of course, due to the frying. So, it's better to boil them. They can be used to make gravies and curries. The famous banana chips of Kerala are made from raw bananas. As they are prepared using coconut oil, it adds up to the health factor.

A plantain provides several grams of fibre to your diet. Fibre is an important nutrient because it helps reduce the risk of heart disease, diabetes and some cancers, such as colon cancer. Fibre also helps prevent constipation by keeping and maintaining your intestinal tract as it should. One cup of boiled green bananas contains 3.6g of fibres. Consumption of adequate amounts of fibre also means that you are less likely to diabetes.

It contains beta-carotene, calcium and vitamin C.

Resistant starch is the starch that is not absorbed into the small intestine, rather, it is passed over to the larger intestine. A research, led by Janine Higgins from the University of Colorado Health Sciences Centre, suggests that resistance can be associated with positive health benefits. The health benefits include:

Reduced fat storage improvement in the insulin sensitivity of the body lowering of the plasma cholesterol and triglyceride concentrations Decrease in glycaemic and insulinemic responses.

Green bananas are high in potassium. A cup of boiled green bananas contains 531 mg of potassium. Our body needs potassium for muscle movement, proper functioning of the nerves, and purification of blood by the kidneys.

Green bananas serve as the perfect food for the 'good and friendly' bacteria. These bacteria, which live in your intestines, consume green bananas and help to achieve a healthier stomach and digestive tract.
Green bananas are a rich source of vitamins like Vitamin B6, Vitamin c and more. These vitamins are extremely important to maintain a healthy body.

Green bananas prevent diarrhoea. Cook them well before consuming. Diarrheal is caused by a bactericidal, viral or parasitic infection. The symptoms of diarrhoea include headache, nausea, fatigue, abdominal cramps, etc. Green bananas help tackle these symptoms.

People who suffer from Type 2 diabetes can use green banana in their diet as green banana contains low amount of sugar. We all know how sensitive the diet of a diabetic patient is. You can include green bananas in the boiled form for best results.

Green bananas, like their yellow counterpart, are a storehouse of health benefits.

LENTILS

TOOR DHAL

Toor dal is also referred to as lentils or split pigeon peas. This traditional Indian dish is often served with rich spices like: Black pepper, cumin seeds and fenugreek, over rice and is a staple in many Indian restaurants and households. Toor dal is a member of the legume family, and this meal is not only delicious, it also HAS A NUMBER OF HEALTH BENEFITS.

Folic Acid

Toor dal contains folic acid, an important vitamin for all women, especially those planning to become pregnant. Folic acid is essential for fetal development and can help to prevent neural tube birth defects such as spina bifida. Getting adequate amounts of folic acid in your diet can help to reduce specific brain and spinal cord birth defects by more than 70 percent, according to the New York State Department of Health.

Protein and Vegetables

The United States Department of Agriculture notes that beans and peas such as toor dhal can be counted in both the protein and vegetable subgroups of the government's healthy eating plan. This is because legumes such as toor dhal are an excellent source of nutrients and plant protein, and they also contain dietary fiber. In essence, Toor dahl represents a low-fat and low-cholesterol alternative. Lentils such as toor dhal provide essential nutrients, fiber and protein for vegetarians as well as those who wish to merely limit their meat consumption.

Carbohydrates

Toor dal is also an excellent source of carbohydrates, which your body needs for energy. When you eat food containing carbohydrates, your body breaks them down into glucose, or blood sugar. Blood sugar is then used to provide energy to your brain, body and nervous system. Unlike simple carbohydrates, which contain processed and refined sugars with little nutrition, legumes such as toor dhal contain complex carbohydrates. Complex carbohydrates are recommended over simple carbohydrates because of their increased nutritional value.

Fiber

Legumes such as toor dal are a healthy source of dietary fiber, which can help to prevent constipation and promote regularity. A diet that includes healthy dietary fiber can also reduce your risk of chronic diseases. Regularly eating legumes as part of an overall healthy diet can lead to a lower risk of heart disease, stroke, certain cancers, type 2 diabetes and cardiovascular disease.

MUNG DAHL

Mung dal, commonly known as mongo, mung, mash bean, mood dal, golden gram, green, and green gram is found in Pakistan, India and Bangladesh. These dals have now become widespread to other parts of the world due to their numerous health benefits. Here are some of the reasons why you should incorporate this nutritious food into your nutrition to gain its full benefits.

Weight Loss

If you have been looking for ways to lose weight, you should add green beans or mung dal to your daily nutrition as it is low in fat. It is an excellent source of fiber, protein and carbohydrates, as well as folic acid and molybdenum. These essential minerals help neutralizing free radicals responsible for cell damage and disease.

Reduces Cholesterol Levels

Consumption of mung dal can help lower cholesterol level as they are high in fiber. Studies show that fiber in beans prevent rising of blood sugar after mealtime. This makes it a great food choice for individuals with hypoglycemia or those with insulin resistance.

Boosts cardiovascular health

Mung dal or green bean are high in antioxidant effects, magnesium, vitamin B6, fiber and folic acid that help improve heart health, preventing the occurrence of diseases such as arteriosclerosis and hardening of the arterial wall. In addition, folic acid and vitamin B6 lower levels of homocysteine in the body, which is the main contributor to stroke and heart attack.

Improves Immune System

Also, mung dal contains vitamin B-1 (thiamine), vitamin-B6 (pyridoxine). Regular intake of food high in Vitamin B-6 is believed to protect you from contagious agents responsible for disease, as well as viral infections.
Although there are no known side effects linked to consumption of mung dal.

It is recommended to avoid all other grams.

CEREALS OR GRAINS

SEERAGA SAMBA RICE

The Seeraga Samba rice is different from the rest of its types because of its texture and taste. It is starchy, has a bit of a corn-like flavour and less fluffy when cooked. The caloric values are high in this variety.

Cultivation

Largely produced in Tamil Nadu, the grain has various sub-categories that vary in size and price. Being low yielding, it is on the pricey side. The variant is also grown in other parts of India and Sri Lanka. The Sri Lankan version is smaller, oval-shaped as compared to its natural grain. It is short-grained, just about one-third of basmati grain size.

Health benefit and nutritional content of Seeraga Samba rice

Seeraga samba rice Helps in fighting cancer: It contains selenium which helps to prevent the cancer of colon and intestine. It has got more fiber and antioxidant which helps to remove free radicals from colon and intestine. It also has phytonutrients which help to fight breast cancer and strengthens the heart.

Helps in lowering cholesterol: The oil in the Seeraga Samba rice reduces the cholesterol. It is rich in fiber, hence, reduces the LDL cholesterol and increases HDL in the body.

Rich in Fiber, it controls the calories in the food and thus stops more intake of food. It also eases digestion and helps to relieve constipation.

PONNI RICE

Ponni Rice is one of the varieties of rice cultivated in vast agricultural lands in state of Tamil Nadu. It is said that the word "Ponni" is derived from local Tamil word which means "like gold". It is the staple rice variety of Tamil Nadu, Karnataka and Andhra Pradesh. Ponni rice is used in Kerala too. It is a medium grain rice variety which is soft and expands lengthwise when cooked and tastes sweet in nature. Ponni rice is exclusively prepared for making vegetarian delicacies and cuisines like curd rice, pongal and lemon rice.

Ponni rice has also several health benefits like it is the most ideal kind of rice preferred by diabetics and high blood sugar patients. It is less in calories and helps in weight reduction. It is also high in fiber, gluten free, low glycemic index, thereby lowering the impact of raised blood sugar and helps lowers cholesterol.

It contains twice as much protein as brown rice. Lowers Cholesterol - Since Ponni rice have fibers, they reduce the absorption...helps mobilize fats from liver. It has a sweet nature, best suited for vegetarian meals- used in making delicious food...

OIL

SESAME OIL

WHAT IS SESAME OIL?

Derived from sesame (Sesamum indicum), a tall annual herb from the Pedaliaceae family, sesame oil is commonly used as a food ingredient and condiment, as well as for medicinal uses. The sesame plant has been cultivated for thousands of years and is believed to be the world's oldest plant used as an oil.

Ancient Egyptians used it for pain as early as 1500 B.C. and, in China, it's been used for food, medicine and ink for more than 3,000 years. While in ancient times sesame and its various forms was particularly valued for its medicinal uses, Greek and Roman soldiers carried it on long marches in the form of a honey-and-seed energy bar.1 It also was believed to be an elixir to extend youth and enhance beauty.

Today, sesame grows extensively in Asia, particularly in China, Burma and India. It is also one of the chief commercial crops in Sudan, Ethiopia and Nigeria.2 Sesame oil is derived from the plant's small, flat and oval seeds, which have a nutty taste and a crunchy texture. There are two types of sesame oil: (1) light sesame oil, made from raw sesame seeds and has a light nutty flavour, and (2) dark sesame oil, made from toasted sesame seeds and has a stronger flavour and aroma.3

USES OF SESAME OIL

Sesame oil has been used for centuries in Asian cuisine. It also has medicinal purposes, especially in Ayurvedic medicine, where it is used as a base oil for about 90 percent of the herbal oils.

In Ayurvedic therapy, sesame oil is renowned for its ability to strengthen and detoxify the body and ensure the proper functioning of all the vital organs. It's also used in sacred and religious ceremonies. Today, sesame oil is a common component of skin and massage oils, hair care products, cosmetics, soaps, perfumes and sunscreens. Sesame oil has great moisturizing, soothing and emollient qualities.

In aromatherapy, it is popularly used as a massage oil and a carrier oil for essential-oils. Here are other uses for sesame oil:

skin moisturizer — Apply it to your skin to keep it soft and smooth and help prevent wrinkles from forming. You can also add it to your bath water to help treat cracked heels and dry knees and elbows. Sesame oil also assists in soothing burns and helps prevent skin-related disorders.4

helps remove toxins from your mouth — It is traditionally recommended for oil-pulling. (However, I prefer using coconut oil for this because it tastes better.)

Natural sunscreen — Apply the oil all over your face and body. You may need to reapply it, though, as the oil is easily removed, especially after heavily perspiring or jumping into water.5

Skin detoxifier — Oil-soluble toxins are said to be attracted to sesame seed oil molecules. Apply sesame oil on your skin, leave it for 15 minutes and then wash it off with warm water.6

Boosts your scalp and hair health — Massage the oil into your scalp and hair to keep your locks strong and shiny. It also effectively helps relieve dry scalp, dandruff and hair loss.

COMPOSITION OF SESAME OIL

Sesame oil contains high levels of natural antioxidants called sesamol, sesamolin and sesamin oils. Sesamin is a lignin with anti-inflammatory properties, and contains vitamin E, which helps keep your skin strong and supple.8

Meanwhile, sesamol possesses over two dozen beneficial pharmacologically active properties, most of which work to improve cardiovascular health. Sesame oil contains 15 percent saturated fat, 42 percent oleic acid and 43 percent omega-6 linoleic acid, with a composition similar to peanut oil. It is also loaded with B-complex vitamins, including thiamin, riboflavin, niacin, pantothenic acid, pyridoxine and folic acid.9
It's rich in amino acids that are essential in building up proteins, and minerals like iron, copper, calcium, manganese, magnesium, selenium, phosphorus and zinc.10

BENEFITS OF SESAME OIL

Sesame oil has natural antibacterial, antiviral and antioxidant properties, and many studies prove its therapeutic and health-promoting benefits. Some of the potential health benefits you can find on sesame in the medical literature are:

Diabetes — A 2006 study published in the Journal of Medicinal Food found that sesame oil used as the sole oil in your diet helps with lowering both blood pressure and plasma glucose in hypertensive diabetics.11

Multiple sclerosis (MS) — In mice studies, sesame oil helped protect mice from developing autoimmune encephalomyelitis, leading researchers to believe that it may react similarly in human patients with MS.12 Other research indicates that it also might be effective in managing Huntington's disease, a fatal disorder that kills brain cells.13

Atherosclerosis — The sesamol in sesame oil was found to have an impact on the atherosclerotic process, in that its fatty acid and non-ester lipid components appeared to inhibit atherosclerosis lesions when mice were put on a sesame seed diet.14

Cancer — High concentrations of sesomol and sesamin in sesame oil have been found to induce mitochondrial apoptosis in colon cancer, as well as in prostate, breast, lung, leukemia, multiple myeloma and pancreatic cancers.

HOW TO MAKE SESAME OIL?

Sesame seeds are pressed and crushed to release the oils. There are many processing methods for this oil, which either involve manually intensive techniques or chemical extraction methods.

Some common techniques are cold pressing, hot pressing or toasting the seeds.20A large number of seeds is needed to produce every ounce of this oil. When buying sesame oil, look for a cold-pressed product, as this method preserves more of the oil's nutrients and healthful antioxidants.

HOW DOES SESAME OIL WORK?

Sesame oil can be used topically or ingested (in moderate amounts). It can also be used as nose drops to help relieve chronic sinusitis, or as a mouthwash or throat gargle to help kill strep and other common cold bacteria.

When applied to your skin, sesame oil absorbs quickly and penetrates through your tissues, up to your bone marrow. Your liver also accepts the oil molecules as "friendly molecules," and does not remove them from your blood. Despite its popularity as an ingredient in many recipes, I do not advise consuming this oil in large amounts.

Even though it's a rancid-resistant oil, its high levels of omega-6 fats can make you cells fragile and prone to oxidation. Getting excessive omega-6 fats from this oil may also throw your omega-3 to 6 ratio out of whack.

IS SESAME OIL SAFE?

Sesame oil is generally safe. It has been evaluated safe for use in cosmetics. In a final assessment published on the International Journal of Toxicology, sesame oil was deemed safe for use as a cosmetic ingredient.21 To ensure that topical application of this oil does not cause any unusual reactions, try applying it to a small area of your skin first.

Because it's a mild inflammatory and has high omega-6 levels, I would recommend consuming it in very small amounts. If you have an allergy to sesame seeds, do not consume or use this oil, as it may lead to allergic reactions.22 I also advise pregnant women or nursing moms to use extreme caution when consuming sesame seeds and sesame oil, as it may have hormone-inducing effects, triggering uterine contractions that can lead to preterm labor or miscarriage.

SPICES

Mustard is not recommended. Consume less salt. It is always good to have less salt in food to help keep body healthy. Ramalinga is not encouraging the intake of salt to ensure the longevity and transformation of the body, towards its full transformation from gross to subtle.

SEA SALT

What too much salt can do to your brain

Too much salt in your diet can have devastating effects on your brain power, and new research reveals the mechanism behind this.

It's a well-known fact that too much salt in our diet raises the risk of cardiovascular disease and high blood pressure.

But it is less known that brain-related problems, such as cerebrovascular disease Trusted Source, stroke Trusted Source, and cognitive impairment Trusted Source, have all been linked to dietary salt.

As the authors of the new research explain, it was suggested that one possible mechanism behind these negative effects involves the so-called endothelial cells inside the cerebral blood vessels.

Endothelial cells line our blood vessels and are responsible for regulating the vascular tone — but a high dietary intake of salt has been associated with dysfunction of these cells.

Although it is known that epithelial dysfunction can bring a plethora of chronic illnesses, it remains unclear exactly how salt-induced endothelial dysfunction may affect the brain in the long run.

This is particularly important given that the brain is heavily reliant on a steady and smooth flow of oxygen to function properly, explain the study authors, who were led in their research efforts by Costantino Iadecola, from Weill Cornell Medicine in New York City, NY.

In their paper, Iadecola and colleagues show how excessive dietary salt affects our gut, immune system, and, ultimately, our brain.

WHAT ABOUT PINK HIMALAYAN SALT?

People claim that pink Himalayan salt is healthier than regular salt.

Pink Himalayan salt is chemically similar to table salt. It contains up to 98 percent sodium chloride.

The rest of the salt consists of trace minerals, such as potassium, magnesium, and calcium. These give the salt its light pink tint. These minerals also explain why Himalayan salt tastes different from regular table salt.

WHAT ABOUT BLACK SALT?

Black salt is a type of rock salt, a salty and pungent-smelling condiment used in the South Asia. It is also known as Himalayan black salt. Popularly known in Bangladesh as bit laban, it is a food additive for incrementing the taste of food. But it is not safe for health. Surprisingly, it is used from five-star hotels to road side temporary shops.

Black salt is collected from the mines or salty soil. It is commercially processed in countries like Bangladesh, India, Nepal and Pakistan.

This salt may cause incurable diseases, because it contains fluoride in toxic amounts. Research suggests that regularly taking this salt may cause fluorosis (fluoride toxicity). Fluoride is one type of mineral. In our body it is necessary about 2-3mg, and it comes from natural water. Where more than one part/million fluoride may cause health hazard, whereas black salt may contain fluoride 160-200 parts/million.

Though fluoride is mandatory for teeth and bone structure, but excessive presence of fluoride in body acts as toxins. Its toxicity can be compared with lead, mercury or radon gas. Fluorosis shows the symptoms like as dental and bone caries, joint pain, anaemia, mucous membrane infection in stomach, thyroid disorders, skin infection and so on.

In India, Fluorosis Research and Rural Development Foundation's survey said that more than 66 million people are affected by fluorosis in India. They also suggested avoiding black salt enriched or added foods for the betterment of health.

ABOUT FAT

Use only ghee/clarified cow butter in seasoning the food, if possible. If not possible, use little Nallennai in tamil, Sesame Oil. Avoid onion and garlic, tamarind and chili. If not possible, take only a little in food.

WHY AVOIDING ONIONS AND GARLIC?

Avoid onion and garlic, tamarind and chili. If not possible, take only a little in food.

The writer is associated with the Department of Pharmacy, Bangabandhu Sheikh Mujibur Rahman Science and Technology University (BSMRSTU). Article published in Daily Star Journal, November 15th 2019.

It is easy to understand why to avoid meat but giving up onions and garlic—that's shocking news, even among the healthy eaters!

"I thought they were good for you."
"I know someone who's been eating raw garlic every day; he's in his nineties and in perfect health."
"My food will be really bland if I skipped those two."
To make it more confusing, most of the Ayurvedic cookbooks have recipes with onions, garlic, and other members of the allium family, such as scallions, shallots, and leeks.

Yes, it is true that onions and garlic have many healing properties, among them:
They lower high blood pressure

They reduce high cholesterol
They are a blood-cleanser
It is anti-fungal, antibacterial
It is a natural antibiotic
It is an aphrodisiac; increases sperm count

Unfortunately, onions and garlic also have negative effects, and as a health-conscious cook you should be aware of them. You see, Ayurveda helps us understand the pharmacodynamics of ingredients on deeper, more subtle levels than modern nutraceutical logic, which focuses on the ingredient content and immediate chemical composition and effects.

Let us first look at the distinct chemical compounds of these bulbous plants. Any cook knows that chopping an onion stinks and stings. Why is it so? Dr. Eric Block gives the answer in his book "Garlic and Other Alliums: The Lore and the Science." Garlic cloves produce a chemical called allicin (2-Propene-1-sulfinothioic acid S-2- propenyl ester), which is responsible for their strong pungency and aroma. Garlic can get into the eyes and mouth even if a clove is just rubbed on the foot, a body length away. Its active ingredient passes right through the skin and into the blood. Prolonged contact with garlic will blister and burn the skin. All alliums produce a sulfur molecule that is small and light enough to launch itself from the cut vegetable, fly through the air, and attack our eyes and nasal passages.

Garlic is a powerful herb and traditional Ayurvedic doctors use it as medicine, but do not recommend it as food for daily consumption. Because it is a broad-spectrum antibiotic, garlic (especially raw) kills not only the bad germs but also the most needed friendly bacteria. Garlic does not discriminate between the "bad guys" and the "good guys" in your gut.
Vaidya Mishra explains that cooked onions and garlic have less of an effect (both therapeutic and harmful), because cooking destroys much of the sulfur. Yet, enough of it remains to still harm the friendly bacteria in your gut, especially if you are among the majority of people who lack a good environment for the bacteria to thrive. If you are one of the few blessed with lots of friendly bacteria and keep a good routine and diet, then whether onions and garlic is good for you depends on how much and how frequently you consume them, and what other foods you eat to buffer and

balance the negative properties. For example, if you consume garlic with cooling vegetables, such as loki or zucchini, and if you are not a high Pitta type, maybe your colon can handle the excess sulfur content, and your friendly bacteria will not be harmed.

As any sulfur-rich ingredient, onions and garlic are very heating. They aggravate Pitta on both physical and emotional levels. For someone suffering from acid reflux, ulcers, colitis, heartburn, intestinal inflammation, skin rashes or redness, etc. eating these two substances will make him feel worse. Once a friend of mine who has had ulcers for many years told me, "My relationship with onions and garlic is this: I eat them, and then they start eating me from within." Other friends with ulcers have told me that it feels like someone's cutting your stomach with a hot knife.

Aside from their burning effects on the physiology, alliums also heat up our emotions. Emotional outbursts are another indication that your Pitta is out of control. Have you noticed that people living in cultures that use a lot of onions and garlic are exceptionally temperamental and passionate? It looks like they are yelling at each other, but they are actually having a normal conversation.

As you can see, Pitta types suffer most from the side effects of these potent ingredients. Kapha types would best tolerate onions and garlic because their intestinal walls tend to be thicker and they also need more heating and stimulating foods. If you are a Vata type, however, you have much thinner, more sensitive intestinal walls and probably like gentler flavouring with less onions and garlic.

On energetic level, onions and garlic constrict the vibrational channels (nadis), thus preventing a person from experiencing mental clarity and higher states of consciousness. Vaidya Mishra once told me that whoever eats garlic and onion will have very strong body, but their spiritual antennas will be blocked.

I stopped eating onions and garlic more than 25 years ago because of my yoga practice. Referring to the ancient texts about yoga, my teachers advised me that if I wanted to succeed in meditation, I had to avoid foods that are overly stimulating or clouding to the mind. During my travels in

India and Asia, I have seen that brahmins and pandits never eat onions and garlic or serve them in temples. And even Buddhists and Zen masters in China and Japan avoid them in order to maintain their spiritual balance.

Spiritual reasons aside, garlic-free dining has become the center of gastronomic dispute, especially in Italy. The debate started in 2007, in the center of Rome at La Trattoria restaurant, where top chef Filippo La Mantia shunned garlic as the basis of his dishes because it is just a stinky ingredient that overpowers the delicate flavours of a preparation.

Again, whether onions and garlic are good for you depends on your friendly bacteria; how much sulfur your colon can handle; how much cooked or raw garlic you consume with what types of spices and vegetables. I choose to stick to the Ayurvedic perspective: use them medicine and avoid them for daily consumption. If you feel overheated or if you like to do yoga, chant, meditate; if you want mental clarity, or balanced emotions, then a diet without onions and garlic may greatly support your spiritual practice. If you have eaten them your whole life, why not experiment without them for a month and see how you feel?

Notes:

The Vedic texts urge pregnant mothers to abstain from onion and garlic and other pungent foods because the child's body is too delicate to tolerate such irritation.

References:

Dr. Eric Block's book "Garlic and Other Alliums: The Lore and the Science"

Bob Beck. Is Garlic a Brain Poison? Nexus Magazine, Feb/Mar 2001. Source: From a lecture by Dr. Robert C Beck, DSc, given at the Whole Life Expo, Seattle, WA, USA, in March 1996.]

Harold McGee. The Chemical Weapons of Onions and Garlic. The New York Times, June 8, 2010.

In Italy, is garlic in or out? USA Today, posted 6/22/2007

BLACK PEPPER

BLACK PEPPER INCREASES BIOAVAILABILITY

Bioavailability is the rate at which a drug is absorbed by the body and successfully reaches the target tissue. Nutrients or drugs are not effective if they aren't absorbed completely. So, by enhancing the bioavailability, black pepper ensures the best outcome from these substances.

Piperine is what carries these substances in their most active form to wherever required. There are 3 possible ways in which black pepper does this:

It speeds up the absorption of drugs from the gastrointestinal tract and reduces the time it takes to travel through the tract.

It prevents the drugs from being metabolized or oxidized when they first pass through the liver.
It does both.

The enhanced bioavailability is extremely beneficial as it hastens the recovery from any health condition.

TREATS COGNITIVE DISORDERS

Just the thought of growing old can be scary. And what's troubling is probably not just the aging but also losing control over your brain, forgetting family, or even yourself. A few foods like black pepper can keep your brain strong and healthy, longer.

ALZHEIMER'S

The pepper prevents Alzheimer's and improves your memory by healing nerve damage or memory impairment in the hippocampus. This might be due to the strengthening of neurotrophins or the prevention of free radicals from damaging cells. The actual mechanism is quite unclear and is yet to be researched in depth.

DEPRESSION

Depression is one of the top-most reasons for suicides in the USA. Chocolates and a big ice cream tub can comfort you but not cure. The food you're looking for is black pepper. The piperine in black pepper acts as an anti-depressant, improves your cognitive ability, and helps you think clearly.

The underlying mechanism is not clear in human-based research, studies involving mice have shown that the anti-depressant effect might be due to the regulation of serotonin, a neurotransmitter believed to affect moods, and dopamine, a neurotransmitter with multiple roles in brain function.

PARKINSON'S

Piperine reduces and stops cell death (anti-apoptotic) and is an anti-inflammatory, which plays a huge role in treating Parkinson's, a degenerative disease that mostly affects physical movement.

EPILEPSY

Medicines used to treat epilepsy might have side effects like CNS depression, which results in an increased heart rate and breathing and even loss of consciousness. Black pepper might be a good choice to treat epilepsy as it has anticonvulsant activity, which reduces the incidence of seizures without causing CNS depression.

PREVENTS CANCER
Cancer is a painful disease to go through, and the treatments make it no better with painful side effects. You can try to mellow down the pain and hasten the recovery with a little assistance from black pepper.
Black pepper has an anti-inflammatory effect that can reduce and prevent the creation of cancerous cells.

Black pepper and cardamom together can boost the strength of natural killer cells, thus showing anti-cancer ability. The two foods also boost your immune system and have an anti-tumor effect.

By helping with natural detox, black pepper consequently prevents the growth of cancerous cells. It might also have the ability to prevent specific chemical that cause cell mutations, resulting in cancerous growth.

PROMOTES WEIGHT LOSS
Your body expends energy even when at rest – this is called basal metabolism. Black pepper, a thermogenic, stimulates this basal metabolism and produces more heat. This can also suppress fat accumulation. Piperine also improves your body's metabolism by increasing the production of the chemicals that use more energy. It also shows antiadipogenic activity, which induces fat cell differentiation and causes weight loss, thus dealing with obesity. And with the enhanced bioavailability of nutrients, black pepper ensures that your diet doesn't go in vain.

HELPS QUIT SMOKING
There are multiple products to help you quit smoking – from patches and gums to electric cigarettes. Some of this non-nicotine equipment make use of black pepper in its vapor form. The pepper used here is mostly the essential oil or one or more extracted irritants.

When you inhale using such equipment, the peppery smoke reaches the respiratory tract and creates a sensation similar to that of regular smoke. This sensation satisfies and reduces your craving and makes it easier to deal with the withdrawal symptoms.

TREATS RESPIRATORY ISSUES
Used in traditional Ayurvedic medicine and lately in modern medicine as well, black pepper can cure respiratory issues like sinus, cough, cold, labored breathing, and asthma.

Its irritant quality softens and breaks down the mucus stuck in the respiratory tract. This mucus is then expelled by sneezing or coughing, which is triggered by the peppery smell. And since the pepper is antibacterial, it prevents infections as well.

STRENGTHENS THE DIGESTIVE SYSTEM
What a strong digestive system needs, is healthy food, and black pepper is a good choice. The pepper strengthens the digestive tract and lessens the time taken by foods to travel the tract. The enhanced bioavailability improves metabolism and stimulates the digestive enzymes. And being a carminative, the pepper ensures healthy expulsion of gas from the body and reduces the formation of excess gas.

Black pepper also improves the appetite via olfactory stimulation. This induces a swallowing impulse, which can be beneficial in older people with dysfunctions such as dysphagia. It also reduces oxidative stress, which is a common cause of cardiovascular diseases, reduced metabolism, gastrointestinal diseases, and stomach disorders. This and the anti-inflammatory factor prevent ulcers and gastric mucosal damage. And with its diuretic and diaphoretic properties, it flushes out toxins and excess water.

A word of caution: Since black pepper increases gastric acid secretion, excessive intake might induce acidity, so take it in measured quantities.

TREATS DIABETES
Black pepper helps prevent and treat diabetes by inhibiting specific enzymes. A study using black pepper essential oil showed that it helped fight type 2 diabetes with its phenolic and antioxidant content.

LOWERS BLOOD PRESSURE AND HYPERTENSION
The piperine in black pepper lowers blood pressure through calcium channel blockade and treats hypertension as well. A study of nitric-oxide-deprived rats showed that piperine could lessen the severity of

hypertension caused by oxidative stress. The phenolics and antioxidants in black pepper essential oil also treat hypertension.

PREVENTS DENTAL ISSUES
Healthy teeth imply healthy gums, which can be maintained by flossing and massaging the gums. And many Ayurvedic mixtures for massaging use black pepper as an ingredient. Such massages can relieve you from a toothache, fend off infections with the pepper's disinfectant quality, and treat dental issues such as pyorrhea, which causes pus or blood discharge.

PROMOTES HEALTHY HAIR
Black pepper for hair care seems like an unlikely choice, but it is effective. It might prevent hair loss and also stimulate hair growth with its anti-androgenic property. However, there's a lack of research on this.

HOW TO CHOOSE BLACK PEPPER?
You can buy black peppers whole, finely powdered, or crushed. Packed ground pepper might be less flavourful and pungent. Therefore, we recommend you buying fresh whole peppers and crush them at home when required. Look for a uniform color in the peppercorns as it might indicate higher quality. Choose organic products as much as possible to ensure no form of adulteration.

Store the pepper in a tightly sealed container and keep it in a cool, dry, and dark place. While whole peppers last almost indefinitely, the crushed ones will remain fresh for about 3 months if stored correctly. Freezing the pepper might enhance the flavour.

AYURVEDIC USES AND RECIPES
Ayurveda uses black pepper for medicinal purposes extensively. It is most famously used in making "Trikatu," a commonly used Ayurvedic herbal mixture.

Trikatu contains equal amounts of black pepper, long pepper, and ginger. This is said to enhance the digestive fire (agni) and help relieve indigestion, improve metabolism, and stimulate proper bile production. The mixture also helps strengthen the lungs and makes way for clear breathing by removing sticky, thick mucus.

Black pepper can be used in multiple Ayurvedic home remedies. Here are a few examples:

TO REMOVE DANDRUFF
Mix black pepper in yogurt to form a paste and apply this mixture on the scalp and rub gently. Leave it for 1/2–1 hour and shampoo. Ensure that you don't use excess pepper as it might burn the scalp.

FOR WET COUGH
Grind 3 g of black pepper with the juice of basil (tulsi) leaves. Take it a few times a day to relieve excess sputum.

FOR DRY COUGH
Mix a ripe banana, 1 tsp honey, and 2 pinches of powdered black pepper. Eat this 2–3 times a day.

For immediate relief from cough, you can sprinkle black pepper on a slice of lemon and suck on it.

TO RELIEVE CONGESTION AND KAPHA
Mix 1/4 tsp powdered black pepper with 1 tsp honey. Eat this mixture on a full stomach.

It relieves congestion through its heating ability, removes the kapha, and stops the cough.

FOR WEIGHT LOSS
Black pepper is commonly used in weight-loss recipes. One such mixture is the black pepper and honey tea. The lemon complements the effects of black pepper by giving your digestion a boost.

CUMIN

CUMIN'S HEALTH BENEFITS

It regulates digestion, cumin has been found being beneficial to alleviate digestive problems. It is also a carminative, which means that it relieves you from gas troubles. Due to its essential oils, magnesium and sodium content, it promotes digestion and also gives relief from stomach aches when taken with hot water. Irritable bowel syndrome is one of the most common gastrointestinal disorders. In 2013, was published in the Middle East journal of digestive diseases, the efficacy of cumin extract in treating gastrointestinal disorders like bloating, and other symptoms of ibs, was revealed.

the very aroma of cumin – which comes from an organic compound called cumin aldehyde, the main component of its essential oil – activates the salivary glands in the mouth, which facilitate the primary digestion of food, next is thymol, a compound present in cumin, which stimulates the glands that secrete acids, bile and enzymes responsible for complete digestion of the food in the stomach.

CUMIN IS RICH IN IRON

Cumin is a good source of iron, a mineral which helps in increasing haemoglobin levels, improving blood flow and also promoting a healthy menstrual cycle.

CUMIN BOOSTS IMMUNITY
As previously discussed, the key nutrients in cumin including iron are essential oils, vitamin and vitamin A which boost our immune system in a number of ways. Vitamin C is one of the most powerful antioxidants that stimulate the function and activity of the white blood cells. It further helps neutralise free radicals that lead to many diseases, including, but not limited to cardiovascular diseases and cancer.

CUMIN HELPS WITH ASTHMA AND BRONCHITIS
The presence of caffeine (a stimulating agent), and the richly aromatic essential oils (the disinfectants) make cumin an ideal anti-congestive combination for those suffering from respiratory disorders such as asthma and bronchitis. it can act as expectorant, meaning that it loosens up the accumulated phlegm and mucus in the respiratory tracts, and making it easier to eliminate them from the system via sneezing or coughing up and spitting. By eliminating as much mucus and phlegm as possible, it can inhibit the formation of additional material and help heal the initial condition that led to its formation in the first place.

SKIN CARE
Cumin helps in protecting skin against fungal and microbial infections due to its disinfectant and antifungal properties. It also aids in reducing signs of premature aging like wrinkles, age spots, and sagging skin. These effects is due to the presence of vitamin e which acts as an antioxidant and combats the free radicals.

PROMOTES SLEEP
It is simultaneously a stimulant as well as a relaxant. Some of the components of cumin essential oil are hypnotic in nature and have tranquilizing effects, which also help relieve stress and anxiety that commonly cause insomnia.

REDUCES THE RISK OF DIABETES

It aids in diabetes prevention by reducing the chances of hypoglycemia. A report published in pharmacological research revealed cumin seeds may help in preventing diabetes. The study which utilized a population of diabetic rats, orally administered a set dosage of cumin seeds for six weeks, during which they were monitored closely. The consumption of cumin resulted in a significant reduction in blood glucose and decrease glucosuria, which is a condition where the urine contains too much glucose, also resulting in hypoglycemia and diabetes. Studies such as this have positive implications for the usage of this seed on the reduction of glucose in human populations.

FOOD-BORNE ILLNESS
The antiviral and antibacterial properties of cumin mentioned above help fight infections and food borne illnesses; it also acts as a disinfectant. The components carvacrol and thymol are responsible for this particular health benefit of cumin.

LOWERS CHOLESTEROL
Cumin has hypolipidemic properties, which helps to control high levels of cholesterol in the body. Other benefits include aiding in weight reduction. Cumin powder mixed with yogurt is one way to get in a daily dose.

PREVENTS ANEMIA
Iron-rich cumin can be a nutritious addition to the daily diet for those with anemia. It may help relieve the symptoms of anemia such as fatigue, anxiety, and cognitive malfunction.

BONE HEALTH
For those people looking for calcium-containing foods to build healthy bones, consider cumin. The calcium in cumin helps in increasing the bone-density, thereby delaying the onset of osteoporosis.

TREATS BOILS
Regular use of cumin in food is thought to help in the prevention of boils, rashes, pimples, and other signs of excess toxic content. Components such as cumin aldehyde, thymol, and phosphorus are good detoxifying agents which help in the regular removal of toxins from the body.

ANTICANCER POTENTIAL

Cumin is known for its antioxidant, chemo preventive and anti-carcinogenic properties. Therefore, it is thought to guard against various cancer, especially colon and breast cancer. in a study published in the nutrition and cancer journal, cancer chemo preventive potentials of different doses of a cumin seed-mixed diet in mice. The findings strongly suggest that cumin seeds' cancer chemo preventive potential could be due to its ability to modulate carcinogen metabolism.

Other research by khadar states that thymoquinone present in its seeds exhibits antitumor, anticancer, antioxidant and anti-inflammatory effects.

RELIEVES SYMPTOMS OF PILES (HEMORRHOIDS)
Cumin is known for its ability to aid in clearing up the symptoms and causes of piles (hemorrhoids). This is due to the presence of dietary fiber, as well as carminative, stimulating, antifungal, and antimicrobial properties that enable it to act as a natural laxative in a powdered form.

FIGHTS COMMON COLD
The essential oils present in cumin help fight viral infections, which are often the cause of the common colds. it also suppresses the development of coughing, since it dries up the excess of mucus. Further, the high content of iron and vitamin c helps to strengthen the immune system and keeps infections from forming or becoming worse.

SOOTHES INFLAMMATION
Cumin extract has been shown to contain anti-inflammatory and antiseptic properties that help in relieving pain and inflammation associated with arthritis

TREATS DIARRHOEA
Traditionally, it has been used as a potent antidiarrheal drug. it helps in giving relief from severe diarrhea.

INCREASES LACTATION
As cumin is rich in iron, it is beneficial for lactating mothers or pregnant women, as well as for women who are undergoing menses. Moreover, it is said to help ease and increase the secretion of milk in lactating women due to the presence of thymol.

Cumin has a remarkable amount of calcium (60mg per tablespoon) which accounts for almost 20 percent of our daily requirement of calcium. Calcium is an important constituent of milk and hence it is very good for lactating mothers.

IMPROVES COGNITIVE PERFORMANCE
Given its good iron content, it may assist in increasing blood circulation to various organs, such as the brain, leading to increased cognitive performance. a study published in pharmaceutical biology provided scientific support for cumin extract's anti-stress, antioxidant, and memory-enhancing properties. Furthermore, it promotes the use of cumin as an important culinary spice in foods given preliminary research on its role in fighting stress and related disorders.

WEIGHT LOSS
According to research published in the annals of nutrition and metabolism, cumin is as impactful as any popular diet pill when it comes to reducing weight and fat.

IRRITABLE BOWEL SYNDROME
it is highly effective in improving symptoms of irritable bowel syndrome (ibs) such as cramps, nausea, bloating, gas, and digestive spasms. researchers at the tehran university of medical sciences published a report in the middle east journal of digestive diseases (mejdd) stating that cumin extract; is a type of herbal remedy effectively used in treating gastrointestinal disorders like bloating and other symptoms of ibs.

REDUCES DRUG DEPENDENCE
The compounds present in cumin may assist in the reduction of the addictive behaviour and withdrawal symptoms of opioid narcotics. However, more research is needed to determine the generalizability and reach of these findings.

IMPROVES MEMORY
Preliminary studies performed on animals show scientific support evidence for cumin as providing anti-stress, antioxidant, and memory-enhancing activities. So, there is a science behind using it as part of your daily dishes to help fight stress and related disorders.

OTHER BENEFITS
Cumin is also thought to have beneficial properties in the treatment of renal colic, weak memory, insect bites, and painful stings.

FENUGREEK

WHAT IS FENUGREEK?
Fenugreek (trigonellafoenum-graecum) is a plant that stands around 2–3 feet (60–90 cm) tall. it has green leaves, small white flowers and pods that contain small, golden-brown seed.

For thousands of years, fenugreek has been used in alternative and Chinese medicine to treat skin conditions and many other diseases.

Recently, it has become a common household spice and thickening agent. it can also be found in products, such as soap and shampoo.

Fenugreek contains the chemicals diosgenin and estrogenic isoflavones, which are similar to the female sex hormone, estrogen. Loss of estrogen can cause menopausal symptoms. so, eating it may help reduce menopausal symptoms like mood swings, depression, cramps, and abnormal hunger pangs. it helps monitor a number of other hormones as well, keeping many other bodily processes in line as well.

LOWERS CHOLESTEROL LEVELS
Research published in the British journal of nutrition shows that fenugreek consumption has efficacy in helping reduce cholesterol levels. it helps reduce the levels of ldl (bad) cholesterol significantly, which can prevent various conditions like atherosclerosis, heart attacks, and strokes. it is a rich source of fiber, which scrapes excess cholesterol off of the arteries and blood vessels of the body. By reducing cholesterol content in the bloodstream, you reduce the risk of formation of blood clots.

PREVENTS COLON CANCER
fenugreek possesses anti-carcinogenic properties, particularly with regards to breast cancer and colon cancer prevention. The steroid diosgenin present in the herb has been specifically linked to colon cancer prevention. Furthermore, various non-starch polysaccharides like saponins, hemicellulose, mucilage, and tannin, and pectin, lower cholesterol levels and inhibit the bile salts from being reabsorbed by the colon. This can bind to the toxins and protect the colon's mucous membrane, which can reduce colorectal cancer and other conditions that can negatively affect the colon.
In some studies, fenugreek has been found to exhibit anticancer effects and may also aid in inducing apoptosis or programmed cell death.

SUPPRESSES APPETITE
The journal "phytotherapy research" has conducted research on the effects of fenugreek on appetite. They found that the natural soluble fiber, galactomannan, found in fenugreek helps suppress appetite by making you feel full.

REDUCES CARDIOVASCULAR RISKS
Fenugreek seeds contain 25 percent galactomannan which is a type of natural soluble fiber that helps prevent heart diseases.

CONTROLS DIABETES
Fenugreek extract helps alleviate type I and type II diabetes. a 2005 pilot study suggests that the addition of fenugreek seeds to the diet of diabetics helped in lowering blood glucose level. Due to the presence of the natural

fiber galactomannan, the herb slows down the rate at which sugar is absorbed into the bloodstream. The amino acid 4-hydroxyisoleucine is found in fenugreek, which regulates the release of insulin. This helps prevent the plunges and peaks of blood sugar in diabetics; 15-20 grams of fenugreek is usually recommended for controlling blood sugar on a daily basis.

RELIEVES CONSTIPATION
Fenugreek adds bulk to the stool due to its high fiber content. This also aids in treating constipation, diarrhea, and relieving minor indigestion.

KIDNEY PROBLEMS
Traditional Chinese medicine recommends the use of fenugreek for patients suffering from various kidney conditions. According to an animal study, fenugreek may help reduce the amount of calcification of kidneys and reduce the risk of developing kidney stones. However, more research would be needed to support the claim.

RELIEVES SORE THROAT
Fenugreek's soothing mucilage can help relieve a sore throat, associated pain, and cough.

EFFECTS ON BREASTMILK PRODUCTION
Breast milk is the best source of nutrition for your baby's development. However, some mothers may struggle to produce sufficient amounts.

While prescription drugs are commonly used to boost breast milk production, research suggests that fenugreek may be a safe, natural alternative.

SOOTHES IRRITATION
Fenugreek seeds contain a gumming substance called mucilage and when mixed with water, mucilage expands and becomes a gelatinous salve that helps in providing relief from irritation.

HEARTBURN

One 2-week pilot study in people with frequent heartburn found that fenugreek reduced their symptoms. In fact, its effects matched those of antacid medications.

INFLAMMATION

This herb has demonstrated anti-inflammatory effects in rats and mice. More research is needed to confirm this in humans.

In addition, some reviews and anecdotal reports from traditional medicine suggest that fenugreek can help with ulcerative colitis, skin problems, and numerous other conditions.

Based on the available evidence, fenugreek has benefits for lowering blood sugar levels, and increasing milk production in breast-feeding mothers.

OTHER BENEFITS

Other benefits of fenugreek include the following:
Treats wounds, inflammation, and gastrointestinal ailments.

It helps in battling free radicals due to its antioxidant properties.

In ayurvedic and Chinese medicine, it is used for inducing labor and aiding digestion.

It helps improve the body's overall metabolism and health.

In external application of fenugreek gives relief from irritated skin and other conditions.

Acts as a febrifuge and gives relief from muscle aches.
Fenugreek is considered to be safe, herbal food. it is used as a spice in many cultures and tastes like bitter celery and maple syrup.

It is recommended to avoid all the other spices along with onion, garlic, asafoetida and chilli.

RAW CANE SUGAR – JAGGERY (GUR)

BENEFITS OF JAGGERY (GUR)
India's most favourite and largest used sweetener is jaggery which has ability to digest food properly as well as cleanse whole body by removing toxins. It is very healthy as it contains high quantity of required minerals, vitamins, iron and etc... Some of the outstanding health benefits of the jaggery are mentioned below:

BENEFITS OF JAGGERY FOR BLOOD
It helps in purifying whole blood if regularly consumed.

PREVENTS FROM BLOOD DISORDERS
It helps in enhancing total blood hemoglobin count and boosts immunity thus prevents from many blood related problems and disorders.

REDUCES RISK OF DIGESTIVE DISORDERS
Raw cane sugar is a very good digestive agent helps in maintaining proper digestive system functioning and improving digestion by reducing digestive disorders.

STIMULATES DIGESTIVE ENZYME SECRETION

It stimulates the secretion of digestive enzymes and gets converted to the acetic acid in stomach thus speeds up the digestion process by reducing overload of digestive tract.

REGULATES PROPER BOWEL MOVEMENTS
Jaggery provides relief from the indigestion, flatulence, intestinal worms and constipation by stimulating the proper bowel movements.

BENEFITS OF JAGGERY FOR BONES
It properly nourishes and strengthens the bones and joints by reducing joints pain and other bone problems.

PROVIDES PROPER NOURISHMENT TO SKIN
Its richness in the vitamins and minerals makes it able to nourish the whole body especially skin. It provides skin smooth, healthy, hydrated and glowing look.

CURES PIMPLES AND ACNE
It makes skin free of wrinkles and spots free by curing problems of pimple and acne.

CURES MENSTRUAL PROBLEMS
It helps in curing various menstrual problems among women by providing relief from the stomach pain during periods.

PREVENTS FROM ANEMIA
Its richness in the iron and folates helps during pregnancy and prevents from anemia by maintaining the normal level of red blood cells. It is a source of instant energy thus prevents from weakness and tiredness.

IMPROVES QUALITY SPERM PRODUCTION
Eating gur with amla powder on regular basis helps in enhancing quality and quantity of semen, reducing weakness, energizing body and treating urinary disorders among men

REDUCES WATER RETENTION

Its high level of minerals content especially high potassium level helps in managing weight by reducing the extra water retention in the body.

IMPROVES BODY METABOLISM
Potassium helps maintaining the electrolyte balance, building muscles as well as improving metabolism thus aids in weight loss.

IMPROVES IRON ABSORPTION
Jaggery is the rich source of iron which should be eaten with the vitamin C rich foods as it enhances the absorption of iron in the body. Vitamin C rich foods are lemon juice, amla, guavas and etc. It is very good source of getting healthy, long, smooth, black and strong hair.

PROVIDES NATURAL BEAUTY TO HAIR
It is considered that applying the paste of jaggery, fuller's earth and curd on the scalp twice a month before shampooing makes hair naturally beautiful and long.

FRUITS

RASTHALI BANANA   **PEYAN BANANA**

These two bananas, Rasthali and Peyan bananas are the only fruits recommended by Ramalinga. These two bananas possessing the fire, the purity and the elixir which the body needs to contribute to its alchemical transformation, from the gross body to the golden body.

IX- VEGETARIANISM AND COMPASSION

ANIMAL FLESH IS FULL OF CHEMICALS

Eating meat has been often called "eating on the top of the food chain. In nature there is a long chain of eaters: plants "eat" sunlight, air and water; animals eat grass and smaller animals.

Now all over the world, fields are being treated with poisonous chemicals (fertilizers and pesticides). These poisons are retained in the bodies of the animals that eat plants and grasses.

For instance, fields were sprayed with the insect killing chemical DDT, a very powerful poison which scientists say can cause cancer, sterility and serious liver disease.
DDT and pesticides are retained in animal (as well as fish) fat and once stored, are difficult to breakdown. Thus, as cows, eat grass or feed, whatever pesticide they eat are retained, so when you eat meat, you are taking into your body all the concentrations of DDT and other chemicals that have accumulated during the animal's lifetime.

Eating at the "top" end of the food chain, humans become the final consumer and thus the recipient of the highest concentration of poisonous pesticides, in fact, meat contains 13 times as much DDT as vegetables, fruits and grass.

The Iowa State University once performed experiments which showed that most of the DDT in human bodies comes from meat.

ANIMAL FLESH FULL OF DISEASES

In his fifth report to the Privy Council in England, we find Professor Gamgee staying that "one-fifth of the total amount of meat consumed is derived from animals killed in a state of malignant disease;"

The poisoning of meat does not stop here. Meat animals are treated with many more chemicals to increase their growth, fatten them quickly, improve their meat colour, etc…

In order to produce the most possible meat at the highest profit, some animals are forced fed, injected with hormones to stimulate growth, given appetite stimulant, antibiotics, sedatives and chemical feed mixtures.

MEET IS FILLED WITH ANIMALS TOXINS

Just before during the agony of being slaughtered, the biochemistry of the terrified animal undergoes profound changes. Toxic by-products are forced throughout the body, thus poisoning the entire carcass

According to the Encyclopaedia Britannica, body poisons, including uric acid and other toxic wastes, are present in the blood and tissue.

Just as our bodies become ill during times of intense rage or fear, animals, no less than humans, undergo profound biochemical changes in dangerous situations. The hormone level the animals blood especially the hormone adrenaline changes radically as they see other animals dying around them and they struggle futilely for life and freedom.

These large amounts of hormones remain in the meat and later poison the human tissue.

MEET IS ONLY DECAY FOOD

Raw meat is always in a state of decay. As soon as an animal is killed, denatured substances, called ptomaine are formed.

These ptomaines can build up in the animal flesh or fish, some are poisonous.

There is evidence to suggest that the human digestive tract did not originally evolve to deal with meat, which passes very slowly through the gut; it takes about 5 days to pass out of the body, whereas, for vegetarian food, it takes only 1 days 1/2.

During this time, the diseases causing products of decaying meat are in constant contact with the digest if organs. The habit of eating animal flesh in its characteristics state of decomposition creates a poisonous state in the colon and wears out the intestinal tract prematurely.

MEET IS FULL OF BACTERIA

Full of bacteria the E coli 0157, a strain of life-threatening bacteria that can cause body diarrhoea and dehydration, is naturally present in the intestines of a cattle. In slaughterhouses and meat cutting plants, the animal's faecal matter can come into contact with the beef and contaminate it. It gets package anyway and get shipped to your supermarket. And the U.S. for example, ground beef products have been found to be contaminated with bacteria. In May 2015, about 1.1 million pounds of ground beef caused 22 illness in Minnesota and the potential for more illnesses in 14 other states were recalled.

The Centres for Disease Control and Prevention (CDC) has estimated that E. coli O157:H7 infections cause 73,000 illnesses, 2,200 hospitalizations, and 60 deaths annually in the United States. The outbreak surveillance data from CDC reported that E. coli O157:H7 infections are decreasing after the peak in 1999.

The very young and elderly, along with those who have compromised immune systems, are considered more susceptible to E coli related illnesses.

COOKED MEET – A REAL DANGER FOR HEALTH

Meets that are barbecued of cooked at high temperatures create the following two types of chemicals that may increase your risk a breast stomach and colorectal cancers.

HCA (heterocyclicamines) are created by cooking meat at high temperatures. Barbecuing, like broiling and pan frying, produces more HCA's than cooking a cooler temperature does. (Baking and roasting require less heat). Researchers have found that small amount of HCA's are also produced in meats that have been cooked until they are well done.

PAH's (polycyclic aromatic hydrocarbons) are deposited on your food by the smoke and flame created by fat dripping onto hot barbecue coals.

FULL OF FATS AND CHOLESTEROL

Study after study clearly demonstrates that beef, pork, poultry and lamb, even the untainted by disease, contain massive amounts of saturated fats (factory farmed animals may have up to thirty times more saturated fat) and cholesterol, thus helping to clog arteries, hospitals and cemeteries worldwide.

This is regular meat-eaters live shorter lives. In a worldwide study, it has found that the Eskimos, Greenlanders and the Russian Kurgi tribes had the highest intake of flesh foods. These groups had a lowest life expectancy - in some cases averaging as low as 30 years.

In comparison, population such as the Pakistan Hunzas, east Indian Todas, Russian Caucasians and the Yucatan Indians live under harsh conditions and eat little or no animal flesh. These populations have the highest life expectancies, as high as 90 to 100 years.

The Hunzas eat almost no animal products, living a vigorous life into their 80's and beyond retirement to unknown, and many pass their one 100th birthday.

FULL OF GENETICALLY ALTERED SUBSTANCE

Animals raised for meat today may not have genetically modified (yet), but they would have been affected by genetic tampering. In the U.S. for example, virtually the entire genetically modified maize crop and large percentage of soya and potatoes are fed to farm animals.

Genetically modified products can cause allergies (skin rashes, nausea and respiratory problems). In severe cases, anaphylactic shock and death occur.

It has been hypothesized that are harmful effects of such American modified foods could be passed on a far more concentrated form to humans (as in the case of pesticides) in contaminated meat type vegetarian-type foods.

A plant-based diet has a far lower concentration of pesticide residues then meat. This is because pesticides accumulate as one organism is eaten by another. When a cow eats grass, or is fed maize, the pesticides inside these foodstuffs are largely retained in a concentrated form in her body fat.

They are then passed on to people in the same concentrated form, when they eat the animal's flesh. Even if farm animals were not fed pesticides directly, harmful residues still accumulate in their body fat as result of " environmental contamination".)

Even processed meat products may be affected. Last March, it was discovered that Kellogg's made veggie corn dogs sold in the U.S. Contained a variety of genetically engineered corn.

ANIMAL FLESH AND CONSCIOUSNESS

Many people believe that, meat-based diet results in more depression, fear and agitation causing more crime and unrest in society. When an animal is killed, it is certainly not going to bless you and the world at large. It is expressing so much hatred, fear, anger and unfulfilled desire. When the animal is dying it carries an innumerable poisonous toxin along with so much pain, suffering and hate recorded in the muscles, nerves, bones, cells etc… so that, when one eats these dead body one is prone to experience the same pain, suffering and hate. Meat leaves so much toxins in the system, so that one starts involuntarily cognising negative thoughts as their own personal experience. You receive things in accord with whatever you are tuning yourself with. You become what you eat as well as what you think and do. This is a Law of nature.

Vegetarianism is an act of love and respect for all living beings through the recognition that they are all our brothers and sisters.

When an animal is killed, it will certainly not bless you and the whole world. It expresses so much hatred, fear, anger and unfulfilled desire. When the animal dies, it carries innumerable toxic toxins with so much pain, suffering and hatred recorded in the muscles, nerves, bones, cells, etc., so that when we eat these dead bodies you feel the same pain, suffering and hate. Meat leaves so many toxins in the system, so that we begin to inadvertently recognize negative thoughts of dead animals that we interpret as ours. You receive things in accordance with what you agree. You become what you eat as well as what you think and do. It is a law of nature.

ABOUT EGGS

The egg is a non-vegetarian food. The basic and essential elements that make up the chicken is what is part of the egg. The egg is an extension of the hen's flesh and, therefore, the egg is not considered vegetarian food. Some people sell and eat eggs saying they will not hatch. This is equivalent to the menstrual cycle of hens. Eating these eggs makes a child helpless and increases the possibility of not having children. Today, to get eggs, in spite of the fact that countries like Europe and America, have banned caged hens, still, in major part of the world, people continue put hens in tiny cages and cause them a lot of pain. The egg obtained under such conditions gives a lot of pain and bad karma to the eater.

Ramalinga has clearly warned us that:

"The worst mistake to make is to put a bird in a cage."

Some people say: **Plants are also living things - Why does the natural law allow us to eat them?**

Ramalinga response is:
"Living things such as trees, herbs and rice fields, etc., have only one sense organs, and that is the sense of touch. The manifestation of life (Jeeva Vilakkam) exists only partially in

these bodies. The seeds from which their lives are born are lifeless like the other seeds, they represent the cause. Without destroying their lives, we use seeds, vegetables, fruits, flowers, tubers and leaves as lifeless food."

In the same way that no pain is caused to human's life when we cut our fingernails and hair and lose our sperm, the vegetable kingdom does not feel pain when we take its fruits, vegetables or seeds.

When we do take all the living plant, with its root or sprout as food, we take the life of the living organism.

WHY ARE THE SEEDS LIFELESS?

Ramalinga replied:

"If the seeds have life in them, they should grow before they are sown in the ground. Even after being sown in the ground, some seeds do not grow. In addition, the seed is the cause."

"It is known, even for young children, that this cause only targets the body. The life force lasts forever, but the body is transitory by nature. The life force that is eternal does not need a cause, but the impermanent body needs a cause. It must be known that the seeds are only inert matter."

HOW DOES LIFE, THE SOUL, ENTER THE SEEDS?

"Once the seed is fixed in the soil, the soul passes into the water mingling with the fertile soil and enters the seed allowing the seed to sprout".

WHY EATING SPROUTS IS CONTRARY TO COMPASSION TO ALL LIVING BEINGS?

The shoot is therefore not a lifeless thing like the seed, the vegetable, etc. Therefore, it is true that the germ should not be ripped off.

Why eating vegetables and fruits is not contrary to compassion towards all living beings?

"There is no impurity in the seeds, vegetables, fruits, etc. because there is no development of the senses and vital energy in them. Therefore, the consumption of the seed, the vegetable, the fruit, the leaflets of the tree, the grass, the rice, etc., is not contrary to compassion towards all living beings".

VEGETARIANISM – THE PURE AND TRUE PATH

In Genesis 1: 29-30 God said: *"Behold, I have given you all the plants that produce seeds that are on the face of all the earth, and every tree that has fruit giving seed; it will be the food for you; and to all the beasts of the earth, and to all the birds of the sky, and to all that moves on the earth, which has a living soul in itself, I have given food of all the green plants. And that was".*

People have often noticed that the only food God originally wanted for humans and all other creatures was vegetation. The fact that humans now eat animals and that many animals eat each other was not part of God's original plan of creation. It is rather the result of the fall of consciousness which happened after the first creation.

DO THE VEDAS TEACH VEGETARIANISM?

The Vedic scriptures teach the path of "Ahimsa Paramo Dharmaha" which means the highest "dharma", the path of no killing, no harming any living being; being a man of peace and love.

In satyartha prakash, Maharishi Dayananda has said that meat eating makes a person's temperament violence prone. Those who eat meat and consume liquor, their bodies and semen get contaminated.

In Christianity, Jesus Christ advocated: Thou shall not kill and love thy neighbour. The views of Jesus Christ in his Gospel of Peace are, "The truth is that one who kills others, is, in fact, killing himself. Whosoever eats flesh of an animal after killing it, is actually eating his own flesh himself. The death of an animal is the death of him who kills the animal because the revenge or punishment for this crime cannot be less than death itself" Again, kill not the harmless animal, nor eat the flesh of your innocent prey; lest you become a slave of Satan. He further said: Vegetarian food will give you life and strength but if you eat dead food (meat) your food will kill you because life begets life and death always begets death.

Saint Ramalinga has said:
"If you want the golden key to unlock the sky, be nice with all life".

No saint, no sage and no writing has ever recommended "himsa" (violence).

In Patanjali's Yoga Sutras and all the scriptures are teaching ahimsa.

"Reduce the harm and minimize the violence. Whatever you receive in your life, let the source be love - it should come with love. Your money should come with love. Your clothes should come with love. Your food must come with love, no violence. Everything should be an offering of love."
Unfortunately, the non-vegetarian diet never comes to us with love. Have you ever heard of an animal that came to you with love telling you?

"Here, please, take my thigh and make your soup"

No, animals do not give us their body parts that way; they even try to escape. They hate us because we are causing them violence. Non-vegetarian food is not a food filled with love.

Ramalinga clearly says:
"Whoever eats the flesh of other beings cannot obtain the grace of the Lord. He also says, "If a person has the siddhi to raise another person from death and if that person eats meat, then he cannot overcome the repeated cycle of birth and death either, he will have to come back in turn"

Thirumoolar and Manichavasagar, two very great Siddha saints, Tamil, condemn the consumption of meat and condemn the meat eaters as Pulaiyars (sinners).

All major philosophies of Advaitam Dwaitam and Visistadvaidam advocate eating only vegetarian foods to ensure spiritual progress.

Jainism also strongly condemns the consumption of meat. There scriptures mentioned that:

"Vegetarianism alone does not bring divinity closer, but it will effectively help to generate human love and compassion for all living beings around us. Vegetarianism is the first step in spirituality."

"People who avoid eating meat and have compassion for all forms of life will be eligible for divine grace."

From the Manu-samhita 5.51-52)
"By not killing any living being, we become fit for salvation."

From the Bhagavat Purana, (11.5.14):
"Those who are ignorant of the true Dharma and, though wicked and haughty, make themselves virtuous, kill animals without any feeling of remorse or fear of punishment. Moreover, in their next lives, these people will be eaten in turn by the creatures they have killed in this world. so is the law."

From Thirukural:
"How can one obtain grace if he develops his flesh by eating the flesh of other living beings?"

From the Mahabharatha (115.16):
"This man, who has eaten meat, later abandons him, gains merit by an action so great that a study of all the Vedas or a performance, O Bharata, of all the sacrifices [Vedic rituals], cannot give."

From the Mahabharatha Bagavad Gita:
"He who is not jealous but who is a good friend for all living beings is dear to me."

From the Bible:
"Do not kill", one of the 10 commandments.
"And to every beast of the earth, and to every bird of the air, and to all that creeps on the earth, all that has the breath of life, I have given all the green plants to feed."

"Blessed are the merciful, for they will obtain Mercy"—Mattew 5:7

From the Koran:

"It is not their meat or their blood that reaches Allah; it is your piety that reaches him "(22.37)" Show mercy to all living beings, as the mercy and love shown to you by the Lord "
- **Muhammad's words.**

The famous saint, Mir Dad, said that anyone who eats the flesh of any living being shall have to repay it with his own flesh. He who breaks another living being's bone shall have his own bones smashed.

Kabir, addressing Muslims, makes it clear that even fasting is in vain if its practitioner lets his tongue dictate the killing of living beings for the sake of its taste; Allah will not be pleased this way.

The Imam of London mosque, Al-Hafiz B.A. Masri, in his book "Islamic concern for Animals", has expressed sorrow about the excesses against animals in the name of religion. In the holy Coran and the teachings of the Holy Prophet Muhammad, it is written that "all acts of torturing of animals, and even keeping birds in cages as sin."

The Imam Masri is himself a vegetarian and advises everyone to adopt vegetarianism.

From buddhism:
"To become a vegetarian is to enter the current that leads to nirvana."

From lord mahavira:

"Show love to all forms of life. whoever wounds his life, he first hurts himself."

From Srilaa.C. Bhaktivedanta Swami Prabhupada:

"Being non-violent towards human beings and being a killer or an enemy of poor animals is the philosophy of dark forces. in this age, there is always an enmity against animals and, therefore, these creatures are always anxious. The emotions of the animals generated before being killed return to human society and this gives rise to ever greater tensions between men, individually, collectively or at the national level."

The Jain's scriptures list 108 forms of violence. Violence in thought and actions, indulging in violence oneself or getting others to use violence or abetting violence by others, are all forbidden. Even to contemplate violence is a sin. Violence is manifested in thought, word and deed. Even the utterance of words which hurt another person is considered as a sin. In a religion where tying up of animals, causing hurt to them, overloading them are even keeping them in cages is considered sinful; the question of eating meat just does not arise.

Those who wish to be happy and secure must learn how to make others happy and secure, otherwise nature has its own strange ways of punishment. just as the description of forests has disturbed the environmental balance and compelled us to launch a campaign for protection of forests and plantation of more trees, we will have to launch a similar campaign one day to save animals and birds which are equally vital for the maintenance of our environmental and ecological balance of nature. Survival of animal world is a matter of our own survival. Delay will be disastrous.

X - VALLALAR'S DIVINE REVELATION OF SACRED HERBALS

These Plants Acting As Nectar, It Is Strongly Recommended That Non-Vegetarian Do Not Consume These Plants; Considering The Fact That Poison And Nectar don't Go Together

KARISALANGANNI IN TAMIL, ECLIPTA ALBA

Thanks to its rich content of copper, iron and vitamin C, it helps control anaemia.

Eclipta alba is an excellent liver tonic which protects and strengthens liver function, increases production of bile and reduces inflammation.

Due to its regenerative effect, it helps cure jaundice and fatty liver. It helps balance acidity, purify blood, control cholesterol, remove bile and phlegm, removes weakness of the body, debility of the mind, diabetes and neutralizes vata, pitta, kapha,

It helps control urinary infections, uterine haemorrhage and white discharge.

It protects and treats eye diseases and maintain clear vision.

Used as tooth powder, it strengthens teeth and gums.
It clears tongue coating.

It helps expel faecal matter from large intestine and cures constipation.

Regular intake helps slow down the aging process and promotes good health.

It helps the transformation of the body into golden body, increases mental light power, peacefulness, builds up spiritual heat to help control excessive anger and sexual energies.

THOOTHUVALAI IN TAMIL, SOLANUMTRIBOLATUM SOLANACEAE, PURPLE FRUITED PEA EGGPLANT:

Thoothuvalai is effective in eliminating phlegm from the lungs, chronic bronchitis, dry cough, wheezing, asthma, loss of hearing.

It relieves body pain and gives strength.

It helps strengthening the nervous system, improves memory power very effectively. Due to its rich calcium content, it strengthens bone and teeth.

It purifies the blood, calms hyper sensibility, takes away pain, regularizes nervous agitation and anxiety, takes away the early symptoms of cancer, thyroid, fever, trembling fever, asthma, balances vata and kapha.

It develops the tissues, purifies through the elimination of excrement, gives strength to the heart and gives a nice glow in the face. It gives contentment and joy, develops listening capacities, develops intelligence and controls anger. It gives a shining and attractive face, increases perception of the five senses and discernment, opens the chakras, helps for good meditation, helps to rise the seven veils, increases the abilities for spiritual studies and increases knowledge of Higher Self.

MUSUMUSUKKAI IN TAMIL, MUKIA MADERASPATNA, MADRAS PEA PUMPKIN

It treats imbalance of impaired Kapha and Pitta.

It is effective in treating rhinitis allergy, running nose, common cold, wheezing, food aversion, tastelessness, odourless, dropsy and all respiratory problems.

It is effective in eliminating phlegm from lungs and cleans the respiratory passages.

It helps control wheezing caused by excess pitta in the body. It helps clear hoarse throat and very useful for dry cough.

It supports ailment especially for lungs and respiratory system.

It cleanses inflamed mucous membrane, reduces irritation, relieves from bronchial spasms and clears inflammation.

It is rich in calcium hence helps strengthen the bones.

PULIYARAI IN TAMIL, OXALIS CORNICULATA, COMMON YELLOW WOODSORREL

Puliyarai removes pitta biles, all types of poison and toxin.

It reduces weight and allergy from food.

It gives good taste and appetite.

It helps cure jaundice, increases red blood cells and removes anaemia.

It regulates over bleeding during menstruation, reduces high blood pressure.

Puliyarai reduces confusion in the mind, brings coolness and calmness.

It strengthens the body as a whole and neutralises the heat coming from muladara chakra, develops the senses, brings rejuvenation and helps prevents early hair greying. It gives power of speech, strengthens the mind. It strengthens the subtle bodies and helps to the secretion of all types of ambrosia.

VALLARAI IN TAMIL, GOTUKOLA OR CENTRELLA ASIATICA, ASIATIC PENNYWORT

Vallalarai's leaves resemble the shape of the brain, so It is no surprise that they can help develop learning and memory power. They also reinforce the nerves, calm the mind, treat depression and reduce sexual desire by helping to transform sexual energy into spiritual power.

Vallarai leaves can reinforce the immune system, reduce tiredness, clear up skin problems.

They reinforce the immunity, cure leprosy, kidneys inflammation and reduce swelling.

The leaves help rejuvenate the cells of the body into light.

They also develop mind clarity, intuition and gives stability of mind necessary for long focus of attention during meditation.

PONNANGANNI IN TAMIL, ALTERNATHERA SESSILIS, DWARF COPPERLEAF

Ponnanganni helps reducing body heat caused by pitta and strengthened the body.

It is rich in protein, iron, calcium, vitamin C.

It has a cooling effect on the eyes, reduces irritation.

It helps improving eyesight and enhances clear vision.

It helps cure piles and spleen disorders.

Using ponanganni regularly gives a glowing skin and relieves skin related problems.

It helps cure piles and spleen disorders.

AAVARAM POO IN TAMIL, SENNA AURICULATA

The essential contents of the flower improve the complexion of the skin and rejuvenate the body.
It helps control diabetes very efficiently.
It helps reduce body heat and cools down the body.
It helps to cure excessive bile (pitta) secretion, blood micturition, irregular menses and ulcer.
It helps purify the blood and removes toxins through sweating.
It helps prevent bad odour and cures skin related problems.

KADUKKAI in Tamil, PORCESSED TERMINALIA CHEBULA, KAAYAKARPAM

It helps decalcifying the pineal gland and oxygenating the blood.

It balances the 5 elements (earth, water, air, fire, ether) in the human physiology

It relieves flatulence and eases bowel movement (constipation)

It acts as a good laxative and cleanse gastrointestinal tract. It induces appetite. It is effective in dyspepsia. It is purgative, astringent. It strengthens the stomach.
It helps in reducing weight by toning up the system.
It detoxifies and rejuvenate the all physiology.

PEAYAN – PLANTAIN ROOT

Plantain root is the perfect kaya kalpa. It is the divine tree of Suddha sanmarga.

It can treat all deficiencies, Peayan has no limit in his effect. It cures the most affected psychic trouble. The jus of the root clears passage of the oesophagi and dissolves kidneys stone. The flower regulates semen and white discharge. It is good for making red oxide. It removes all kind of poison (venin, radiation..,) small pot.

It develops physical attraction, augments digestion and purgation and regulates the prana, constructive power.

It softens the mind and creates a motherly feeling of loveliness and liveliness.

It Contains ozone power, ambrosial effect. It opens the chakras. It helps develop intelligence and creative power. It is the manifestation of grace light. It helps connect with Rudra heart centre. It controls causal heat and Protect from all evils, Symbol of eternity.

XI - THE STORY OF CREATION THE EVOLUTION OF THE SOULS - FROM ATOM TO SOUL

In his "Upadesha", Ramalinga explains his enlightened view about the self, the soul and the evolving psychic being. He has clearly told that the Lord of the heart as the Divine Himself has become each soul as one individual centre among the many centres of manifestation.

"How shall I address Thee, O my Lord, who hast showered grace on me and taken me into Thy possession and rule? Shall I address Thee as the inseparable great light of my heart? Or as the Father of my soul? Or as the Mother of my soul? Or as the bliss? Or as the Lord of my soul? Or as the unique Amrita that has brought up and developed my soul? Or as my Friend? Or as the Unique Essence or Source of me as a being of existence?"

Here, can be seen that in the fully evolved psychic being, the Divine abides as its Lord, the Divine Presence as the Origin of one's soul and as the cause for its growth and development.

"O Lord! Thou hast become the soul of soul in the harmonious and excellent Golden World of Truth-Knowledge by Thy Play of Grace, giving insatiable bliss".

O my soul! O soul of my sweet soul! O my consciousness! O consciousness of my consciousness!"

"O Light that shines as the Soul of my soul of form!... O God of Vast Grace-Light who has become Peru Veli, the Vastness of Formless Space (Supramental Vastness) and the (Spaceless) Infinity that contains or manifests the said Vast Space at the

summit super-mind, and Thou transcend into the Infinity of existence Beyond."

"O universal Lord who playeth in the harmonious Golden World of Truth-Knowledge! By Thy Play of Grace, thou hast become Light in and of all the souls or beings."

"O Lord who has become my soul, come, come! O Lord who has become a sweet Soul within my soul, come, come! O Lord of my soul come, come!"

"O Soul of my soul come, come to play! O Thou who abideth in my heart, come, come to play! O My Lord, O Husband of my soul, come to play!"

In the above stanzas, Ramalinga clearly, speaks of the Lord of the Heart as the Divine in one's soul and that the Divine Himself has become each soul which is one individual centre among the many centre of His Manifestation. Both the psychic being or evolved soul, and the Divine Presence in the soul are addressed. The Divine Presence is also referred as the Divine Consciousness. Souls of soul means also in effects the individual Self above the head, that is to say, the individual divinity or the Divine portion presiding over the soul with its deputy within the heart in the field of evolution. As Ramalinga is expressing it, this individual Self is always one with the Supreme Divine, the Supreme Self in all beings which is at once transcendental, universal and individual Self, that is the Soul of soul.

"O Lord, O Ambrosia in the heart! O Ambrosia which is the beginning less origin and relation of my soul!"

"O self-existent original Light without beginning and end!... The Light that shines in all living beings."

"O God of the light of Cit Ambalam, that is to say, the comprehending super-mind! O player of Purity! Thou abideth in my heart for ever...Thou hast become the Mother, Father and benevolent Guru of my soul..."

"O precious Gem of Light! Thou art the Soul of the persistently living soul, full of bliss."
"O vast Grace-Light that has made my heart as the Sabha, the field of play of Truth-knowledge where it resides, giving me Thy refuge."

O Grace-Flame of Truth! Thou hast manifested the White Light so as to make the Light of the soul manifest and the inner Light to grow."

"O Lord of Truth! Thou art present in Ajna, holding the soul centre, deep behind the mind, as possessed by the heart of love and hast manifested everywhere at all levels of being, the inmost, inner, outer and outmost."

"O stable Light that has manifested in the inmost hearts and in the inner and outer levels and also in the outmost level of nature!"

In the above stanzas, Ramalinga refers to the Divine spark, soul-essence or the Christ in the Christian tradition, in all the living beings and creatures. It is the Supramental Light that possesses the heart, mind and soul and make them the field of Thy play; In fact, it manifests in all levels of being, from the innermost to the outermost, from the soul to the body. According to Ramalinga, the soul centre can be reached or realised in the centre of the brain. Ramalinga gives importance to Ajna centre, amid the forehead, as it is the most conscious centre in man where the divine flame Agni burns. Ramalinga insists that Ajna should be contemplated with a heart full of love and compassion to realise the light of our soul, our true nature.

Ramalinga describes the four-fold disciplines according to the inmost, inner, outer and outermost levels of being. Ramalinga makes a four-fold distinction in the levels of the individual being in *"Pinda"*, the human system with its body having its basis in the subconscious and of the corresponding of *"Anda"*, the universal nature.

"The Divine Light shines in four levels, through the inmost, inner, outer and outermost.

1 - In "Pinda" (the human system), *"Anma"* (the soul or divine spirit in man), that knows the Truth of everything which through the phenomenon of attention is directing his awareness on the object of knowledge, is **the inmost**;

2 – The jeevan or the evolving psychic being put forth by the divine spirit or soul-spark, is **the inner being** with a consciousness that knows the use of a thing;

3 - The instrumental nature, *"karana"* (or mental and vital instruments or faculties), with its consciousness which knows through discrimination about the name and form, qualities, good or bad of a thing, is **the outer**;

4 - The body and its senses, comprised of the bodily sense organs-Indriyas such as eyes and its perceptive knowledge that perceives a thing by perception alone, without mental discrimination as to the name, form and qualities good or bad of a thing, is **the outermost**.

So too in *"anda"* (the universal nature), Agni is the inmost, corresponding to **the inmost** soul, sun is the inner corresponding to the **inner Jeevan**, moon is the outer corresponding to the **outer being**, and stars are the outermost corresponding to the **outermost of being**...

Now the causal manifestation, *"Kaarana"*, of the Divine Light takes place in *"Pinda"*, in the human body, at Ajna, the mid centre between the eyebrows, Ajna as the soul centre;

And for "*Anda*"(the universal), in "*Paramaakaasa*" (the supreme Ether or sky) as the supramental world – the Divine Light here in "Paramaakaasa" is of the nature of Light within the Light.

The causal-effectual manifestation takes place in Sarvayoni, in the Womb of all created beings and all manifestations in the "*bindu*"(light) of lightning and in the "nada"(sound)of thunder, bindu being the focal point of the light and nada, the vibration of sound. Both bindu and nada are making the causal-effectual relationship which brings forth creation; lightning and thunder are here as a metaphor for the outer phenomenal of nature or its effectual manifestation.

"Ramalinga says that The Light of the Universal Soul or Spirit is the" *JnanaSabhai* or *Cit Sabhai*", the field or world of Truth-Consciousness, the comprehensive Super-Mind;

The Light within that Light is the Divine Spirit, God the supreme Being, the One-in-One or the Supreme Infinite Light-in-the Universal Light.

The dance or play of movement of this inner Light of the Divine is called the dance or play of the dance of the World of knowledge "*Jnana Akasha Natanam* or *Ananda Natanam*", the will of the Divine Knowledge in manifestation which is the blissful dance of the divine dancer, "*Nataraja*", the Supreme Siva.

So too in Pinda, the human system and/or the subconscient and the material inconscient "*Anma Akasha*", the sky or space of the Soul of souls whose inmost part is called the Golden Sabhai, the Golden field of Truth-Knowledge and Jeeva Akasha, the sky or space of Jeeva or Jeevas (the inner being Jeevan or evolving psychic being) that is the Rajata Sabhai or silver Sabhai (the luminous silver whitish field by way of comparison).
Thus, the Divine Spirit or God has integrally manifested by its integral Conscious Force in the effectual, causal and causal-effectual levels of manifestation and especially at the said important nine places, four in the Pinda (Pinda, i.e. the field of evolution) and five in the Anda (i.e the

universal planes including *"paramaakaasa"*, the Super-Mind, the Super-Causal source)"

Paramaakaasa, the transcendent and Universal Super-Mind is the supreme cause for all creation. In the universe it is Agni (the cosmic fire) that is the inmost cause, present at Ajna (third eye) in the individual level of soul.
The Mind (i.e. Moon) indicates the causal-effectual or manifestation (Kariya Karanan).

The effectual manifestation (Kariyan) of the inner being jeevan, into the outer levels representing by the sun in the universal nature.

Concerning the Super-Causal Source of Paramaakaasa, Agni, the sun and the moon, the three luminaries taken together are depicted as the effectual manifestation in Anda, the universe; between them, Agni becomes the causal *"Karanan"*, the moon becomes the causal-effectual or manifestation *"Kariya Karanan"* and the sun becomes the effectual *"Kariyan"*.

AGNI

In Upadesha, Ramalinga is pointing out that Agni, which is hidden in the earth, represents the inmost divine principle of the Universal Nature. Agni of the Universal corresponds to *"Aanma"* (the soul) or the Aanmaakasa in the pinda that is in the heart of man and in the sub-conscient. Agni is also described as formless causal with the powers to give knowledge and enlightenment as well as the burning fire consuming karma at Ajna level (i.e. power of creative and dynamic manifestation), golden, perfect and whole in the possibilities of manifestation with all the 64 *"kalaas"* or principles of existence, all-pervading and becoming the light of the soul (i.e., as its being and having the soul's consciousness as its field of play of knowledge and Power.

Thus, this description of Agni fits with Aanma Aakaasa, the sky or space of souls which is also called the Golden Sabhai.

THE SUN

Ramalinga gives all details about Agni, the stars, the moon and the sun:

The Sun has a form that illuminates light and gives heat without burning; it represents the effectual aspect of creation "Kariyan" with its 16 kalas or its own principles of existence. With its round shape, luminous sphere, Brahmananda Vyapaka is pervading into the physical universe and extending into the earth and its orbit. The sun has five colours and represents the Jeeva Consciousness of evolving psychic being, the field of play of knowledge "Sabhai". The Light of the Jeeva is the Lord or the Light of its being.
The five colours of the sun are:

1-White – "Adi Shakti" – "Anugraha" (Grace of evolution)
2-Green – "Para Shakti" – "Tirobhava" (Veiling of involution)
3-Red – "Iccha Shakti" – Force of Destruction
4-black (i.e. deep blue) – "Kriya Shakti" – Force of Maintenance
5-Gold – "Jnana Shakti" - Force of Creation

THE MOON

The moon is form-formless (Rupa-Arupa), one side of its sphere being luminous while the other shadowy, full and new moon. It acts as the causal-effectual or manifestation "Kariya Karanan". It is reflecting the light (Shoba) but not heating. With its 12 kalas and 4 kalas given to the stars, its light is pervading in the earth and is orbiting around the sun and extending in the all universe. Its colour is of mixed green and white. Its field of play or influence is mental consciousness "Sabhai". The mental light is its being.

Ramalinga refers to the covering of the 64 kalas of Agni, as if by ashes (i.e. involution) and of which eight kalas are now manifested. He further adds that the sun, standing as the symbol of Jeevan, the evolving psychic being, has given 4 out of its 16 kalas to moon of the mind; this signifying the evolutionary progress or ingress of the evolving psychic being into the mind. In turn, the moon of the mind has given 4 out of 16 kalas to the stars which represent the outermost being of "indriyas" or senses and the physical body. Thus, the evolution appears to be represented by the symbol of Agni, the Sun, the Moon and the stars in the inmost, inner, outer and outer-most levels of human being in the field of terrestrial Nature.

Agni has not yet exhausted all the 64 kalas or potentialities of manifestation. It has revealed or released into manifestation only 8 kalas so far up till now. Therefore, the possibility for further evolutionary progress is implied. Ramalinga further clarifies, that all the kalas of Agni, manifest and unmanifest, sun and moon have combined to form the material body (pinda) of 96 kalas or tattvas in the field of ignorance.

THE CREATION OF THE 7 DAYS OF THE WEEK FROM THE MIXING TOGETHER OF THESE THREE LIGHTS : SUN, MOON, AGNI.

SUNDAY: Arises from the coming together of the light of the Moon with the light of Agni

MONDAY: Arises from the coming together of the light of the Sun with the light of Agni.

TUESDAY: Arises from the coming together of the light of the Sun with the light of Moon.

WEDNESDAY: Arises from the coming together of the light of the Moon with the light of the Sun.

THURSDAY: Arises from the coming together of the light of the Sun with the light of Mercury.

FRIDAY: Arises from the coming together of the light of the Moon with the light of Mars.

SATURDAY: Arises from the coming together of the light of the Sun with light of the Moon and the light of Agni.

THE EMERGENCE OF CREATION THROUGH THE 96 TATTVAS

The 96 tattvas "aaraarukaattiya" are the 96 instruments of the soul to mingle with God.

According to very ancient siddha system, as revealed by Ramalinga, the human physiology and the universe are composed of 96 tattvas; they are the 96 constituents which constitute the all creation; They are the elementary principles that govern this creation and the fundamental elements which act as the basic building blocks for this complex creation.

siddha fundamental principles never differentiated man from the universe. According to them, "nature is man and man is nature, and therefore, both are essentially one. Man is said to be the microcosm and the universe the macrocosm.

Vallalar has revealed the true meaning of the world Tattvas:

"Tat" means this, and this is equal to Siva. Tvam describes Siva's character or qualities.

Lord Siva is the supreme reality. He is eternal, Formless, Independent, Omnipresent, One without a second, Beginningless, Causeless, Taintless, Self-Existent, Ever Free, Ever Pure. He is not limited by time. He is Infinite Bliss and Infinite Intelligence.

Lord Siva pervades the whole world by his Shakti. He works his Shakti who is the conscious energy of Lord Siva. She is the very body of Lord Siva.

As the potter is the first cause for the pot, the stick and the wheel are the instrumental causes, the clay is the material cause of the pot; Similarly, Lord Siva is the first cause of the world. Shakti is the instrumental cause. Maya is the material cause.

Lord Siva is the God of Love. His Mercy for all his creatures is infinite. He is the Saviour and Guru. Through the 96 Tattvas, Lord Siva is engaged in freeing the souls from the thraldom of matter. He assumes the form of

Guru out of his intense Love for mankind. He wishes that all should know Him and attain the ultimate state of bliss in the complete Union with Thee. He watches the activities of the souls, helping them in their onward march. The Lord with His Omnipresent Grace, endowed the soul and body with the 96 tattvas, allowing the soul going through them and become aware of the presence of the Light of God within itself, the source of all Knowledge.

According to Ramalinga, there are three aspects of Siva:

1 – The lower aspect of Siva who dissolves the world and liberates the Jivas from their bondage.

2 – The higher form of Siva is called Parapara. In this form Siva appears as Siva and Shakti "Ardhanarisvara", Param- Jyothi.

3 – Beyond these two forms Siva, He is the Param or the ultimate, the absolute undifferentiated Supreme God.

From there the all creation stems through the sequential unfoldment of the 96 Tattvas as shown below:

ALMIGHTY GOD	ARUT PERUN JYOTHI	VAST SUPREME GRACE LIGHT
DIVINE MOTHER	ARUT SHITHI	
The ultimate Primal One who creates the vast universe from Pure Consciousness, Sath Chith Ananda	SUDDHA NATHAM	SUDDHA SIVAM
It appears from the union of Siva and Shakti	SUDDHA VINDHU	SUDDHA SAKTHI
The primal unvoiced sound	PARA NATHAM	PARASIVAM
Light and Wisdom	PARA VINDHU	PARASAKTHI

THE 5 SIVA TATTVAM

When Jnana shakti is acting, it is called Sivam or Siva Shakti.	NATHAM	SIVAM Siva alone is the efficient cause of all creation, evolution, preservation, concealment and dissolution
When kriya shakti is acting, it is called Shakti	VINDHU	SAKTHI Siva brings forth the worlds and all living beings through his dynamic power, Shakti.
When the two are acting simultaneously at 50% each, it is called Sadasivam	SATHASIVAM	Shath Chith Anandam Absolute and supreme state of bliss consciousness
When Kriya Shakti is acting more than jnana shakti, it is called Isuram.	ESWARAM	The expression of unconditional love through all living beings
When Jnana Shakti is acting more than Kriya Shakti, it is called Suththaviththai.	SUDDHAVITHAI	To experience unconditional love through Supreme Compassion for all living beings

The 7 Vidhya Tattvam

MAYAI   Maya meaning "she who measures" the peculiar power by which the One reality appears to become limited and measurable, quantifiable through the illusion of separation of subject and object. Here, the universal Being becomes pasu, the bound consciousness/being or anu (atom/particle). This is due to the play of creation. This mark the beginning of the impure "asuddha" order of ontogenesis.

KALAM   The time of living in this body is programmed in our soul by God, according to the quality of our past actions.

NEYATHI   God is giving a certain quantity of karma to bring with us in each incarnation. This quantity of karma given by God is determined in accordance with our capacity to manage it.

KALAI   The 5 steps on the path to God realization, the path of the soul raising towards God.

1 – Nivirthikalai
According to our sincerity, determination and dedication to God on our sadhana, God will be freeing us from attachments.

2 - Pirathittakalai
Establishment of a state free from desire.

3 - Vidya Kalai
The soul gains the knowledge, wisdom and experiences the Mercy of God in 3 steps: 1-The guessing about the existence of God is driving us to search for Thee; 2-gaining knowledge through the holy scriptures; 3-gaining the experience of our soul, the experience of God through our spiritual practice.

4 - Shantikkalai
Having reached a state free from liking and disliking and hate, our mind and soul is filled with peace.

5 - Shanti Athithakkalai
Having crossed the experience of peace, beyond peacefulness, our soul is mingling with God.

VITHAI	God is giving us spiritual knowledge which we receive through inner inspiration and intuition.	
ARAAGAM	Consciousness in action	
PURUDAN	Purusha, The principle of individual consciousness or subjectivity.	
ASUDDHA MAYA SHAKTI	**PRAKURITHIMAYAI**	**THE BEGINNING OF THE IMPURE MAYA**

THE 4 LEVELS OF THE MIND

MANAM	The origin of the constant thinking activity
BUDHI	**Researching organ**: what is this, what is good, what is bad, what is that; It is correlated with cognition and understanding.
CHITHAM	It is the transpersonal, subconscious mind in which the seeds of karma reside, past memories and old concepts of the reality; It is the basis of our ordinary consciousness; higher intelligence.
AGANGAARAM	It is related with the stimulating and discriminating aspect of the mind.

THE 5 ORGANS OF ACTION: "KARUVIDAL"	Mouth "Vaai"
	Hands "Kaigal"
	Feet "Kalgal"
	Anus "Eru"
	Sex organ "Karuvai"

THE 5 SENSORY ORGANS OR COGNITIVE ORGANS: "AIMPULANGAL"	Taste "Chuvai"
	Sight "Oli"
	Touch "Uuru"
	Hearing "Oochai"
	Smell "Nathram"

THE 5 ORGANS OR TOOLS OF GAINING KNOWLEDGE: "AIMPORIGAL"	Body "Mei"
	Mouth "Vaei"
	Eyes "Kah"
	Nose "Mukku"
	Ears "Chevi"

THE 5 ELEMENTS: "MAHABHUUTAS"	Earth "Nilam",
	Water "Niir"
	Fire "Neruppu"
	Air "Kaathru"
	Space "Vaanam"
THE 60 THATHVIGAM	EXTERNAL TOOLS OF GAINING KNOWLEDGE
5 PRITHIVI KARYAM - EARTH ELEMENT BODY STRUCTURE	SKIN
	BONE
	VEINS
	FLESH
	HAIR
5 APPU KARYAM - WATER ELEMENT BODY STRUCTURE	Water
	Blood
	Bone Marrow
	Brain
	Semen
5 TEJU KARYAM – FIRE ELEMENT BODY ENERGY	Hunger
	Sleeping
	Fear
	Sex
	Laziness
5 VAYU KARYAM – AIR ELEMENT BODY MOVEMENT	Running
	Walking
	Standing

	Sitting
	Lying

5 SPACE KARYAM/SPACE ELEMENT – BODY – MIND ASUDDHA MAYA SHAKTI	Jealousy
	Anger
	Desire
	Obstinacy
	Envy

5 VASANATHI – EXPRESSION	Vasanam – Speech
	Kamanam – Smelling
	Danam – Giving
	Visarkam – Elimination
	Anandam – Happiness

THE 10 VAYUS OR GASES

Prana Vayu	It is located in the head and chest, and governs intake, inspiration, propulsion and forward momentum.
Apana Vayu	It is located in the pelvis region and governs the elimination and the downward and outward movement.
Vyana Vayu	It is located in the whole body and governs circulation on all levels, expansiveness, pervasiveness.
Udana Vayu	It is located in the throat and governs growth, speech, expression, ascension, upward movement.
Samanan Vayu	It is located in the navel and governs assimilation, discernment, inner absorption, consolidation.
Naga	It causes the action of belching.
Kurma	It controls the movements of the eye lids.
Krikara	It regulates the function of sneezing.
Devadattan	It produces yawning when the body is depleted with oxygen.
Dhananjayan	It produces pranayama sounds

THE 10 MAIN ENERGY CHANNELS, NADIS

The 10 Nadis, are the main subtle channels in the human physiology. They carry the light and information's throughout the whole physiology. Any obstruction in any of them will generate all types of diseases.

IDAKALAI

Idakalai nadi is connected with Prana Vayu.
The colour of Idakalai is black. Vayu "Vadam" moves from this nadi. This nadi begins from the big toe of the right leg, then it reaches the left side of the liver. From there, it divides into two branches, one branche to the left thum and the other to the left Poikai. Then, from the Poikai, it again divides into two branches, one to the left nostril and the other to the anus
Any disruption in the free flow of energy through this nadi will result in diseases like dyspepsia, piles, jaundice, anaemia, dropsy, gonorrhea etc.,

PINKALAI

The color of the Pinkalai is yellow. Pitham (fire) travels through this nadi. It begins from the big toe of the left leg, to the right side of the liver. Then, it divides into two, one of which ends in the right thumb and the other through the right poikai reaches the right nostril "suryam" or sun. Then, from the lower jaw to the moolam
Pinkalainadi associated with Apana vayu. It begins from the big toe of the left leg to the right nostril. If there is any disruption or disturbance into the free flow of informations through this nadi, problems related to the abdomen like loose motion, constipation, worms, continuous gastric problems, seetham, stool with pus cells, dryness, syphilis and excess perspiration etc., will occur.

SHULUMUNAI

Shulumunainadi which is red in colour, begins from the Moolatharam up to the centre of the eyebrow and vice-versa.

Shulumunainadi in association with Vyana Vayu. If Vyanavayu get stock in the head due to obstruction in the shulumunainadi, the following diseases may manifest as : pain in joints, sprain, trauma, stomach pain, blood poisoning, head related diseases, eczema, leprosy, cough, tuberculosis etc.,

GANDHARI

Gandhari nadi functions in association with Nagan Vayu. It starts from the left eye and goes through the lower part of the ear, through the spine and reaches the foot – heel.

Gandhari nadi in association with Nagan Vayu, reaches the throat from the right eye and will stay there when distracted or perturbated. In that condition, it will create disease such as : fits, fever, cold, phlegmatic, poisonous paralysis, kuvalai, tuberculosis, shivering piameham and cough.

ATHI

Athi nadi functions in association with Kurma Vayu. It begins at the moolam region (anal), moves upwards and reaches the right ear and finally reaches the right nostril

Athi nadi in association with Kurma Vayu, starts from right ear and end in right eye when imbalanced or disturbed. When imbalanced it causes diseases such as : neuralgia in head, head diseases and diseases in lips.

SINGKUVAI

Singkuvai nadi function in association with Uthana Vayu. It begins from moolam (anal), then it reaches the naval pit, there it divides into 10 branches and finally reaches the uvula. Its colour is dark bluish (like rainy cloud)

Singkuvainadi which functions in association with Uthana Vayu is disturbed or imbalanced it accumulate on the tongue. It will creates diseases such as : diabetic, sexual diseases, piles, neuralgia, malaikan, fistula, excessive pain, ezhai, araiyappu, inner pain, kuvalaikayam and mikuveekam.

ALLAMPUDAI

Allampudainadi function in association with Krikara Vayu. Its color is red. It begins from the anal, reaches the left ear upwardly and finally ends on the left side of the nose.

PURUDAN

Purudannadi function in association with Samanan Vayu. It begins from the heel and reach the right eye like a string.

When Purudannadi which functions in association with Samanan Vayu is perturbed or imbalanced, it will accumulate in the right eye and will create diseases such as : phlegmatic kapha, rheumatism, sweating, heat related ailments, delirium, angerness, edema, gastric problems, fever, unconsciousness, indigestion, shivering and eye problems.

SANGHINI

Sanghininadi functions in association with Devadattan Vayu. It begins from the penis or the vagina to the moolam (anal). Then it moves upwards to the chuliyadi from where it is divided into 10 branches. Some of the branches reach shulumunai or Amirtha place in the brain. Its colour is crystalline.

When Sanghininadi which functions in association with Devadattan Vayu is disturbed, it will enter into the penis and from there will move upwards. This imbalanced is the cause of these diseases : meham, disease due to excess heat, cough, changes in voice, gastric problem, varatchai and phlegmatic disease..

KUKU

Kuku nadi functions in association with Dhananjayan Vayu. It starts from the coccyx, moves upwards and reaches the base of the heart. There, it branches into 10. One of these branches reaches the ladam and ends at moolam (anal). The color of this nadi is green.

Kuku nadi in association with Dhananjayan Vayu, when imbalanced will linked with abanan and reaches the brain.

This causes phlegmatic diseases, veechuvalli, fits, sweating, thosam, prathapam, unconsciousness and hiccup.

VAKKU - 4 LEVELS OF SPEECH

SUKUMAI	It is the highest form of sound. It zooms forth from the Supernal Ether (paramamvyomam) where all the sound vibrations that build the various worlds pre-exist in an undifferentiated state.
PAISANTI	It is the sound vibration heard in the Causal worlds. A sage whose consciousness is concentrated in the causal body is able to "glimpse" a Truth in a vision or a revelation. Knowledge is acquired in the inner mind by sight without the use of the reasoning faculty or sensory data.
MATHIMAI	It is the sound as perceived in the subtle or the Pranic world. A good example of this would be the thought-forms held in our mind.
VAIKHARI	It is the lowest form of sound and it signifies outward expression. This is the spoken word emerging from the throat.

YEDANAI - DESIRE

As the root cause of suffering

DHARAYEDANAI	Desire for a life partner
PUTHIRYEDANAI	Desire for progeniture
ARTHAYEDANAI	Desire for material things

THE 3 GUNAS

The 3 Gunas are the three basic characteristics or attributes that exist in all things, including your body and mind.

Sattva binds us to attachment with happiness, rajas binds with attachment to activity and tamas binds us to attachment with delusion. As long as we are influenced by any of the three gunas, we remain in bondage of Maya. In order to reach Samadhi or Enlightenment, the first step is to increase sattva and decrease rajas and tamas. Next, the ultimate goal is to become unattached from the 3 gunas and see the reality beyond Maya.

A person who has transcended the 3 gunas is indifferent to the duality of life like pain and pleasure. He/she is undisturbed by the gunas and knows that the gunas are part of Maya, and not of the universe's sole reality which is the Self.

SATHVA
The Guna of Purity and Harmony

Sattva manifests itself as purity, knowledge and harmony. It is the quality of goodness, joy, satisfaction, nobility and contentment. It is free of fear, violence, wrath and malice. Sattvic quality is pure and forgiving. It is the guna that people want to increase in order to reach the state of Samadhi or Liberation. Increasing sattva is possible by reducing rajas and tamas, both in your mind and in your body.

You can do this by eating sattvic food such as fresh fruits and vegetables, whole grains and legumes. sattvic foods are fresh and pure and grow above the ground, receiving their positive energy from the sunlight. By practicing yoga and living a non-violent lifestyle, surrounding yourself by positive people and performing activities that bring you and others joy you increase the sattvic elements in your mind and body.

RAJASA
The Guna of Passion and Manipulation

Rajas represents itself by passion, action, energy and motion. Rajas is characterized by a feeling of attachment, a longing for satisfaction and desire. If you want to decrease the level of rajas, avoid consuming rajasic foods like fried and spicy food and stimulants such as caffeine.

THAMASA
The Guna of impurity and ignorance

Tamas manifests itself as impurity, laziness and darkness. It is the consequence of ignorance and it prevents all beings from seeing the reality. In order to decrease the tamasic elements in your mind and body, avoid eating tamasic foods (e.g. alcohol, meat, processed food), indulging (e.g. overeating, over sleeping, etc.).

EVOLUTION OF THE SOUL

Ramalinga has observed in his "Peru Vinnapam" that the soul in course of evolution has its foundation or roots in the material unconscious, in the inconscient darkness itself, due to its original descent by involution or fall. From that state of darkness, by the action of Divine Grace, the soul is lifted up to begin the evolutionary journey from existences of matter, such as hill and stone, into plant life, animal life and human life. Ramalinga was aware of a six-fold embodiment when his soul came down into the physical world of matter and enter into the physical body formed in his Mother's womb to take birth as a child – a physical body which he himself had prepared in advance, right from its embryonic stage or even before by sending his soul's emanations to enter into the egg-cell and sperm-cell of his parents for the purpose of conception and growth in the womb; his soul at that time remembered its old moorings in inconscient darkness in which it remained originally in a state of swoon for an immeasurable time till it was redeemed by the Divine Grace initiated into the evolutionary process of birth in life.

Ramalinga observed that "atmas" or individual beings are individual portions of "Sat", the Supreme Self. The atmas or souls, are the centres of Consciousness based in unity for manifestation of the Consciousness-Force into or as the Wisdom and Knowledge of the Divine Grace. In order to evolve and make progress as jeevas, they require physical bodies "Bhuta Kariya Deha". If the jeevas do not so evolve in and through their physical bodies, the manifestation of their souls will be obscured. Ramalinga explains the logical necessity of the evolution of the souls in and through the physical bodies; the souls cannot continue to evolve without the body.

In the first creation, brought forth by the Divine Grace, through the manifestation of successive fall in involution, the souls due to ancient impurity of ego, failed in their attempt to follow the Laws of Nature as determined by God in order to attain their true nature, the state of Supreme Bliss lived in a total fusion with the Supreme Grace Light in a body of light. In the second creation through the manifestation by successive ascent in evolution, the souls got manifold various physical bodies and enjoyments "dehabhoga" due to the manifold variations in the modes of attempt and approach of their egos.

The relevant forms that are taking the jeevas "Paguti Uruvi" in each sequential stage of evolution suggesting individualised and specific bodies in the nature itself, from the grossest to the subtlest.

Anma Akasa or the soul of space is the sky of soul atoms which the Grace Shakti (energy) of the divine brings forth into existence in Pinda, the worlds of the sub-conscient and inconscient. Pinda in ordinary language represents the human body, deep within which is found the soul-atom which is the divine spirit in man. Golden Sabhai is the apprehending Super-mind that is the sky of souls in the sub-conscient and inconscient materiel world.

"Jnana-Sabhai" or "Cit-Sabhai" represents the comprehending Super-mind which is the highest true origin and cause of the universe; It is referred to as "Parama Akasha" or "Jnana Akasha". In the human body, the Ajnacenter, point in the mid of the eyes-brows, center which Ramalinga considers as belonging to Anda, the universal that is referred as Cit-Sabhai or Jnana-Sabhai. Thus, the heart center, which is Pinda, the subconscient and inconscient material nature, where Anma Akasha, the sky of souls exists and arise, can be taken as indicating correspondingly the Golden Sabhai in the human body.

THE MECHANICS OF EVOLUTION AND INVOLUTION OF THE SOULS

Ramalinga's in "Shristi Jnana" from the treaty of Upadesha, speaks of the Divine and the souls in the sky of spirit. It compares the souls in the spiritual sky with the physical atoms in the physical ethereal sky.

He says that Akasa, the physical space or space of ether is beginningless. Likewise, its cause which is "Paramakasa" (the supreme supramental sky of spiritual substance) is also beginningless.

The sky of spirit is the essential form "swarupa" of the Divine. Again, the gas (air) or gaseous state of the physical ethereal space is also beginningless. Just as gas or gaseous state in the ethereal sky is beginningless, so too in the spiritual sky of the Divine is "Arut Shakti", the Grace Power of the Divine (Cit Shakti) which is also beginningless.

The physical space of ether is wholly filled up without any gap by "anus" the atoms and atomic particles of physical substance such as neutron, proton, electron and aggregates of atoms called the molecules. So too the Sky of Spirit "anmaakasa" which is verily the Divine being is full of "anus", the souls which are the children of the One Spirit. These "anus is called atma - the soul.

The Divine Being is the Supreme Spiritual substance which is represented by the Ether of the physical space; and the "Cit Shakti" the Consciousness - Force of the Divine by the next physical element, gas "vayu" as a form of power.

In the Tamil language "anu" means the minute physical substance as well as the soul spark. The One Divine Existence has become the soul spark of the individual being and the physical atom.

"The atoms of the physical space "bhutaakasa anu" are of ordinary and special kinds. They fall into 7 classes. They are namely:

1- **Val anu** ", the nascent, the newborn or young atom, the basic atom as known to science.
2- **Drava anu**", the liquid atom or molecule of liquid atoms.
3- **Guru anu**", the heavy atom, the atom of a heavy element of solid matter or molecule of heavy atoms.

4 "**Laghu anu**", the light anu, the atom as gaseous element, which is of light weight,
5- "**Anu**", the atomic particle, the electron as distinguished from val anu, the atom of science.
6- "**Paramanu**", the subtler atomic particle such as the photon,
7 - "**Vibhu anu**" the all-pervading atomic particle or substance of ether possibly represented by neutrino or graviton.

These "anus" or atoms are of manifold distinctions which can broadly fall into three groups namely:

1 - "**Kariyan anu**"-" **Apakva**", the effectual or impure atom,
2 - "**Kariya-karanan anu**"-" **Pakva–apakva**", the causal – effectual or pure – impure atom,
3 – "**Karanan anu**"-"**Pakva**", the causal atom or atomic particle or pure atom.

Likewise, in the presence of the Divine as Sky of Spirit "Anma Akasha", souls too become of three types namely: impure, pure-impure et pure.

They become of three types of souls because of the Grace Shakti (acting) in the presence of the Divine, just as the three broad classes of atoms or atomic particles of the physical space are due to the presence of gas or gaseous state therein."

"The earthly gross physical matter (solid) is the first of the five elements which is constituted by basic atom (val anu, the nascent or young atom as the basic atom of science). Within it is anu (the electron) is a much valued light, the photons of visible physical sight produced or emitted by high-energy electrons of the nucleus in orbital motion; within that light is another light which is yet physical light, the photons of invisible light called as massless photons of x-rays and gamma-rays.

Within that merited inner physical light rather than from supra physical light such as mental light or spiritual life, is the space, the ethereal physical space, which is caused by the massless neutrinos or gravitons.

Within the natural or phenomenal space is another space, which means subtler inner space, but yet physical, possibly formed by gravitons and extending into or overlapping the subtle – physical space. In that space the lord plays in dance giving the physical rhythm of music of the ethereal physical space"

-TiruvadiPerumanai, stanza24

Anu is defined by Ramalinga as "bhutakarya anu", the effectual or derivative physical atomic particle and that it is the same as the heat of the sun ray which is to be taken as the electron. If the electron is the effectual atomic particle, then it follows that photon of visible and invisible light acting as the causal-effectual, and the neutrinos or gravitons the causal. Thus Anu (the nascent or new-born atom), paramanu (the subtler atomic particle such as the photon), and vibhu anu (the all-pervading atomic particle or substance of ether possibly represented by neutrino or graviton).

Are respectively the effectual, causal-effectual and causal atomic particles.

"Val anu" the nascent atom is the basis for the aggregation of various kinds of atoms or atomic cells resulting in the growth of plant giving different colors and tastes.

"Likewise, by the will of the Divine, the Grace Shakti, once extended Herself in the sky of spirit, and the souls "anmas" at once came into existence to do the five-fold functions of creation. The sky or space of spirit became full of children "santhana" because soul sparks "anma anu" of the Divine manifested themselves into existence. Thereby, the five – fold functions of creation, maintenance, destruction, involution and evolution will not be impeded at any time.

In spite of the fact that, with the Grace of God, the souls-atoms where made perfect children of God, they have fallen into low state of ignorance, not because of their ignorance, not because of their inherent force of nature, but because of a causal force of artificiality in manifestation, meaning involutionary force of descent into ignorance by the formation of ego-consciousness.

Ramalinga has said that, in the first universal creation which took place by the Divine Grace (i.e. referring to the manifestation in involutionary descent) the jeevas because of their ancient impurities, having failed in their efforts to attain the state of Supreme Bliss in the way devised by the Divine Grace, a second universal creation (possibly in evolutionary ascent) has come to take place providing manifold enjoyments on the level of the world and body according to the differences of efforts or aspirations of the ancient ego-consciousness of beings.

The secret truth of this may be understand by going into the nature of God and the soul.

THE ESSENTIAL NATURE OF GOD AND SOUL

Although God is identified with both a form and non-form, in his original nature "Swarupa-Laksana" it is said that God stands beyond the concept of divinity.

God is not "para", which is subject to change; It is not "Sadasiva", the name given to the one who is with or without form; He is not the one who has no form; he is not the one who has a form; He is extraordinary and inexplicable. It is designed to be with a form, formless, with a form and without, because of the imagination made accessible by His Grace. When the true nature of God is realized by the student of truth, He will reveal Himself beyond all manifestations of forms and names and will stand in the fusion of the One with the realized.

Ramalinga Vallalar as well as Thirumular characterizes God with eight attributes. God is contrary to the soul, not subject to the influence of the three gunas or attributes. These three gunas are: "sattva" (strength of purity, silence and creativity), "rajas" (force of activity or dynamism), "tamas" (impurity, stagnation, inertia and destruction), which are the products of "Maya" (illusion - ignorance). Although he is not subject to the action of the three gunas, who are unclean, He is said to be the One with the eight Pure Gunas. The writings of "Saivagamas" quote the eight Pure Gunas of the Lord as:

1 – Being self-dependent or self-sufficient "tan-vayattanadal"

2 – As being immaculate "tuya-udambinanadal"
3 - Having an innate intuitive and wisdom "iyarkai-y-unavinanadal"
4 - Being omniscient "unardalmurrum"
5 - Being free by nature of all the impurities which veil the soul "iyalbagavé pacangalin ningudal"
6 - Being of infinite Grace "peraruludaimai)
7 - Being omnipotent "mudivil-arraludaimal"
8 - Being in enjoyment of boundless and supreme bliss "varambil-inbamudaimai"

In order to be a little more precise about the nature of the Lord, it is said that He is characterized as:

"Sat" (Satya) the truth that never changes and "Cit" (jnana) consciousness and "Ananda" bliss.

The Supreme Bliss of Blissful Consciousness is said to be the nature of the Lord.

The relationship between the Supreme Lord and other spiritual entities is one in identity in difference. That is, by His Omnipresence that He stands in identity with the world and the souls; by nature, He stands different from them; by his graceful help, He stands One with them, while being different from them.

THE BONDS OR ATTACHMENTS OF THE SOUL

Pasa is the impediment that holds back the soul. Pasa is of three distinct qualities:

1- "**Anaava**" meaning the ignorance which is called egoism;
2- "**Maya**" is the material cause of all that is created.
3 - "**Karma**" meaning action. It is divided into two, good and bad actions - it is the cause of repetitive births.

ANAVA

"Anaava" is egoity, the primal bondage for the souls. It is eternal and beginningless. It is said that Anaava mala is to the souls as the verdigris is to the copper. If Anaava mala is removed, the souls will be restored to their essential nature as intelligence. Anaava is one; but by virtue of its infinite capacities, it thwarts the three potencies of the soul.

Thirumular and Ramalinga Vallalar identifies the ego-sense as "Anaava". This ego-sense is due to ignorance. Only to help the soul out of this ignorance God associates it with "Maya". In association with "Maya", the soul also accumulates the third one, karma. Thirumular calls this "anaava" as "irul" (darkness). The later, "Saiva Siddhaantins", would characterize anaava-mala" as worse than darkness; because, in the case of darkness it conceals only the objects which are in its fold, but reveals itself. In the case of "anaava", it is not only concealing that which is in its fold but also itself.

MAYA

Maya is the seed of the world; all manifestations come out from it and return into it. It said to be of two kinds:

1 – "suddhamaya" (the pure maya) and 2 - "asuddhamaya" (the impuremaya). They help the souls to take birth, to undergo experiences and finally get liberated.

WHAT TYPE OF GRACE IS THIS MAYA TO CAUSE ANOTHER IMPEDIMENT TO THE SOUL WHICH IS ALREADY IMPEDED WITH ANAAVA?

Thirumular comes out with an example to answer this objection: The washer men use the saline soil to remove the stains in cloths. Here, adding dirt to a cloth, which is already dirty is not to make the cloth dirtier but to make it cleaner. Similarly, adding Maya, another fetter, to the already ailing soul is not to restrain it but to help with an instrument to gain knowledge. Therefore, it is nothing, but a technique played by the Lord to help the soul improve themselves. It is only because of the Maya that the soul's natural potencies of knowledge, desire and action are activated.

KARMA

Karma is action of the mind, word felt and spoken and body. Thirumular warns us: don't think that only the deeds of the body are taken into account. Do not behave in such a way that your lips utter one thing, mind thinks another, and the deeds does the third.

Karma is brought about by the activity of one's body. But how is the body itself brought into existence? What is the cause of the body? The body is the result of deeds done in a previous life. Just as the seed and the sprout follow each other, the bodies and actions come in a series and as cause and effect of one another from time immemorial like a perpetually flowing stream "pravaahaanaadi". Hence, there is no saying which is earlier, and which is later of these two. Thirumular has resolved this debate regarding whether karma precedes birth or birth precedes karma. He said that it is birth, with the subtle body, which precedes karma. Let consider these verses from the Thirumandiram:

"Of the two bodies that the Lord created
If suuksma (subtle) is to be explained,
It is the "puriyasta-kaya" (body of eight constituents) made of
Sound, touch, sight, taste, smell, intellect, mind and ego-sense
Of the eight, five serve as a sense organ
And three serves as internal organs;
This paasa attached causes sentience in the souls
Thus, the Lord binds them and unbinds them."

Because of its association with the subtle body, which is a product of Maya, the soul becomes sentient and starts doing. This helps the Lord to bind and unbind the soul with the gross body. Therefore, the gross body is the result of the subtle karmas (the likes and dislikes) of the soul in its subtle body.

CLASSIFICATION OF KARMA

The karma is generally classified into two: good and bad (nal-vinai or punya and tii-vinai or paapa) and both are called "iru-vinai" (the two deeds). In accordance of the two deeds the souls will enjoy heaven or suffer in hell.

Karma is distinctively classified into three: (praarabdha, sancita and aagaamya) Of these three, "praarabdha" is that karma from previous births which has started manifesting its consequences in the present birth. It is inescapable, however, many tried to escape it. Therefore, it has to be experienced and thus, only eliminated. "Sancita" is that past karma from previous births which will not manifest until a future birth and can be overcome and destroyed only by compassionate service to all living beings and jnana. "Aagaamya" is the karma, which is created now by our present acts, which will mature in the normal course of events. It is open to us, so to act accordingly as to make our future or mar it.

RELATION BETWEEN THE THREE MALAS

In the following verse, Thirumular explains the relation between the three malas:

"Aanava, Maya and karma are like
The kernel, bran and husk to the soul, allowing not
The soul to reach the Lord wrapping it;
Rid of your pasa and adore God."

PASU

That which is bound by "pasa" is "pasu". It is also referred by Thirumular by names such as "Aanmaa, aadan, uyir". Let us first explore the nature of the soul according to Tirumular. There are various views that the soul is nothing but the gross body, the senses, the subtle body, the prana (vita air), brahman, the internal organs, etc. the verses of thirumular clearly state that soul is different from the aforesaid and it is the enjoyer of the results produced by these organs.

According to Ramalinga, the souls are in number. These souls are not created entities. If it is held that the souls are created then it leads to a contradiction; because that which is created is not eternal and it would also be difficult to explain why God having no need, has created the souls. Hence, Ramalinga holds that the souls are eternal and that they are entangled in the chain of births and deaths because of their bondages – aanava and karma.

THE NATURE OF THE SOULS

It is said that the soul is eternal and intelligent. Though the soul is intelligent, it remains ignorant without even knowing its potency of intelligence because of its attachment with the fetter aanava. Aanava is so called because it minimizes the triadic potencies of the soul to the size of an atom "anu".

The soul is attributed with two important characteristics. The first one is that the soul will never be on its own. It is always dependent. In the state of bondage, it is dependent on pasa and in the state of liberation it is dependent on Pati.

The second characteristic of the soul is that it reflects the nature of that on which it depends. When it depends on the unintelligent existence – "asat", i.e., on aanava, it reflects the qualities of it. When it is in the company of the intelligent existence – "sat", i.e., Pati, it reflects the qualities of Him. Hence, the soul can associate with both, "sat" and "asat", Thirumular calls it "satasat". He compares the soul with crystal, which reflects the thing kept nearby.

In summary, the cause of the loss of knowledge is the identification with the body and the object of experience, loosing track that all manifestations are nothing but an expression of the underlying source, Arut Perun Jyothi – The Supreme Grace Light.

WHO ARE YOU?

"If you are asked, "who are you in this physical body?", The answer shall be, "I am the soul", Anma or Atma of the form of atom; this soul-atom (i.e.

the soul-spark or divine-spark) which has the radiance of 10 million of suns…"

Anma referred above is the soul-essence, the divine spark or spirit. The ethereal space, Akasha is anaadi, which is beginningless, because its causal source is the Divine of Paramaakaasa, the supreme world of space, the beginningless Source-Grace-Shakti of the Divine which is also anaadi.

Just as the ethereal space "Akasha" is full of atoms without gap, so too Aanma akasha, the sky or world of souls in the divine being is full of soul-atoms which are called Anma, spirit or soul; Anma-Akasha, the sky of souls "Santaanamaya" is full of children (i.e., soul-atoms of the Divine).

THE STATES OF THE SOUL

Depending on the association of the soul, there are three classifications or states of the soul. These states of dependence are called "avasthas". The three "avasthas" are:

1 – "kevalaavastha" is the state of the soul in association with aanava alone or identified with the ego-sense. This is the primary state of the soul.

2 – "sakalaavastha" is a state of the soul when it is associated with the other two malas, maaya and karma. This is the intermediate state.

3 – "suddhaavastha" is a state when the soul gets rid of these three malas and stands in association with Pati, the Lord. This is the final state.
This is the final state. Thirumular puts these states in a nutshell: one who realized himself is a "suddha"; the one who knows nothing is a "kevala"; and the one who knows with distortion is a "sakala". These three states are called "kaarana-avasthas" (the causal state).

XII - STATES OF CONCIOUSNESS

PLANES OF ASCENT OF THE SOUL THROUGH THE 17 STATES OF CONSCIOUSNESS

For the proper understanding of the achievement of the soul in the human body, one has to know the various stages of spiritual experiences. The soul of the aspiring individual undergoes different stages of experiences. The waking, dreaming, sleeping and intuitional consciousness which gradually become more and more perfect. The desire, attachment, lust and the shackles fastening the soul are loosened and lost sight of higher state of experiences. At Parathuriyam-Supra-Mental consciousness, self-realization is achieved. At the stage of Suddha Sivasakram, the aspirant visualizes the Supreme Grace. He becomes eligible to enter sanmargam. His body of love becomes converted into the body of Grace and enjoys God Supreme Bliss.

The human beings leading a mundane life, without even a thought a thought of its transient nature, are said to be in the normal wakefulness "Jeevasakram". Human beings are alert only for trivial things; they are cautious for the acquisition of wealth, gold, of land, of women, of wine, of name and fame by all means without discrimination.

STATES OF CONCIOUSNESS

PLANES OF ASCENT OF THE SOUL TO SUDDHA SIVA VELI

Ramalinga has listed 17 levels or states and planes of experience in all, leading finally to the world of Ananda of Bliss and immortality. These 17 planes or states come under six main groups.

I – JEEVA STATES

1ˢᵗ STATES OF CONSCIOUSNESS – JEEVASAKRAM

The human beings leading a mundane life, without even a thought about its transient nature, are said to be in the normal wakefulness

"Jeevasakram". Human beings are alert only for trivial things; they are cautious for the acquisition of wealth, gold, of land, of women, of wine, of name and fame by all means, without discrimination.

In that first state of consciousness, the soul is active from its position, between the eyebrows. The soul is intelligent; but, unfortunately in that 1st state of consciousness, the soul does not know about its potency of intelligence. The self, the sense of "I" of experience is identified with the object of experience which is covering the soul. To help the soul to come out of ignorance, the Lord, out of His Grace, has provided the soul with instruments by way of creating the world out of "Maya". But these instruments, the tattva-taatvikas, cannot enlighten the soul, forgetting the purpose of the instruments, engage itself in the worldly activities, completely lost in the gritty grip of the fetters (the veil of egoism covering the soul).

Siddha Thirumuular depicts this graphically in the following verse:

"The ploughman ploughed; the heaven poured;
By the ploughing, Lily blossomed;
Comparing it with his wife's eye,
The ploughman ceased to plough it further."

The ploughman ploughs his field to cultivate a particular crop and removes all weeds. Otherwise the weeds will have an effect on the growth of his intended crop. Though the lily is very beautiful and likeable, ultimately it is weed. Instead of weeding it out, the ploughman compares it with his wife's eyes and leaves it to grow. Thus, he made the mistake of losing his purpose. Here, the ploughman stands for the soul. Ploughing is the soul's efforts to get rid of the "malas" illusion or covering value of the self. The pouring of the heavens stands for the Divine Grace. It is out of the Divine Grace alone that the world is evolving. The world is represented by the lily flower. The soul, instead of detaching from the world, lost itself completely identified in and by the worldly activities forgetting the original purpose. Tirumuular calls such a soul a severely fettered soul.

Here, another example from Saiva Siddhanta:

Once upon a time, there was a prince, caught up in ignorance of his parentage, joins some gypsies, loses his independence and dignity and allows himself to be brought up in gypsy way, unbecoming of a prince. He does not realise that he is a prince and that his father is a king, until the king finds him, takes him away from the gypsies and restores him to his rightful place. Similarly, the soul forgets its essential nature, gets lost in the world of the senses, loses its intelligence and suffers, on account of not knowing itself and the Lord. When the soul as a result of following a path of Truth and Purity, becomes fit, and the Lord who is eternal, pure intelligence and Omnipresent Grace assumes the form of a preceptor, teaches it, destroys the efficiency of the mala so that the soul may get rid of the suggestion of the senses, and restores it to its essential nature.

To understand the nature of the fetter and of the tattvas, Thirumular is giving a very profound metaphorical analogy:

"The cuckoo bird leaves its egg in the crow's nest;
The crow hatches it, nurses it. The young cuckoo,
Suspecting nothing neither dissociates nor asks why,
It allows the crow to nurse it out of ignorance."

In this verse, the crow is Maya; the cuckoo is the soul. It is out of the Divine Grace that the soul realises its mistakes and gets them right. When the Divine Grace descends on the soul, it gets rid of the malas and attain liberation.

"in the state of liberation – the souls do penance on their part;
And are in full receipt of Divine Grace; purified of the tattvas;
And rid of the karmas; stands in true devotion;
Immersed in the Transcendental Bliss."

In association with the 96 principles of the body or Tatvas "AaraaruKaattiya".

This first state of consciousness, waking state of consciousness is allowing us to function and think, but unfortunately, without being aware of the source of action. Therefore, the soul remains unconscious of its own potentialities and remains ignorant of its True Nature. The Lord with His Omnipresent Grace, endowed the soul and body with the 96 tattvas, allowing the soul going through them and become aware of the presence of the Light of God within itself, the source of all Knowledge.

THE 2nd STATE OF CONSCIOUSNESS – JEEVA SWAPNA

The second state of consciousness – Jeeva Swapna, the dreaming state of consciousness that is associated with the center of the throat which is activated during dream. Here, the soul lives in association with the jnanendriyas and karmendriyas, 25 tattvas or life's principle.

THE 3rd STATE OF CONSCIOUSNESS – JEEVA SUZHUTHI

The third state of consciousness is associated with the insouciance of sleep. This state of consciousness represents a barrier on the path of deathlessness since, according to Ramalinga the realization of deathlessness is depending upon our ability to sleep less, meaning no more than three hours a night and never sleep during the day. During sleep, the soul descends from throat to heart "Anaata-chakra", leaves association with the 22 Tattvas or principles of life as seen above, and remains with 3 Tattvas only: Praana, Citta and Purusha.

II-NIRMALA JEEVA – PSYCHO-SPIRITUEL STATES OF CONSCIOUSNESS

This are the subliminal, psychic and psycho-spiritual experiences in the initial conditions of purity in the inner and outer being of man, realized in the Nirmala states of jagrata, Swapna and suluthi.

THE 4th STATE OF CONSCIOUSNESS, SUDDHASAKRAM

The 4th state of consciousness represents the perfect state of awakening. At this stage of evolution, on the path of Sanmarga, the seeker in the search of

God, becomes aware of the Truth, he becomes aware of his true nature and at the same time, he becomes aware of the impermanent and transitory nature of the world. When this perfect awakening is attained, he can start perceiving the existence of the Supreme Lord.

THE 5th STATE OF CONSCIOUSNESS SUDDHASORPANAM

The 5th state of consciousness represents the entry into the subliminal and having psychic realization of God in the heart: In these stages of realization, one is realizing one's inner mind, the inner vital and the inner physical within their soul. It is a state of self-realization lived within the soul and in the inmost of the heart. The domain of the aspirant on the realization of the Self is "Nirmala Jagrata" or "Suddhaorpanam".

THE 6th STATE OF CONSCIOUSNESS SUDDHASUZHUTHI

At the 6th state of consciousness, gradually the aspirant enters a state of perfect and conscient carelessness. at this level the aspirant is aware of nothing but God. Ramalinga says that at this level, no lust sits in the one who has reach Suddhasuzhuthi state of consciousness. He is dreaming to see the Lotus Feet of the Lord and feeling and inseparable union with His Feet in his untiring search for Him.

III - PARA VELI - SPIRITUAL MIND LEVELS

"The Vast Grace-Light, the Supramental Grace-Light has determined the pure, free and wide space of pure mentality (cosmic mind) to be held and contained by the Space of Para Veli (Spiritual mind) which is above it. This Para Veli is realized in the Sahasrara above the head by transcending the pure and free mental plane, the cosmic mind of the lower order of the worlds. The gradation of the lower worlds are mentioned in "Jyoti Agaval" as the earthly fields off matter and its five elements with their natural qualities and states of evolutionary perfection and the presence of life-forces and mind-forces in them, then the Space of the physical universe as an extension and formation of the wide cosmic Subtle-physical Space, then the Space of the cosmic Vital universe and its formation and extension as vital plane in the physical universe and then the Space of the inspired arts and sciences (par example, the Space of the cosmic Vital mind and Heart, then the Space of cosmic Pure Mind realized at Ajna as spiritualized mind. This cosmic Mind leads beyond to Para Veli, the Space of Spiritual Mind. This Space of Spiritual Mind, Para Veli, is the dynamic spiritual planes in the overhead consciousness as experienced above the body in the Sahasrara (the 7thcakra at the top of the head). The experience of these planes of the Spiritual Mind open the door into cosmic consciousness with one's realization of the cosmic self and one may remain witness to or actively participate in the dynamic spiritual movements of Truth-thought, Truth-vision, Truth-vision, Truth-intuition, etc...., without losing the peace of the Spirit or soul. They are comprised of the three planes, seventh to ninth, namely: Spiritual Higher Mind, Illumined Mind and Intuitive Mind.

THE 7TH STATE OF CONSCIOUSNESS–PARASAKRAMOR SUDDHATHURIAM

"Is a plane of infinite Peace and Silence into which the thoughts, Truth-thoughts descend from above,"

It is the silent spiritual Mind in the overhead that one can experience the static Brahman, the "Nirguna Brahman" by exclusive concentration on it as a goal. But it is not the final goal, as it is believed and thought among the spiritual masters belonging to the Vedic tradition, but rather a partial manifestation of the Supreme Divine. SUDDHATHURIAM corresponds to the Nada center according to the Book of Upadesha, p.54.

The realization of the Spiritual Higher Mind is the first overhead plane where one becomes aware of the Self, the One everywhere and knows and sees things through an elevated thought-power and comprehensive mental sight...as in a large strong and clear day light. In the Higher Mind, we are aware of the sea like downpour of masses of spontaneous Knowledge which assumes the nature of Thought... and capable of including at once a mass of knowledge in a single view. It has a cosmic character. It is the plane of Truth-thought. Suddhathuriam is the perfect experience of the dawn of the Divine Spark within the consciousness. The lust and the veil which have been covering the soul hitherto for generations by the influence of the devil power of the ego, asuddhamaya, are shed one after another and the soul is gradually cleansed by the spark of light emanating from the Supreme Light of Grace. The soul is bound by the shackles of Purusha, individual consciousness, however, the melting mood and the spontaneous impulse of love for God, overwhelm the aspirant.

THE 8TH STATE OF CONSCIOUSNESS - PARASORPANAM

Ramalinga has not been elaborated by Ramalinga. Elsewhere in Upadesha, it is indicated like Parabindu, lower center. Further these spiritual Mental planes are already familiar in the ancient Tamil spiritual literature such as Thirumandiram of siddha thirumuular who is believed to have lived 3000 years ago, and in the modern literature of Sri Kumara Deva of the 18th century in his poem "Vijnaana Saara". These two sages indicate gradations to the Super-Mind in their literature. This plane is considered as a plane of Truth-Vision or revelation.

THE 9TH STATE OF CONSCIOUSNESS, PARA SUZHUTHI

"O Supreme Divine, thou art in the ninth level which is the middle of all the 17 levels or Spaces, and Thy Divine Nature comes into manifestation by transformation of one's own nature into Thy Nature Sivamayamaaki."

Elsewhere in Upadesha, Para Suzhuthi is indicated as Paranada lower center. This state of consciousness corresponds to the Intuitive Mind. Its four Intuitive Powers are:

a) A sight that sees without seeing, the Truth-Vision;
b) A hearing that hears without hearing, the Truth-hearing or inspiration;

c) The Intelligence or Intuition that knows or seizes the Truth-significance of things immediately without the processes of mental understanding, Truth-intuition; and d) The discrimination that discriminate without the mental process of discrimination, the Truth-discrimination. The four-fold powers of intuition are described in "Mahadevamaalai" as having their true source in the high-seated world of Truth-Knowledge, the Super-Mind, which is a world indicated as a world beyond the Vedas, beyond sound of words, and beyond the nine levels but as the world or state in between one and two, as One in one and Two-in-one which are the first and second poises of Truth-world Space.

"O Light of discrimination that discriminates without the mental process of discrimination in the sages who are poised ever in the true, proper and rightful state of eternal existence, O Intuition that intuitively knows rare inner state in between the one and the two, the comprehending and apprehending poises of Super-Mind, Cit Sabhai and Por Sabhai; O vision that sees without seeing and which is a state beyond the nine levels and which is also beyond nadanta, the state of potential Sound of words. O Inspiration that hears without hearing and which is poised at the summit or end of Vedic knowledge and beyond the mode of actions." - **Mahadeva Malai 7-5-46**

IV - SIVA OVERMIND LEVELS

This is a gradation of three planes of Siva Jagrata, Siva Swapna and Suzhuthi levels of experience indicated in Upadesha, as dikraanta, adikraanta and dwaadasaanta. The twelfth represents the summit of the Siva Veli. Beyond that is the Suddha Siva Veli, the Vast World of Truth-Knowledge which is Super-Mind. The three planes or spaces of Siva Veli or Over-Mind are indicated as

1) Para Veli or more properly as Para Turya Veli, dikraanta which is going into all directions; Omkara Peetam;

2) Parampara Veli, adikraanta or without direction, hence total and all-encompassing – kundali state– Vishwagraasa state of seizing into experience the whole universe;

3) ParaaparaVeli, Parigraha state of veiling – Upasaanta state of intense and great peace. They respectively signify selected over-mind, global over-mind and over-mind gnosis. We have already seen that the ParaaparaVeli or space which is the border between para and apara, the higher and the

lower worlds, leads to Param, the Heaven of tertiary Super-Mind, and beyond that is Paraa Param, the apprehending Super-Mind which in turn leads to Paramparam, the farthest Heaven of the Comprehending Super-Mind. The triple Heaven comes under one homogeneous Sky or Space of Truth-Knowledge called Chidambaram.

"The Over-Mind is not strictly a transcendental consciousness…Though it looks up to the transcendental and may receive something from it…It is more properly a cosmic consciousness…" "…It stands behind every particular in the cosmos and is the source of all our mental, vital or physical actualities and possibilities which are diminished and degraded derivations and variations from it."
- **Letters on Savitri – Savitri 1954 edition p.922**

THE 10TH STATE OF CONSCIOUSNESS – SIVA SAKRAM

This plane of experience is the field of movement of the many gods and goddesses, each taking and receiving from above one aspect, power or quality of the Supreme and Universal Divine, the Supramental Ishwara, and develops it to its utmost and thus creates a world of its own. Thus, they create many worlds of their own and move in all directions "dikraanta" of cosmic Space.

This State and subsequent state of Consciousness are governed by the Grace of the Lord Supreme. The possibility of enjoying these Divine stages depends upon the extend of the descent of Grace in the soul. There are thousands of verses yearning for the Grace to pervade in him; the sanction is not so simple as it appears. It was perhaps miraculously easy for Ramalinga Vallalar to be blessed with all these experiences. Many souls of this world have attained this stage and only a few could ascend further. Most of them were either overpowered by the extraordinary brilliance of the soul and mistook it for the brilliance of the Supreme Grace or were disappointed by their inability to proceed further. At this stage of Sivasakram also known as Gurusakram, the aspirant is able to perceive the Supreme Grace in the form of Light. The descent of the Divine Grace in the individual is gradually profuse. There three forms of Supreme Light which will beneficially act upon the human body of the purified soul for the infusion of Grace. The tremendous power of the Sun is offered to fill in through the eyes of the enabling aspirant, to do all wonders at will. The Supreme Grace Light dawns in the sanctified intellect of the aspirant empowering him to disseminate the soothing principles of Grace. The illumination of a higher power called "Parai" is disbursed in the mind of the aspirant, enriching him to gain supremacy in the domain of the Supreme Grace Light. These Three different kinds of rays supply the necessary energy for a divine photosynthesis in alchemizing the fundamental elements of the humane frame in which the perfect soul is enshrined. At this stage, the soul is saturated with compassion and the body appears to be an incarnation of immeasurable love for all living beings.

THE 11TH STATE OF CONSCIOUSNESS, SIVA SORPANAM

"O Supreme Divine who are seated in a single seat of Space in the eleventh level of experience."

At This SIVA SORPANAM or GURU SORPANAM State of consciousness, the aspirant dreams of the divine embrace.

Parampara Veli, Paramparam (in a derivative sense here as Parampara Veli); Adikraanta (Upadesha p.54), that which transcending all directions and hence becoming a directionless all-encompassing cosmos; Viswagraasa that is the swallowing up or seizing of the whole universe, having the total universe in experience for enjoyment; Kundali State or Circle, the universal coiled energy (Upadesha p.103); Kundali Loka of Suddha Maya or Kutilai (Upadesha p.36, 54, 103; Vyakhyana p.123, 94).

"Para Veli, Spiritual Mind as opening into the selective over-mind, is self-determined by the Vast Grace-Light to be contained and held in the next higher plane of Parampara Veli of over-ruling governance, the global over-mind."

THE 12TH STATE OF CONSCIOUSNESS, SIVA SUZHUTHI OR PARAAPARA VELI

In the SIVA SUZHUTHI state of consciousness, is experienced as a state of supreme tranquillity, where the soul is neither conscious of its own self, nor ignorant of it. Here, the Supreme Grace Light flows into the body, preparing it for the next higher sublime stage of SUDDHA SIVA SAKRAM.

Ramalinga refers to a collapsible door of this Paraapara plane that has been so self-determined by the Divine who is Vast Grace Light that it can be shattered into pieces and that this plane contains or holds the one below it, the Parampara Veli or the global over-mind.

This Paraapara plane is, in effect, representative of the summit overmind comprised of five planes. Ramalinga calls them, the pure plan Parai – the Suddha Maha Maya that is the Over-mental Maha-Shakti. They are generally referred as the highly pure and conscious planes of Maha Suddha Param beginning from its first plane onwards and as the five-fold pure planes of Paranaada beginning from its first plane onwards. These five planes are also grouped by Ramalinga in the ascending order into three levels:

1) ParaaparaVeli – possibly the gnostic over-mind and "Ananda" (happiness) over-mind together;

2) The middle veli, the middle Space or Parampara Veli or Global over-mind

3) Tat Paaramaamveli, that is Sat over-mind which is the first of the great and pure planes of Maha Suddha Param or the five-fold Paranada.

"The Divine Feet of the Lord, dance without dancing, as it were, the Supreme Dance of Bliss (Anandaateetanatanam) in the Divine Vast World of manifestation of Parai, the Cosmic Maha Shakti and also has become her heaven "Param" and has manifested as Paramparam (Global over-mind) in that heaven.

V - SUDDHA SIVA VELI – ARUL VELI – THE SPACE OF GRACE

Arul Veli, the Space of Grace; Arut Perun Jyoti Veli, the Space of Vast-Grace-Light; Satya Jnana Veli, the Space of Truth-Consciousness; Chidambaram Veli, the Sky or Space of Truth-Consciousness, Ubhaya Veli or Ubhayaambaram, the biune infinite; the universal self-extension in and of the infinity of the Divine Being; Arivup Peru Veli, the Vast Space of Knowledge, Dwaadasaanta Peru Veli, the Vast Space beyond the twelfth plane or center of experience; Jnana Natana Veli, the Space of Dance of dynamic play of Knowledge-will in world founding movement; Samarasa Satja Jnana Veli, the world of Harmony of Truth-Consciousness.

The Vast Grace-Light has self-determined the Paraapara Veli, the over-mind gnosis or summit over-mid to be contained by Peru Veli, the Vast Space of Knowledge above, which Vast Space is homogeneous.

Ramalinga denotes Ajna, the mind center, the door access to the soul and center of Fire, as Chit Sabhai anga, Chit Sabhai dwara and even as Cit Sabhai itself, as it is the way to part of the rue Chit Sabhai, the comprehending Super-Mind.

Suddha Siva Veli, the Supramental Vastness is described as the pure Vast Space that contains all the spaces and is secretly hidden within them and which the Vedas have been vainly searching for those spaces, such as Para Veli, (the spiritual Mind and lower over-mind Space), Nadu Veli (the middle Space or Parampara Veli or Global over-mind), and Upasantaveli (the Space of intense peace and repose signified also as a void Space) with its seven Spaces, the Spaces of over-mind.

THE 13[Th] STATE OF CONSCIOUSNESS, SUDDHA SIVA SAKRAM

"O Supreme Divine! The thirteenth state or plane is a plane of indestructible and unlimited Bliss in the Space of Knowledge."

"I became uniquely separate from Him in the auspicious state of Suddha Siva Jagrata, the tertiary poise of Super-Mind."

"The Lord and myself became of one mould of body and He drew apart giving me His blissful body."

"In the objective embracing of the Divine, I attained a deathless body by receiving the pure Light."

"After realizing Guru Turya State (or Siva Turya, a state of Grace, 'Arul Nilai' – a state of transition into the Truth-World) I have attained the state of Samarasa Sanmarga in an embracing union with my Lord of Grace in Podu, the world of equal self-extension, I got blissfully His mould of body."

"When the Dancer of Cit Sabhai, my beloved Lord, embraced me outwardly (in the physical), I got the golden body which He had impressed on me and I became blissful."

"When I embraced the beautiful and golden body of the God of Grace Light who is my Lord-Husband, there pervaded everywhere the infinite Light; when He embraced me there, I became the Infinite bliss of Satcitananda. I have entered into that high and divine session of Samarasa Sanmarga Sabhai, the tertiary session of Truth and Harmony of Knowledge, and remained with my divine Lord-Husband in close union."

"When I embraced the unique Form of my Lord in the plane of Sudha Siva Jagrata (the tertiary poise of Super-Mind or Samarasa Sanmarga Sabhai) I experienced the unmodified true nature of Bliss of the Divine in the uniting contact and oneness of Truth-Form and Truth-Taste or Truth-Sense. This Bliss has *the sense of sweetness as of honey and the form of luminosity as that of the light of precious gem."*

THE 14TH AND 15TH STATE OF CONSCIONSNESS, SUDDHA SIVA SORPANAM AND SUDDHA SIVA SULUTHI

In the ascent, *"the soul having realized itself as a center or soul-form and soul-movement of the One transcendent and Universal Divine, reaches and joins Him (14th state) and gets blissfully fused and ripened in Him and becomes Himself in the (15th state). "I became Himself" I realized myself as a soul-center of the Divine and became Himself enjoying the state of biune Oneness with Him, a state of I-He in Him. O Lord of Knowledge-Play and Vast-Golden-Light whom I have become"*

In the descent of manifestation too there is a simultaneous two-fold movement of consciousness by which the Transcendent and Universal Divine becomes Myself as a soul-form and vice versa such as self-issuing as myself and self-returning as Himself.

"In Ponnambalam He became Myself (15th state) I became Himself (14th state)" "Becoming myself, He becomes Himself as my Lord."

The Divine enjoys a state of biune Oneness with the soul, a state of He-I in Him. The 14th and the 15th states have to be considered together both in the ascent and descent and may be expressed simultaneously as I-He, as I am becoming Himself and He is becoming Myself, both states being fluid and interchangeable, each implying the other. Both the 14th and 15th state put together would thus mean:

I realized myself as a soul-form of the Universal Divine who or which is the stable Conscious Self or Soul-Essence and as such also the relation of a free difference in unity with Him, as I-He in ascent or return; as He-I in descent.

"I reached and joined Him in Suddha Siva Swapna State (the 14th state). I bore the rapture of the ripened state of Suddha Siva Susupti (the 15th state)."

"I saw Him with my eyes (13th state), I ripened in Him (15th state) and became one with Him in self-identity (16th state)." The 14th state is also implied in the 15th state.

"The Light which has become myself, becomes Himself (i.e. in descent becomes Myself-Himself) within me in unity."

"He became Myself, became Himself (i.e. in descent He became Myself-Himself."

In a song Ramalinga explains in detail and where the Lord is addressed as the Ambrosia of Medicine. "That Ambrosia of One-in-One (i.e. of the Cit Sabhai) has become the Two-in-One and in fact three, four, five-in-one and so on. Thus, the process of manifold becoming of the One-in-One is indicated.

"The One-in-One has become the infinitely manifold crores of existences."

"The Lord, The Father has made himself, his Grace-Shakti and Myself as one."

THE 16TH STATE OF CONSCIOUSNESS, SUDDHA SIVA TURYAM – COMPREHENDING SUPER-MIND

"O Supreme Divine! The high-seated level of experience is that of the integral and perfect blissful existence."

"I have become one with Him in the state of Suddha Siva Turya."

"He became Space of Vastness of Heaven (summit or first poise or 16th Space). He plays in the excellent Heaven of Knowledge. He became the King, the Lord, abiding and sorting in me (in a play of loving relationship)

"Without anything else to confront, He became Himself the Universal All (1st Poise); He became myself (2nd Poise); drawing apart from the one unique formation or union of Himself and myself, He gave me His Blissful Form (3rdPoise)."

"O Divine Father who has made Himself, His Grace-Shakti and me into one existence."

"I became uniquely separate from Him in the unique and good state of Suddha Siva Jagrata."

(3rd Poise of Super-Mind or Samarasa Sanmarga Sabhai, the 13th state of Consciousness or Space)

"(As a soul form) I moved unto Him (the support of my being) in Suddha Siva Swapna state."
(2nd Poise of Super-Mind or Por Sabhai, the 14th state of consciousness or Space)

"I became one with Him in self-identity in Suddha Siva Turya State."

(1st Poise of Super-Mind or Cit Sabhai, the 16th state or Space)

"In the state of Suddha Siva Turyaateeta I became the infinite and eternal Self of Satcitananda (Sivam) which is birthless and has become All and yet is beyond All."

THE 17TH LEVEL OF CONSCIOUSNESS, SUDDHA SIVA TURYAADHEETHAM (SUMMIT-SUPER-MIND AND BEYOND)

The 17th state called Suddha Siva Turyateeta is the Ananda Loka itself or at least the summit Super-Mind called Samarasa Satya Jnana Sabhai or Samarasa Sivananda Sabhai as opening into the Ananda Loka above.

A few of its realization are explained to a certain extent as follows:

To realize integrally in experience the triple bodies of perfection, namely Suddha deha or pure physical body, Pranava deva or the subtle body of Sound Om, and Jnana deha, Knowledge body or Causal body, free from the limitations of time, place and circumstances and to process in full freedom the Supreme Power of ruling mastery over the universal and individual principles of being and becoming and as example of that power, the power of reviving the dead into bodily life, transmutation of the baser substances into silver and gold and realizing the identity of substances of all things.

Further elaborating on the goal of his Sanmarga, Ramalinga says:

"The realization of Sarva Siddhi, the all -perfection or integral perfection is the inseparable goal of Suddha Samarasa Sanmarga, the Path of purity, harmony, the right and truth, even as grace is inseparably one with the Divine Spirit…There

are three steps on the Path. They are the realizations of 1) Cit Sabhai (here, denoting the realization at the Ajna center of the soul or psychic being and the Divine in the soul, Ajna being the mind cum soul-center which is derived from the world of Truth-Knowledge); 2) Por Sabhai (the Golden Sabhai or apprehending session of Truth-Knowledge and 3) Suddha Jnana Sabhai, the true and pure Cit-Sabhai also called Suddha Cit Sabhai, or the comprehending Super-Mind or Vijnana. The experience of the body of perfection is too unique and special to be mentioned here in detail. All about it will be revealed openly by the Divine when Suddha Sanmarga prevails."

Ramalinga holds the goal of the Great Blissful Life before mankind in his prose works "Jeeva Karunnyam" thus:

"The great life of Bliss is to become the Self of all-existence and to possess the integral and perfect Bliss of the Divine who is Sat and Cit and has become all the bodies, instruments, worlds, states of experiences and enjoyments through the Presence and the Power of Grace-Shakti, His conscious Force and thus experience for ever the state of bliss without impediment of time, place and circumstances...The glory of these who have realized the integral and perfect Bliss of the Divine is as follows: They shall have transformed the impure gross physical substances of their effectual body such as skin, nerves, bones, muscles, blood, semen etc..., and their corresponding causal cells of impure nature (asuddha prakriti kaarana anu) to attain a golden effectual body of immeasurable purity and refinement (Suddha bhuutakaaryadeeha). They will have also a pure causal body physical body (Suddha bhuutakaaranadeeha) which will

appear as a golden form of body to the sight only, but will be unseizable to the touch like ether, and an ether like body of Knowledge (jnana deha) which will be unseen…"

From the above passages, it is possible to construe that Ramalinga had pointed out the possibility for all mankind to attain the Great Blissful Life in the 17th state, as opening into the Ananda Loka, as the ultimate goal of human life along with the attainment, here on earth, of all-round perfection and the transformation of the triple body into deathlessness by the power of the Grace-Light, the Love and Bliss of the Divine and thus, becoming one with all the bodies. The knowledge of deathlessness according to Ramalinga, as we have already seen, includes the knowledge and self-creative power of creating all substances of whatever kind, including bodily substances, particularly the five sublimated or divinized elements of un-obstructing physical physical-matter, non-flowing water or liquid, soundless fire, non-burning air or gas, and deathless ethereal substance. So, a constant and progressive renewal, change and growth of these divine substances of the body are implied in such a transformation.

Ramalinga made it very clear that the experience of even the high poise of the world of Truth-Knowledge resulting in "Suddha Jnana Siddhi" (comprehending Super-Mind with its powers of action, of transformation and fulfilment) is not enough. Ramalinga has pointed out that one should be further established in "Samarasa Suddha Jnana Sanmarga", the harmonized powers of Truth-Knowledge and the resulting fulfilment, characteristic of the summit poise of Super-Mind.

This implies that all the poises of the world of Truth-Knowledge should be possessed together and simultaneously in a harmonized experience. This has been already hinted at by Ramalinga when he declared,

"I possess both the Cit Sabhai and the Por Sabhai", O Lord I enjoy in me simultaneously together, the powers and movements of Thy Divine Play of Knowledge – the Will of

Citambalam and Ponnambalam giving me deathlessness of body and bliss according to your predetermination."

Thus, the integral possession and realization of the Super-Mind with its triple poise is the key for the transformation and the perfection of the whole being and of the body into its deathless and blissful state. This should be possible by firmly establishing oneself in the Ananda Loka or at the summit of the Super-Mind as opening into the Ananda Loka. However, the above background seems to explain the extraordinary quick transformation of Ramalinga, in mind, life and body.

XIII - SCIENCE OF DEATHLESSNESS – TRIPLE SIDDHI & TRIPLE BODY

In his book of "Upadesha"& "Peru Vinnapam", Ramalinga write on the deathless and indestructible triple bodies of the physical, subtle and causal and on the triple "siddhis" (Divine Power) of karma Siddhi, Yoga Siddhi and in their supramental significances.

TRANSFORMATION IN SUDDHA SANMARGA

What is Suddha Sanmarga? Suddham means transcending the exclusiveness of any one thing. As suddham comes before the word Sanmarga, it means that it transcends all the religions and spiritual philosophies. Sanmargam has four significances according to four stages. The highest stage which is the highest goal of Suddha Sanmarga is the state of Suddha Siva turyateeta that is the Summit of the Super-mind where the world of Truth-Consciousness opens into the infinite and eternal world of "Ananda" above, the state of Purely Supreme Divine Bliss. It is the 17 levels level, the highest state of realisation according to the gradation of ascent or evolution.

1 - SUDDHA DEHA OR GOLDEN BODY – 13th STATE OF CONSCIOUSNESS -SUDDHA SIVA SAKRAM

Suddha deha or Swarna deha is a pure physical body with a great measure of purity and transformation which becomes manifest as a golden physical body. With that realisation of the first stage, everything is turned into its values; the physical body, feelings, consciousness and knowledge are based on the principle of Paratva (transformation of the physical body) under the direct influence of super-mind in a supra-mental realisation. It is the initial transformation of the physical body into a relative deathlessness with a long period of life up to the age of Godhead Sadasiva. Ramalinga depicted 5 levels of ascent for the golden body:

1rst level: The 5 carats golden body of Brahma can live up to 436.000 years of age.

2nd level: The 6 carats golden body of Vishnou can live up to 864.000 years of age.

3rd level: 7 carats golden body of Rudran can live up to 1.296.000 years of age.

4th level: 8 carats Golden body of Maheswara can live up to 1.728.000 years of age.

5th level: 9 carats Golden body of Sadasivam can live up to 4.324.000 years of age.

The Suddha deha is also called the first stage being the result of the super-mind-directed psycho-spiritual transformation which may be called the first stage of supramental transformation. Ramalinga tells that, when he embraced the Golden body of the beautiful Lord, all the powers and forces of darkness were dispelled away and replaced by the Supreme truth-Light which is the Blissful Grace-Light and that it has become a Golden body, partaking of the amrita of Supreme Grace Light. The one who has attained the golden body looks like one of 12 years old; free from thirst, food, sleep, shadow of body, evacuation of waste material, urination, perspiration, senility of old age, greying of hair, disease etc…, hair, neither excessive nor deficient in growth.

One who has attained the Suddha deha or Golden body state has the capacity to demonstrate many siddhis or divine powers "Karma Siddhis":

1- "**Anima**", to make an insignificant or small thing like piece of straw to become a very large like the mountain Meru;
2- "**Mahima**", to make a big thing like the Meru mountain to become small like a piece of straw;
3- "**Garima**", to dissolve or reduce the Meru mountain, a very heavy mountain, into nothing.

Its poorva or first stage of transformation, the lowest level of transformation can be somewhat expressed at the least to be the attainment of Suddha deha, that is the attainment of a pure physical body or golden body, here in a relative sense comparatively to the absolute and integral purity of the body corresponding to the ultimate stage of realisation.

When Ramalinga received the golden body "Suddha deha", he prays to the lord, seeking His refuge, to overcome and cross over the dark nether ocean of the inconscient darkness, even though he observed having attained the golden body of deathlessness filled with Light and Amrita of Bliss. Obviously, the "suddhadeha", 1st stage of transformation was not the final transformation as it seems there were still attacks from the inconscient though they could not succumb or overcome him to or by death. In the earliest "Vinappam" Ramalinga mentioned the difficulties of death, disease, aging senility, fear, afflictions and sufferings. Due to the still uncleared off physical ego-consciousness of the body, he surrendered himself to the Divine completely praying to make this physical body itself an eternal body living a life of bliss on the earth. In response to his prayers, it seems that the Lord directed Ramalinga to marry the Grace-Shakti in order to overcome the difficulties reach the highest state of perfection. Ramalinga married the Grace-Shakti after having announced it to his disciples and become one with the Divine Mother. Through the blessing and help of the divine Mother, Ramalinga finally scores victor over death and attains all siddhis usually referred to as triple siddhis namely karma siddhis or karma jnana siddhis, yoga siddhis or yoga jnana siddhis, jnana siddhis or Atma jnana siddhis and tattva jnana siddhis.

According to Ramalinga's experience of transformation of body and his often-repeated declaration, the full emergence of jnana deha, the supramental causal body of knowledge into the physical is the sin qua none of the deathless transformation of body. Once it emerges in its fulness, it quickly and spontaneously completed the supramental transformation of the subtle and physical bodies namely pranavadeha and suddhadeha and make them deathless too.

2 - PRANAVA DEHA OR BODY OF SOUND

The body of sound or Pranavadeha, "KaaryaKaaranarupa" or middle conscious soul, "Parampara deha", full wisdom in between lower consciousness and higher consciousness. It is actually the transformation of the body in a body with the purity of Gold, ranging from 16 to 108 carats that looks like 5 to 8 years old. Pranava body can be seen but unseizable to touch.

One who has attained the Pranavadeha state has the free will and power to perform 64 Siddhis. By his free will and power, he can revive into bodily life persons deceased and buried within a period of 12 to 108 years death. The yoga siddhi opens one into Pranavadeha or subtle body which gives to the physical body a still greater golden purity than the Suddha deha of the first stage and it has the causal-effectual form of body "Kaarya Kaaranaruupa" and lives up to the age of Brahma, 311,040 billion years.

3 - JNANA DEHA OR BODY OF WISDOM

Kaaranarupa, the soul mingling with the One soul of all souls and becoming one with God. In "Jyoti Agaval" Ramalinga tells about the trans formatory changes occurring in his body possibly around the year 1871-1872 which lead to the attainment of a deathless body. According to Ramalinga, a deathless body is constituted by the divinised five elements, namely, deathless ethereal substance, non-ignitable air or gas, non-flowing liquid, soundless fire and non-obstructing matter. The changes are about the plasticity and suppleness of bones, muscles etc..., condensation of blood and concentration of semen in the chest as one drop, blossoming of petals of brain and the influx of intermittent nervous current etc..., The plasticity and suppleness of bones, muscles, skin, all the seven kinds of cells of the body and the corresponding causal cells of impure nature so as to change the body into a golden effectual physical body of immeasurable purity and refinement. It had made the body wholly suppliant or plastic that it became a non-obstructing penetrable physical body into which all the five elements, radio – active rays and even instruments of weapon can pass through harmlessly without obstruction and without injury to the body and that this body could not be killed by such elements rays and weapons nor by god of death nor by any violent means. It will not be cooled by coolness of water and cannot be immersed by or in water even if tried to immerse it. It will not be heated by heat of fire, in spite of burning it, it will not feel the heat or get any mark of burning within it. It will not be moved by movement and contact of air. It will not be separated by the inter-fusing ether or space in the body, it will not be separated by ether or space. Such a body will move not merely in a field of supporting medium "adhara" (support), but also in the (support less) "niradhara". The instruments of sense-knowledge like eyes and instruments of sense-action like speech will not get attached to sense object of sight, speech etc…, but if out of compassion for others, sense of perceptions have to be experienced, even obstruction like wall and mountain cannot cover the eyes; the eyes can see all objects and contents in and of all the worlds and of the individual bodies within and without; whenever one is, their ears will hear the sound of speech from all the worlds and individual bodies. Rooted in one's own place of living, their tongue will taste all the rasas or tastes. Where the body remains, there itself, the skin of their body will experience all the sensations of touch; likewise their nose will sense all smells; their hands, remaining where they are, irrespective of time and distance, will reach to give to persons at whatever place of distance; so too, their legs remaining unmoved, without physical movement, will walk and reach to all destinations; Likewise their speech will communicate with all the persons wherever their position; rooted to their own place, their senses can enjoy the objects of senses at any place whatsoever. Their faculties and instruments of mind will be free from attachment to anything whatsoever. If by compassion for others they want to get interested in and attached to any being or all beings to know wholly all of their thoughts, will and modifications thereof Sankalpa Vikalpa, they can in a minute or moment of time, simultaneously know, judge and decide about them. Their knowledge not being of objective character; but if by compassion they want to have objective knowledge of things and beings, they can do so instantaneously about all the worlds, beings, qualities, experiences and results. They are free from gunas or qualities "gunas" of lower nature nor will they be influenced within by the three gunas: sattva, rajas and tamas; without, the gunas will not affect the instruments and faculties of their minds and senses; within, they will not be covered or veiled by Prakriti, power of primordial nature; without their nature will not be attached to the gunas of lower nature; within, they will not be affected by the principle of "Kaala" time, "raaga" desire, "vidya" knowledge and agency of being purusha and all others principles and their operative powers of functioning "tatva" and "tattva kariya". They will not be modified by Maya, the obscuring power of lower nature. They shall have transcended Suddha Maha Maya, the greater and purer Nature, the Conscious Force of Summit-over-mind and manifest themselves as beings of knowledge-nature. They will be free from food, sleep, sexual impulse and fear. Their body will be free from the defect of dirt and impurities, perspiration, shadow, greying of hair, shrinking of skin, aging senility and become deathless in and of the physical body. Their body will not be affected at and time and place by cold, heat, rain, thunder and other natural elements, nor it can be troubled or tormented by the lower vital beings such as "rakshasas, asuras, bhutas, pisachas nor by the higher vital beings, gods or devas not by munisor men of austerities and tapas nor by human beings and dwellers of hell, nor by animals, birds, creeping creatures or reptiles and non-movable things. Their body cannot be cut by instruments like swords and knives. It is within the natural powers of their body to have the vision of all the atoms, cells, becoming as large as the worlds and all the worlds becoming as minute as the atoms, cell.

Jnana siddhis which are related to the causal body gives power over 64.000 forces or Shakti and with these forces at one's command, one can perform 647 crores,6.647.000.000 of manifold various great siddhis "Maha Siddhis". By his free will and power, the large multiple numbers referring to a total and integral and simultaneous power of knowledge and will do all deeds of perfection called siddhis. His body, the causal form of body "Kaaranarupa" will give immeasurable purity to the physical body, by which it can live eternally without any limit of time Kaalaateeta. The causal body in itself is all pervasive "pooranavyapaka", and though it emerges, it will be unseen. One will have all achieving powers "Sarva Maha Shakti" with complete freedom of will "Sarvawatana". He will have the power of Shabdamaya darshan, the vision of sound, which signifies, the harmonisation of Light and Sound, the vision and inspiration of the Truth. He will have the "paraaparatva principle", the direct supramental truth and power as the basis of his physical body, consciousness and knowledge because of the emergence of jnana deha into the physical body. In Tamil the word "Paraapara" has a lesser and higher significance. In its higher sense it means Paraa Param, the farthest Heaven, the apprehending Super-mind and in its lower sense it means the border between the highest and the lowest, Para and apara, knowledge and ignorance. Here, in the context of description of the causal body as all-pervading and all-powerful, "Paraaparatva" shall mean necessarily the supramental principle itself. This Jnana Siddhis however leads to the pure, integral and triple forms of Siddhis namely: Suddha Karma Siddhi, Suddha Yoga Siddhi and Suddha Jnana Siddhi which are attained correspondingly in both the lowest and highest poises of Super-mind (the Heaven beyond the Heaven, the farther Heaven denoting apprehending Super-mind), its tertiary and apprehending poises. Ramalinga calls the Super-mind by names such as Suddha Siva Veli or Suddha jnana Veli or Arivup Peru Veli, the Vastness of Knowledge.

Ramalinga observes that one of the chief aims of the "Samarasa Suddha Sanmarga is to have the integral realisation at once and simultaneously of all siddhis such as the siddhis of the triple bodies of Jnana deha, Pranavadeha and Suddha deha which are free from all limitations of time, place and circumstances and beyond all impediments, the siddhi or power of free will over all principles in the cosmic and individual existence, the siddhi of reviving the dead into bodily life, the siddhi of transforming or transmuting baser metals into finer metals such as silver and gold, The Siddhi of identification with the essence and substance of things "Vastu Pratyaksha Anubhava Siddhi". The chief aim of the Suddha Sanmarga can be known if one realises the state of "Suddha Siva Turyaateeta", the summit of Super-mind as opening into the world of Sat Chit Ananda.

When all these siddhis including all the siddhis of the triple body integrate absolutely in the field of Samarasa Suddha jnana, an eternal deathless physical body, the triple deathless and indestructible body is realised with fivefold universal powers of creation, maintenance, destruction for renewal, for purification, control and for recreation, involution or veiling and obscuring consciousness of others in order to hide oneself from them and act impersonally on them, evolution or unveiling and clarifying the consciousness which is called "anugraha" or act of Grace will be performed by the immediate power of their thought and will; the five universal godheads of the above said universal functions: Brahma, Vishnou, Rudra, Maheshwara, Sadasiva will do their respective functions at the command of a graceful look from the corner of their eyes.

Their knowledge will be God's Knowledge; their action will be God's action; their experiences become God's own; with all-effectuating power of will, deathless in and of the body for all time, free from the defects of ego, lower nature and lower modes of action and free from the painful experiences of these three kinds of impurities, they will become manifestations of the Divine Grace. Even an insignificant material object of inanimate and inconscient nature will awaken into life or consciousness by the graceful look of their eyes and perform the said five-fold functions. The grandeur and glory of their divine realisation will necessarily cover or include all the realisations of the six traditional disciplines namely Vedanta, Siddhanta, Kalaanta, Bodhanta, Nadanta and Yoganta; but it transcends and exceeds all of them. Such is the greatness and glory of those who have attained the integral and perfect Bliss of divine life.

Ramalinga has shown, demonstrated and opened the way to all mankind, to this most sublime and divine path giving access to the highest pinnacle of spiritual development lived in the state of Supreme Bliss.

"The spiritual gain that one should truly know of and attain in and by human birth is the goal of realising the perfect and great Bliss of the Divine who is of "Sat" Nature and also of "Chit" Nature that manifests by its Force of Grace all the worlds and planes of existence, all things, all beings, all ways of discipline, all results and effects; and of realising the matchless great divine life that is to be lived without any impediment, whatsoever of time, place and circumstance" – **Ramalinga – Jeeva Karunyam – prose p.64.**

SACRIFICE OF DEATHLESS BODY BY DEMATERIALISATION

The one natural and common question that is generally asked is as to why Ramalinga should have dematerialised his body and disappeared, if he had attained deathlessness of body?

In the cases of "siddhas" who have finally disappeared by dematerialisation, the process might be that of a progressive subtilisation of the substance of the body towards the ethereal substance so as to make their final disappearance into Grace-Space which seems to be the "Supramental Space", as it described in Suddha Sadhakam or that of the unity of soul and body-consciousness – as camphor put into fire – resulting in the dissolution or an upward breaking of body's substance upward… to higher plane – Sri Aurobindo on "The Divine Body"

So as to reach into the yonder heaven Param which seems to be the supramental heaven and that such substance dissolved in Param will get crystallized – as salt from sea water – and form itself as a body for its further evolutionary progress in the next birth. It is evident that in either case the process is attended with an upward aspiration to reach the Heaven or the divine abode, bodily, with an attitude of rejecting the world of birth and death and sorrows. Their overwhelming aspiration was to quit this world of death and sorrow seeking refuge in a heaven abode or even in the Grace-Space of Truth-World ; god of death was not very much concerned with them, as they did not attempt to face and conquer death here in its own realm.

But Ramalinga's case is quite opposite to the above. He willed for an earthly fulfilment by a life of deathless body which is to be lived here itself. Even his dematerialisation was intended for a terrestrial fulfilment as it is seen from his last writings and spoken words, as it occurred in a strange background – in a process of manifestation of God of Light at his place and God's identification with enlarged physical body, for his avowed purpose of entering into all physical bodies universally by and through such a dematerialisation of this transformed sleepless, deathless, golden and enlarged physical body in its state of Truth-Knowledge. Ramalinga said on his time, in future I will enter into all the bodies, for making it a possibility on the earth for man to get the powers of resurrection in case of death and of transformation of even the aged into youth, and of fixing the forces of his body's deathlessness into the earth-nature for the benefit of man in his evolution towards deathlessness of the body.

Evidently in the light of this understanding, the deathless substances of his body to dematerialise could not have escaped or gone up into the yonder heaven but should have been distributed or scattered as potential seed sown and fixed in the very earth-nature or rather more possibly and properly in its base and foundation meaning the inconscient, so as to make it possible for man to attain deathlessness of body one day and to get powers of transformation and resurrection to begin with. The very characteristic and subtle vibrations at his resort at Mettukuppam seem to emphasise the validity of such an inference.

For all the others who dematerialised and disappeared apparently by a different way and method, we do not find positive internal evidence from their writings as to the attainment of deathlessness of the body were involving transformatory changes in its physical substances and structure, or to their clear and categorical affirmation of it or to an integral realisation and possession of all the poises of Truth-Knowledge, or to the various stages of transformation including the crucial stages of attacks from the inconscient darkness or to the vision of a direct manifestation of the Divine on earth and the consequential evolution of man into a divine superman. At best, these may be the cases of realisation of some level or levels in the lower or tertiary super-mind attended with partial transformation of body. One such case of dematerialisation is that of the poet and saint Maanicka Vaachakar who had the intensities of Bliss overwhelming him; he got an amrita-oozing body; Amrita got stored up even in the root of hair; it coursed in the hollows of bones. In this context, he observed: *"O Lord! At last Thouhast made me realise myself as one being in existence and hast made me, a being of the Supreme or Transcendent Bliss and Grace as also of the universal delight; and the Supreme Bliss and universal delight enter into my individual being."*

In another stanza, the saint has declared: *"O Lord! Thou hast made me a being" "The Divine who eternally abides in my heart has become my own self and has entered into my soul and body pervading everywhere imperishably without fail."*

"Because of and by His Grace, I have come to worship his feet…O Truth! I have realised the Home, this day by seeing or realizing Thy Golden Feet…Thou hast come as the Truth-Flame of Light manifesting Truth-Knowledge and dispelling away all falsehood."

Maanicka Vaachakar became free from disease and aging into senility. He even sensed that the luminous divine substance had cancelled the decaying nature of the body. He referred to his ripening body of flesh and melting bones, the flesh and bones tending to become plastic and supple, because the Lord entered into his body to make a golden temple. And in this context the saint observed:

"O Lord of Bliss and Light! I have seized Thee firmly."

The saint aspired and waited possibly in his oldest day to be called up into the Heaven above, "Siva Loka" so as to leave the body behind. However, instead of death, it is said that he dematerialised his body and disappeared into the Light. Ramalinga referred about Maanicka vaashakar in one of his songs, saying that the saint became one with the Grace-Space, the Supramental space on dematerialisation.

Coming back to Ramalinga's triple deathlessness body experience, his bones, muscles and skin became plastic and supple; his blood condensed; these imply change in substance of all the cells of his body and a change in the structure of vital organs as well. He attained a triple indestructible body with the power to resurrect the dead.

COLLECTIVE EVOLUTIONARY SIGNIFICANCES OF RAMALINGA'S DEMATERIALISATION AND SUPERMAN CONSCIOUSNESS

Ramalinga's words suggesting his "Avatar Consciousness"

"O Father! Thou hast made me one with Thyself and Thy Grace-shakti; the Lord has taken my life and soul, substance and body; I play on earth the Grace-Play of the Lord, My Father; All my actions are the Lords own. Know that my nature is the Nature of my Father, the Supreme Lord. All the words I speak are verily the words of the universal Lord Himself. O God of Light! Thou hast declared that "I" and "Thou" are One. Thou hast crowned me with Thy direct crown of Light. O Father! Thou hast given me Thy sceptre of Grace-Light and asked me to rule over. Thou hast enjoined me to take upon myself all the difficulties of the beings of the world in order to remove them and thereby rejoice. I bear the great name and title

as the true and dear Son of the Lord Chit-Sabhai, the Supra-Mental Divine. (Ramalinga added to his original name Ramalingam Pillai the title of Chidambaram as a prefix). O Lord! Thy devotees on the wide earth will consider me as Thyself; O Lord! Thou hast given me the power to perform the five-fold universal functions so that the multitudes of beings of the world shall get into the Path of light, my way is Thy Way, O Lord! My Way is the Sanmarga (The Path of Truth, The Right, Harmony and Purity) that abolishes death; I have received the Grace of the Lord who has brought me in this time "Yuga" or Age so that I shall make all people of the world who are impure and dark within and even with a deceitful show of outward purity, get corrected or mended so as to join the way of Sanmarga and become happy by attaining the heavenly life, the blissful life of deathless body, here itself… By the Grace of the Universal Lord of Truth-Knowledge even the shawl I wear will resurrect the dead into bodily life of flesh. I have got the triple indestructible bodies of Sudha deha, Pranavadeha and Jnana deha in order to give myself freely in play everywhere."

Ramalinga wanted to enter into all material physical bodies universally. Ramalinga last words were: I am in this body; in the future, I will enter into all physical bodies and to identify or associate and connect them with own deathless body in a state of Truth-Knowledge to share his powers of transformation and deathlessness with all – and that too in an age when there had not taken place then as now, the universal descent and manifestation of the Light. This could not have been possible unless he sought a solution for death at the very root of matter which has its basis in the inconscient darkness. This too, he could not have done all alone by himself, unaided by the Divine who directly manifested thereat, and became one with his enlarged body. It is quite likely that as a result of that process and as His instrument and with His help, Ramalinga did dematerialised and scattered the transformed elements of his deathless body in the Ether realm of the inconscient having the intention to fix into the earth-nature the possibility of body's deathlessness for man. Such a background alone will justify the nature of his promises and assurances given, on the eve of his retirement into seclusion, -promises given almost in a tone and vein of what might be called "Avatar Consciousness", when considering more particularly the promises of his coming back into bodily form and giving boon of deathlessness to those who are purified prepared, and conditions of purity to the unprepared and the promises of the happening of miracles of resurrection of the dead into bodily life, after the manifestation of the Divine on earth. Further his dematerialisation considered by us to have taken place in the inconscient as a mode of fixing deathlessness to the earth-nature must have been relevantly called for in the circumstances to fulfil his avowed divine mission of annihilating death which he expressed in the following terms and passages, befitting and proper only to an "Avatar Consciousness".

Ramalinga never called him an Avatar, much less allowed his disciples to designate him even as a swami. However, this humility apart, it is apparent that in his last three years of earthly life, he lived continuously in the fullness of a Supra-Mental state. In his poems, Ramalinga clearly expresses that he was the instrument through whom the God of Light, the Vast Supreme Grace Light was going to come and manifest on earth. He said:

"From now on, the Universal Lord of the Play in Compassion begins His New Age for the happiness of the whole world when the Vast Grace-Light shall manifest progressively by and through me and only His days of happiness are ahead."

In a public notice to his disciples on November 25th 1872, he observed that:

"the One, the Supreme and Universal Divine, is making a move to manifest so that all the people of the world may generally and commonly get the great benefit of the state of Sanmarga (the state of Truth, the Right, the Good and

harmony) and live an eternal life and that the members of the sanmarga shall be full of faith to receive in that hour of manifestation the spiritual gain and shall fully cooperate in the discipline of worship."

In an earlier message to the disciples on 26th of December 1870, Ramalinga observed that:

"Have true faith, that because of one person, infinitely multitudes of people will be benefited. It is true that you will be benefited by me. Patiently await for some time till I come out within a few days in your midst by the Divine Will...Thiruchittrambalam (Be Blessed with the Divine Truth-Consciousness of the truth-World."

RAMALINGA'S VISION OF THE EARTHLY EVOLUTION

In the poems "Suddha Siva Nilai" and Ulakappeeru or boon of the world, Ramalinga specially mention the nature of collective evolution and evolutionary changes that are to come with the manifestation of Vast Grace-Light on the earth. In the poem "Ulakappeeru", Ramalinga sees in vision that with the advent of the God of Vast Grace-Light, the worldly minded people will shed their impurities and become God-like; the strong-bodied become cultured; the fools become wise; in the all of nature the purity, refinement, delicacy and qualities will excels by throwing out defects; even material prosperity becomes the order of the day removing the wanting and craving of the people; the earth and the universe will take to the reign of Grace; the path of Truth, the Right and Harmony (i.e. Suddha Sanmarga) will prevail over the other ways of spiritual discipline; and by Divine Play, the mind and heart of men become purified and clarified in consciousness; the poisonous creatures come to live without poison in them; plant life will become to be luxuriant and will have incessant growth; inimical creatures like serpents and birds will come to live in harmony together; the impurities of nature will be washed away and the purity of good nature will subsist and will be sustained; many discriminating hearts minds will become clarified in consciousness and the Play of the Divine Will manifest in them; The whole world will take the "rule of Grace" and will proper; even the dead will resurrect to bodily life; those who died in grief will be seen free from grief after death; devotees will sing, dance and worship the Supreme Grace-Light; The liberated ones will become aware of the Truth of being and will experience bliss; The perfected human beings of divine perfection attained by transformation will partake of the bliss of clarified Amrita. These visions of collective evolution on the earth will be seen as manifestations of the God of Vast-Grace-Light in the awakening process of the Light reaching towards the poet and entering into his heart – his heart representing the heart of the sub-conscient which is symbolical of the earth and its evolution.

In the poem "Suddha Siva Nilai", Ramalinga observes that the heavenly gods and godheads such as Brahma and Vishnu are gathering and are waiting at the gate to fulfil the will of the Lord, when the Lords will be coming and manifest with the blissful Sakti (Siva Kama Vali) here on this earth to play his will in the near future. In other words, all the gods and godheads will also come to the earth to fulfil the will of the Supreme in His direct manifestation here. The eternal and omnipotent Lord will play here on the earth for ever in time without break. Again, in the poems 12-33, Ramalinga promises *"the coming of a new race"* and in 12-34 "The great life of deathlessness body". Ramalinga promised that this is the time that the Eternal and Universal Lord is coming by Himself to play openly, as on an open road, the manifestation of His Grace Light, and that in order to get into a new and pure race of good people who will have bodies free from aging senility, greying of hair and death, by taking to the most refined and divine food of Amrita, Ramalinga exhorts the people to attain this state here and now as the universal Lord is planned to manifest. This is the time for the Omnipotent Lord of perfect will and action to come as to transform even the old and weak people of wrinkled skin into youth and make the dead resurrect into bodily life."It is truth that the Lord is about to come and that the veils of ignorance would be removed…If you persevere with aspiration and effort you can receive the gains accordingly…The Lord has now given by His Will as a first step this Mahamantra so as to express and manifest openly its Truth.

ARUTPERUNJOTHI-ARUTPERUNJOTHI
THANIPPERUNKARUNAI-ARUTPERUNJOTHI

In the same speech, Ramalinga answered to a question as to whether spiritual discipline was any more necessary, in view of the fact, that the Supreme Divine Himself was coming or manifesting here on the earth. He answered that with the advent of the Divine and by His Grace the dark green screen (the veil of identification with the illusory aspect of life, desires and attachments having forgotten The source of all life, the source of existence), will be removed, this even for the ordinary people of ignorance without their effort and aspiration for it and they can live, as far as possible, in conditions of purity. However, Ramalinga advised that one can live in certain states of purity after the removal of the vital veil, but in order to get the higher spiritual gains such as powers of universal functions and spiritual realisation, one has to progress only by a good effort of discipline, and therefore they, the disciples should continue the spiritual discipline so that when the Divine will manifest on earth, they could readily get the higher spiritual gains also. – **from Upadesha p.132.**

XIV - COMPASSION PART I

LIVING A LIFE OF COMPASSION TOWARDS ALL LIVING BEINGS

Only the Act of Practicing Compassion towards All Living Beings Is the Act of Worshipping God

Those who got human birth in this world should understand and obtain the benefit for the soul, which is attainable through this birth, within the available time span.

What is the benefit of the soul – what is the reason of our being here in this human for me?

To understand what is meant by the benefit for the soul: One should understand truly that the benefit for the soul is to live a unique great life at all times, at all places and in all ways without any sort of hindrance, obtaining the Absolute Natural Bliss of God, who by His Power of Grace has made all the universes, all the worlds, all the things, all the living beings, all the ways of living, all the usefulness and also made them to manifest, exist and enlighten them.

How to attain that great life where one lives with unhindered natural bliss?

It is good to know that it can only be obtained by the action of Grace which is God's Natural Manifestation.

By which means the grace which is god's natural manifestation could be obtained?

Grace which is God's Natural Manifestation can only be obtained by leading a life of compassion towards all living beings and that not even a little of it can be obtained by any other means,

How is it that God's Grace can only be obtained by leading a life of compassion towards all living beings and not by another means?

Grace is God's Mercy which is God's Natural Manifestation. Compassion shown to fellow human beings means the sympathy or their souls' natural manifestation. It is therefore, possible to obtain the Mercy of God by virtue of displaying sympathy to human beings. Since this is the experience and certainty that God's Mercy cannot be obtained by any other means but only by being compassionate to all human beings, it is good to know that no other proof is required in this regard.

As leading a compassionate life to living beings is the only way to obtain Grace, it has to be known that true and pure spiritual path and the virtuous path "Sanmargam" means to live a life full of compassion towards all living beings.

In the contrary, the untrue and sinful path or the path of nescience is a life lived without compassion towards fellow human beings.

When the act of compassion to living beings manifests, true knowledge and love will blossom along with it. This in turn, will result in the manifestation of benevolent forces of nature. Due to these benevolent forces, all that is good is emerging.

In the contrary, when compassion to living beings disappear, true knowledge and love cease to exist resulting in the disappearance of benevolent forces of nature and because of this all that is evil will emerge. Therefore, it is to be understood that virtue is nothing but showing compassion to living beings and vice is the absence of this quality.

It is good to know as the sworn truth, that enlightenment coming out of leading a life of compassion towards living beings is the expression of God Himself and the outcome of bliss expressed Enlightenment of God and the bliss coming out of leading a life of compassion towards living beings is the Divine Bliss.

Those who have attained the state of liberation and are experiencing Divine Bliss for a long period and have attained a state of perfection during their lifetime are the liberated souls. Only those liberated souls will realise God by their knowledge and experience the union with Thee.

What does it means, by leading a life of compassion towards all living beings?

This is the way of worshipping God by leading one's life through the process of the melting of souls. This happen when one soul is melting with another soul for the sake of other human beings. One feels what the other feels; I am one with the other.

When will the melting of the soul towards other beings occur?

It should be known that the melting of the soul will occur when one sees, hears or comes to know of the suffering of other living beings due to hunger thirst, disease, desire, poverty, fear and the suffering when being killed.

What Is the Right to Have Compassion towards Other Living Beings:

All living beings are created by the Almighty God with the same characteristics and they form an integral part of Natural Truth. Hence, human beings are all brothers with the same right. The melting of the soul occurs, when one of the brothers sees another human being, whom he considers as his brother who is grieving or come to know that he shall be grieved due to some calamity, his soul gets melted out of sympathy for him spontaneously. Therefore, one must learn that the melting of one's soul for the sake of another human being when he sees him in distress or comes to know that he is going to be distressed is an age old spiritual rights.

Some people, even on seeing other living beings suffering, do not have compassion towards them and are hard-hearted; why don't these people have the right to brotherhood?

Some people do not exhibit compassion towards fellow human beings even after having seen and known that the human beings who are grieved and will be grieved are their brothers. It so happens because the knowledge of the soul that acts as an eye, through which the sufferings of the people could be perceived, has lost its brightness due to an inner disease called fallacy or untruth. Besides this, the ancillaries to the soul such as the mind and other related faculties which are only subservient and function as a mirror to reflect what the soul perceives. If what the soul perceives has become dense tending to block the reflection, this aspect is leading to the loss of proper perception. In view of this truth, it is to be known that whosoever expressed compassion towards fellow human beings are the persons who have the enlightened spiritual vision.

The sufferings of the living beings due to hunger thirst, fear etc., are the experiences of the subtle inner instruments (karanam) and the sense organs and the working organs (indriyam); they are not the experiences of the soul. So, is there any special benefit in being compassionate to living beings on such grounds?

In this physical body, except the existence of the Soul as the 'Life Force' and the manifestation of God, in the form of knowledge of the knowledge, the mental faculties and the sense organs, are inert instruments, having no capacity to know anything on their own. These inert things, will therefore, not be able to experience the joys and sorrows. In the same manner, we could not say, that the red soil experienced the pleasure and pain, as it could not be said either, that the mind experienced happiness and misery. Human beings construct houses made of red soil for their physical existence. In the same way, the human body is a small house made of the mind and the organs of senses by God for leading human life. One who resides within that house will experience the joys and sorrows of life not the house. Moreover, when the eyes which are diseased and subsequently got the power of vision impaired, happen to see human sufferings through spectacles, only the eyes will shed tears not the spectacles. Hence, it is to be known that the inert instruments such as the mind etc are only subservient to the Soul and those inert instruments will not experience the happiness and unhappiness, only the Soul will experience the same.

When the human beings are rejoiced, the mind is cheerful; when they are grieved, the mind gets weakened; should it, therefore, be understood that the mind only experiences the happiness and grief?

It is not to be understood like that, the healthiness and the physical fatigue of the body of a human being, who resides within a house made of glasses, gets reflected within the house and appears outside through the glasses. The brightness as well as the fatigue of the eyes gets reflected outside through the spectacles one wears. In the same way, the joys and sorrows of the Soul, caused by happiness or sadness, gets reflected through the mind and the sense organs and visible outside. It is, therefore, to be understood, that the Soul experiences the happiness and pain, and to know and experience the pleasure and pain, the mental faculties and the organs of senses are instrumental to the Soul.

Many human beings created by god suffer a lot due to hunger, thirst, fear etc.; why?

Since these human beings were stony hearted and had no intention of leading a life of compassion in their previous bodies, and chose the vicious ways of living, they suffer a lot due to hunger, thirst, fear etc. as per the Gracious order of God.

Human beings did have previous bodies; how is it?

A family man who has come to a rented house, to lead his life, should have lived in another rented house previously but could not have lived without a house. If he faces any crisis in the present house also, he will go and live in another house. In the same way the Life Force (Jeevan), that has come to reside in the present body, by paying food as rent, should have lived in another body previously, after having paid the same sort of rent, but will not exist without a body. In case of any trouble in the present body, also he will go to reside in another body. Therefore, we ought to know, that human beings had bodies before, and will have bodies after the present ones are lost.

The sinful deeds committed by human beings in the previous bodies will come into existence in the present body also; how does it happen?

If a family man disobeyed the order of the house owner, and had invited bad and vicious people to the house where he lived previously, and entertained them, the same people will follow and befriend him, even if he leaves the old house and occupied another one. Likewise, if a human being had not acted in accordance with the order of God, and by following the vicious path, willingly committed sins in the previous body, those sinful deeds will follow him even if he takes a new body, and will be with him in the present body also.

If it is the 'will of god' that makes those human beings who in their previous birth had deviated from the 'life of showing compassion' to human beings and followed the vicious path to be grieved in their present birth due to hunger, thirst, fear etc., will it not be going against the divine commandment to show compassion to those human beings and provide food etc., in order to alleviate their misery?

It is not so. The king, through his servants, feeds even the criminals of the worst kind, who were fettered and imprisoned for having disobeyed his orders. In a similar way, God feeds even the sinners who antagonised Him, because of their total disobedience to His commandments, and are kept as slaves in the hell in various ways, through his sub–ordinate deities. The king dismisses those servants who have disobeyed his orders and committed simple offences of various kinds, from service. He also prevents them from receiving any material gains and sends them from the place of service to any other place to enable them to acquire the 'Right Knowledge'. Consequent upon their loss of job, they lose their happiness and food etc., and move around the country in search of food etc. and suffer. On seeing their miserable condition, the kind-hearted people provide them with food and other needful things. When the king comes to know about this or sees this happening, he will not be angry with the donors but will appreciate them as good and compassionate family men.

Similarly, all Powerful God, by His Powers "Shakti" precludes the human beings who have not acted in accordance with His Will and committed simple crimes from enjoying physical as well as material comforts of this world, enabling them to acquire the right knowledge, removing their being from their present body to bring them into another body. Since those human beings have lost their physical comforts and worldly enjoyments, they move from place to place in search of food etc… and suffer. If kind-hearted people, on seeing their miserable state of existence, give them food, God will never be angry with them but will be too happy to know that they are Merciful People and bless them to be happy and prosper more and more. Hence, it should be truly understood that the Gracious Law of God always acknowledges the quality of exhibiting compassion by human beings to fellow human beings

It must be learnt that only due to the practice of compassion to the human beings there is discipline in this world; if there is no compassionate life, not even a little amount of the worldly discipline will exist; how?

When human beings do not display compassion to other human beings, true knowledge and love will disappear. When they do not exist, benignity, the feeling of spiritual oneness and benevolent attitude will cease to exist, and due to the non–existence of these human qualities, the discipline of the weaker human beings will be obstructed and destroyed by the envy of the stronger human beings. Ultimately, even the conduct and discipline of the stronger human beings, will also get degenerated into 'baseness' in nature, resulting in the change and destruction of the conduct of the one by the other, out of their pride. In the forest where animals such as Tiger and Lion live, there is no worldly discipline at all due to lack of compassionate life among them. Similarly, the worldly discipline will not exist in the place where people live without compassion and this is to be understood.

The heavenly discipline exists due to the life compassion by human beings and in the absence of the same, the heavenly discipline too will not exist; how?

When there is no compassion express to living beings, Grace will not find its expression. When Grace does not get expressed, 'State of Divinity' cannot be attained when the state of Divinity is not attained nobody will enjoy the Bliss of salvation (MukthiInbam) and in the event of non–attainment of salvation by anybody, heavenly discipline will not exist at all.

As compassionate life is not prevalent in wide -spread manner, only the beings who follow the 'vicious path' have increased, this situation has led to the existence of immorality as a way of life everywhere; how?

The hard hearted people who had no compassion to living beings, according to their hard hearted deeds have taken birth, some as dwellers of

Hell, some as the inhabitants of Ocean, some as inhabitants of Forest, some as Wild Animals like Tiger, Bear, Lion, Yale, Elephant, Wild Oxen, Goat, Pig, Dog, Cat etc., some as poisonous creatures like Snake, Scorpion, some as hard and vicious creatures like Crocodile, Shark etc., some as carnivorous group of birds like Crow, Vulture, etc., some as impure plants like strychnine tree, milk hedge etc. It is to be learnt that the practice of showing compassion to living beings is not only an important instrument to obtain the Grace of God but also it is the partial manifestation of that Grace itself. As the act of showing compassion to living beings is the natural manifestation of the Souls, those human beings who do not have that natural manifestation will never get the manifestation of God both within and without themselves.

What is the important objective of practising compassion towards human beings?

The Souls are a part of the natural truth (Eyarkai Wunmai). They are also the rightful place for the co–existence of Grace which is the Manifestation of nature (EyarKkai Vilakkam) in the form of knowledge of knowledge, and for the Souls to become human beings and multiply, the bodies made of elements are the prerequisite. In case, the Souls do not incarnate in human bodies and get multiplied, the manifestation of Souls will be concealed, and because of this concealment, the Grace will not manifest, and this kind of circumstances will lead to a state of non–existence of knowledge (Moodam), and this situation will keep the Souls in bondage (Bandham). It is, therefore, absolutely necessary to have bodies made of elements. As the primary cause for the bodies made of elements is Maya (Illusion).The Maya, because of the various Illusory effects (Illusions), such as Hunger, Thirst, Disease, Desire, Poverty, Fear and the agony of getting killed, the bodies will be endangered frequently. The human beings, by the Grace of God have been given enough freedom and knowledge to be extremely careful against those dangers and try to avert the same with the help of intelligence derived from mental faculties and sense organs. The human beings by making use of this freedom, should get rid of those dangers for their bodies and make efforts to obtain the spiritual benefit. In the case of human beings who suffer because of their inability to safeguard themselves against the dangers caused by Hunger, Thirst, Disease, Desire, poverty, fear and the pain of getting killed due to the role of destiny or carelessness on their part, the human beings who are privileged enough to get rid of those dangers must take pity on those human beings and eradicate the same.

COMPASSIONATE ACTIVITIES LEADING TO 'HAPPINESS OF THIS WORLD' (ABARA JEEVAKARUNIYAM)

Apart from the acts of kindness relating to the alleviation of sufferings caused by Hunger and the pain when getting killed, relieving of human beings from all other kinds of sufferings is Abara Jeeva Karuniyam. It will, therefore, lead only to a little amount of worldly happiness.

COMPASSIONATE ACTIVITIES LEADING TO 'BOTH TEMPORAL HAPPINESS AND ETERNAL BLISS' (PARA JEEVAKARUNIYAM)

The compassionate activities performed in the case of alleviating the sufferings of human beings who suffer due to hunger and the agony of getting killed by someone are known as Para Jeeva Karuniyam. Hence, by the Grace of God, the practitioners of compassion of this kind, will gain this worldly pleasures and illimitable Bliss arising out of their divine power to perform miracles (Siththis) and also the never ending Bliss of obtaining liberation (MukthiInbum) from the cycles of birth and death. Those human beings who in spite of having enough knowledge and privilege to save other human beings from the danger(s) which they might be facing because of role of destiny and their carelessness have not done so but betrayed them will not obtain the Grace of God to enjoy the happiness of this world and the Eternal Bliss of gaining Mukthi. Moreover, they will also lose whatever worldly luxuries and liberties they enjoy in their present lives as dictated by God in the scriptures (Vedas). In the case of human beings who do not have sufficient knowledge and freedom to safeguard themselves against the dangers caused by Hunger and the pain while they are getting killed due to their fate or carelessness, the human beings who are in a position to redress those grievances should alleviate the sufferings of those human beings out of compassion without betraying them. It is, therefore, to be learnt that this is the important objective of performing compassion. Having true faith in this concept, the act of performing compassionate activities of feeding the human beings who starve and preventing the human beings from getting killed in order to enable them to experience happiness is the supreme form of Benefit.

Why, as per the divine law, among the dangers caused by hunger, getting killed, thirst, disease, desire, poverty and fear which have to be averted; only the acts of averting the dangers caused by hunger and getting killed are quoted significantly?

There are two kinds of compassionate activities, one is Abara Jeeva Karuniyam and the other one is Para Jeeva Karuniyam. As the acts of averting Hunger and preventing somebody from getting killed are the activities that fall under the category of Para Jeeva Karuniyam, the same are mentioned significantly.

THIRST (Thaham)

Moreover, those persons who are kind enough to get rid of the hunger of the human beings, who suffer from hunger, will not be unwilling to provide water to them, to quench their thirst. To give water, much effort is not required, as water is found in Lake, Pond, and Canal etc. By thirst only reversible damage will happen to the body and the body will not be affected in a serious way, but by hunger irreversible damage will happen to the bodies.

DISEASE (Pini)

Those who are sympathetic enough, to alleviate the suffering because of hunger, will also be kind enough to get rid of the sufferings of those who are diseased. When hunger intensifies, diseases increase and only by means of proper food, the diseases are cured. Though, other medicines are given to get cured from the diseases, only proper dieting is required for the sustenance of the body. The body can be maintained with diseases for so many days, but the body cannot be sustained even for a single day without food

DESIRE (Itchai)

Those who have compassion to feed those who are hungry with food, will definitely have the compassion to remove the sufferings due to Desire. If human beings are really hungry, they would desire nothing but food. Those who have satisfied their hunger by intake of food, they could compromise themselves without getting their desire fulfilled. The body can be sustained with desire for many days but with hunger, it cannot be sustained for a single day.

POVERTY (Elimai)

Those who are merciful to alleviate the hunger of the human beings, who are hungry with food, will also be kind enough to eradicate the poverty of those human beings, who do not have the liberty to do the same for themselves. There is no other poverty, worse than that, of suffering due to hunger. Poverty could be reversed after a few days, but hunger could not be reversed like that. The body can be kept alive with poverty but not with hunger.

FEAR (Bayam)

Those who are kind enough to alleviate the hunger, will naturally be kind and helpful, to get rid of the 'fear' of those who suffer, due to the cause of fear. Nothing is as fearful as the fear caused by hunger and the fear of getting killed. In some ways, one can get rid of fear, but there is no other way to get rid of hunger. One can keep the body alive with fear, but the body cannot be sustained with hunger. The pain and the sufferings arising out of the state of being hungry, and the pain and suffering resulting from the state of being killed, are similar in nature. Hence, it is to be known, that the important objective of leading a life of compassion towards human beings, is to alleviate the suffering caused by hunger, and saving them from the agony of getting killed.

Why? Although the main objective of showing compassion is to alleviate the suffering caused by hunger and the suffering when getting killed, the act of removing the hunger is emphasised?

When a human being comes to know that another living being is going to be killed by hunger, out of compassion removes the hunger and enables the living beings to be alive, will, naturally be compassionate enough to alleviate the sufferings of the living beings who are getting killed by any other means. Those who do not help in getting rid of the pain of getting killed, will not have enough sympathy to remove the sufferings of those who suffer due to hunger. The killing that happens because of hunger, will be alleviated only by the offering of food, not by any other means, whereas the killing caused by enmity etc., could be prevented by many ways and means. Hence, it must be learnt that the suffering experienced, when getting killed, is included in the suffering caused by Hunger, and the same is stressed frequently. Moreover, the persons suffering from thirst, disease, Desire, poverty, and Fear forget all those sufferings when affected by the pangs of hunger and go in search of food. Even the criminal sentenced to death by the orders of the king, on the charge of murder, forgets his fear and distress and tries to get rid of his hunger when he is hungry. The persons who are diseased, and for the elderly persons, after getting informed by the doctor that their death is certain, forget their sorrows and pains, when affected by hunger, and try to get their hunger alleviated. It is to be learnt that one who is willing to provide food for hunger out of compassion, will never allow the human beings to be in distress and get destroyed by any other means, and because of this reason, the charitable act of alleviating the suffering due to hunger is often emphasized.

If it is true that 'hunger' harms and destroys the bodies of all living beings, the hunger of all the beings must be known and alleviated. If one starts doing this act, will it not be impossible to know and alleviate, the hunger of all the seven classes of beings namely 1) celestial beings (devars), 2) human beings, 3) dwellers of hell, 4) animals, 5) birds, 6) reptiles, 7) plants, created by god ?

The celestial beings do have more freedom than that of human beings, and they also have the capacity to alleviate the hunger on their own. Hence, it is not necessary for others to think about their hunger, but it is necessary to know that even the divine beings (Devars), will suffer when they are hungry and sympathies with them.

The Dwellers of Hell are not in the places where we could reach and alleviate their hunger. As they are in some other places and their hunger are taken care of and alleviated by punitive authorities of God, we need not think about their hunger but it is necessary to have pity for them, considering that they will also suffer when they are hungry.

The Trees and Grass are not destined to have any freedom. In the case of species of plants that are grown by the human beings by their own efforts, and for their own use in their lives, it is necessary for them to water those plant species, to satisfy their hunger, whereas the other species of plants are fed in accordance with the Law of Grace, and kept alive. As it is not our freedom to know about their hunger and provide food but the freedom of God, it is not necessary to think about them but necessary to feel pity for them, considering that the plant(s) species will also suffer for want of food.

The living beings that crawl on land and water, reptiles, birds and animals get their food supplied to them, in accordance with their destiny by the law of Grace. The living beings eat the food and get their hunger satisfied. It is, therefore, not our freedom to provide proper food to them, but the freedom of God. But it is necessary for the human beings, to provide food and satisfy the hunger of those animal species, such as cow, ox, he-buffalo, and goat, horse which are reared by people according to their freedom and for their own use in their lives.

In the case of human beings, whether they are men or women, the loss and the agony that are experienced by them, due to hunger, the benefit and happiness which are gained when hunger is satisfied, are similar and common in nature. Besides this, 'the knowledge of the Soul' that understands the losses and sufferings because of hunger, by means of well-developed mental faculties, like the mind etc., and through the sense organs, like the eye etc., is also similar in both cases. The food provided to the human beings, by the Gracious Law, in accordance with destiny alone is not enough to live and keep the body alive, they have to subsist also by the food earned by them, by their own efforts, intelligence and freedom, and earn their own food (AahamiyaAahaaram). The human beings have been given full freedom by the Grace of God. At the same time, the Grace of God have also enforced the law, that makes the human beings suffer for want of food, because of their destiny, in order to get their hunger satisfied, making them dependent on one another, so that, one who provides food out of compassion to alleviate the hunger of the other, may also guide him to follow the right ways and efforts, so that, he who gave food, may obtain liberation (Mukthi) and supernatural power to perform miracles (Siththis).

Taking a human body is not as easy as taking the bodies of other living beings. In the human body, both the manifestation of Soul and the manifestation of Grace get expressed to the full extent. It is not certain whether another human body could be obtained again in the event of losing the present one. The human body has been taken only to attain the 'Eternal Bliss of salvation'. Ever since the days of first creation, only the human body has been created by the consent of God with supreme intelligence.

It should, therefore, be understood that God has dictated that only the human beings should show the act of compassion to living beings with steadfastness and get their hunger satisfied.

How come! The food provided by the gracious law of god in accordance with the destiny of living beings like animals and birds etc., is enough for them, but in the case of human beings alone they are required to earn their own food in addition to the food provided to them by the gracious act of god?

God has ordered that the human beings, by intake of food made available by the Gracious act of God (Praratha Aahaaram), according to their destiny, should overcome the experience resulting out of their deeds of the past (Karmas), and by intake of food earned by their own efforts (AahamiyaAahaaram), should strengthen their body, the sense organs and the subtle mental faculties (Karana Indiriyam).And by adopting the righteous path of practising compassion (Sanmaarkkam), should enjoy the Bliss of gaining supernatural powers (Siththis) and liberation (Mukthi). Hence, it is to be learnt that both the food provided according to their destiny, and the food earned by their own efforts are necessary to the human beings. The bodies of the living beings like Animals, Birds, Reptiles and Plants are the bodies created as punishment bodies. It should, therefore, be understood that the food according to their destiny would be provided to them without any break by the power of Grace of God, and they do not require to earn their own food by their own efforts.

Why? At first, it was mentioned that the act of showing compassion is common to all living beings.

In the life of showing compassion to living beings, the important aspect is to provide food and alleviate the sufferings due to hunger of all the human beings.

In the event of the possibility of living beings getting killed by other causes, similar to that of hunger, it should be prevented as far as possible, by all the ways and means to keep them alive and happy.

If the living beings happen to suffer due to some other reasons, like disease and fear, if possible, the sufferings should be removed.

In the case of living beings like animal, birds, reptile and plant etc...., their suffering due to fear and Their suffering due to fear and the suffering when getting killed should be averted by any ways and means.
As far as wild and ferocious living beings are concerned, one may cause them to suffer by fear and they should not be made to suffer by getting them killed.

It is to be known that all those kinds of activities are connected with the acts of showing compassion to living beings, and that is why it has been commanded by God, that the human beings should show compassion towards all the living beings.

Some of the living beings that are earned and kept by people for getting their assistance in their lives, do eat the meat of the other beings (thamasa aahaaram). Hence, whenever people get the hunger of such beings alleviated, can they be given the same kind of food to satisfy their hunger?

It is to be learnt that the act of killing one living being to satisfy the hunger of another living being out of the flesh, is not acceptable to God and it is not considered as the path of showing compassion. This practice is out and out against nature.

All living beings are part of Natural Truth and they are also the place for manifestation of God in the form of Grace. When the natural manifestation of God is hidden, the nature of living beings (Jeeva thanmai) will be non-existent. The Natural Manifestation of God is in no way different from the Natural Manifestation of living beings. Both, the natural manifestation of

God and the Natural manifestation of living beings do exist in all the bodies. It is, therefore, to be understood that the act of killing a being to satisfy the hunger of another being is fully against the principle of practicing compassion towards all living beings.

Animals like tiger and lion kill other beings and by eating the flesh of the other beings they get the happiness of getting their hunger satisfied. Can we believe that, the Happiness Is Due To Partial Natural Manifestation Of God And Full Manifestation Of Nature Of The Living Beings ?

No, We can't. In the event of intake of food made of flesh and meat (Thamasa Aahaaram), the Partial Natural Manifestation of God, who is the perfect reality and the natural manifestation of Soul, which is a portion of the perfect reality, do not express itself, just as Light cannot emerge from darkness.

Why, is this food called thamasa aahaaram (dark natured food)?

If this kind of food is obtained by causing suffering and conceals the manifestation of Soul, which in turn prevents the manifestation of God, this food is called Thamasa food.

The satisfaction and happiness gained because of intake of this kind of food leads to the manifestation of joy; of which manifestation is this ?

It should be learnt, that, it is the manifestation of the beginingless illusion of the Soul that is bereft of knowledge (Pasu) and the inner mental faculties.
What is called pasu?

The Soul that is bereft of its knowledge because of its connection with three impure characteristics namely Arrogance, Illusion and karma (the effect of deeds done in the past) is called PASU.

How does the pasu (the soul without knowledge) get manifested?

When the brightness of the sun appears through the darkness of the clouds which veils the sun, even the darkness of clouds gets illuminated and manifested. Similarly, even though the impure and illusory inner instruments (Asutha Maya Karanam) and the Tamasic quality (Ignorant State) are Dark natured, they also get manifested by the supreme effulgence which they veil. From this, it is to be learnt that the manifestation one gets because of intake of meat/flesh (Thamasa Aaharam) is the manifestation of impure, illusory, inner instruments (Mental Faculties) only.

PLANTS ARE ALSO LIVING BEINGS

Vegetation like trees, grass, paddy etc., are also considered to be living beings; if the human beings by causing pain to them, intake the same as food, are they not thamasa food (food obtained by torturing other living beings). Is the resultant happiness, not the happiness of impure mind and subtle mental faculties?

The vegetation like trees, grass, paddy etc., are also living beings. By causing pain to them, if they are used as food, they are also partly Thamasa Aahaaram and the happiness derived out of this food is also the happiness of impure and subtle mental faculties. But it is not so.

The living beings like tree, grass and paddy etc., have only one sense and that is the sense of touch. The manifestation of Life (Jeeva Vilakkam) exists only partly in those bodies. The seeds from which their lives come into existence are lifeless like other seeds. We could sow the seeds ourselves and get them grown as living beings. Without destroying their lives, we make use of the seeds, vegetables, fruits, flowers, tubers and leaves as food which are lifeless, but only the cause for the origin of life. When we do not take the entire living plant(s) as food, but only their products like seeds, vegetables, fruits etc., no pain is caused to them just as no pain is caused while removing the nails, cutting hair and the coming out of semen from the bodies of living beings.

Moreover, the plant species have no mental faculties like the Mind etc. Hence, it is to be known, that the acts of taking only the products of living plants as food will not be considered as killing life or causing pain to them, and it will not go against the principles of practicing compassion towards all living beings. Therefore, the happiness arising out of the intake of such food is the manifestation of God as well as life.

The seeds which are produced by the plants like tree are originally lifeless but becomes a cause for entry of life force into it; how?

If seeds have life in them, they should grow even before they are sown in the land. Even after being sown in the land, some seeds fail to grow. Moreover, the seed is the cause. It is known even to young children that this cause is to get the body only. The life force is lasting forever but the body is Transient by nature. The life force, which is everlasting does not need any cause, but the impermanent body needs a cause. It should, therefore, be learnt that the seeds are mere inert matter only.

How does the soul enter into the seeds?

It is to be learnt that, when the seeds are sown in the soil and watered, according to the gracious law of God, the atomized Souls join together and get into the soil through that water and mingle with the fertile energy of the soil and enter into the seeds.

Some say that sprouts should not be plucked out at all; if that is the case, how can it be said that seed, vegetable, leaf etc., may be eaten?

Once the Seed gets fixed in the soil, the Soul goes through the water into the soil mingles with the fertile energy of the earth and finally gets into the seed and enables the seed to sprout. The sprout, therefore, is not a lifeless thing like the seed, vegetable etc. Hence, it is true that sprout should not be plucked out.

VEGETARIAN FOOD

Even though the killing of life is not involved while intake of seed, vegetable, fruit etc., is there the same kind of impurity which exists in nail, hair, semen etc.,

There is no impurity in them as there is no development of senses and life energy in them. Hence, the act of intake of the seed, vegetable, fruit, leaflets of the tree, grass, paddy etc., is not against the practice of compassion towards all living beings.

FOOD MADE OF MEAT IS NOT THE NATURAL FOOD

Is not meat the natural food for the ferocious animals like tiger etc?
It is not their natural food habit but an acquired habit that became hereditary during the course of time. It is, therefore, possible to change their food habit and make them eat only pure and vegetal food (Sathva Aahaaram). A good man, in his house, brings up a cat and a dog. He prevents them from going out and eating impure food in other places. At the same time, he gets them used to take only pure food, from the very beginning of their lives, and due to this habit, they continue to take only pure food and live on that food. Hence, it may be learnt that, as there is nobody to train the ferocious animals like tiger, lion etc., to get them habituated in eating only pure food, they go on taking only impure food because they are so habituated. It should, therefore, be truly known that the act of killing one living being for the sake of feeding another living being is neither in accordance with the Grace of God nor it is the practice of showing compassion to all living beings.

It is possible to obtain two kinds of Bliss in the life of showing compassion towards living beings viz. 'this worldly happiness' (AbaraInbam) and 'the ultimate happiness' (Para Inbam).

WORLDLY HAPPINESS (AbaraInbam)

The happiness arising out of the compassionate act of alleviating the sufferings due to Desire etc. is known as Worldly Happiness. It is to be known that they are some of the pleasures experienced during this worldly life.

What are those pleasures?

There are human beings who suffer for want of clothes to wear, place to reside, land to plough, wife to derive bodily pleasure, money or any other material which is required to do what they want. In this case, out of compassion, when they are given clothes to wear, place to reside, land to plough, women to get bodily pleasure, money etc., to do what they wish, those who have received them experience the happiness that comes from within themselves and get the same manifested in their faces and on seeing their happiness, those who have given also get their happiness manifested. It should, therefore, be known that this manifestation of happiness appears only partly in God's domain but perfect in the mental faculties of human beings and that is why it is known as worldly happiness (AbaraInbam)

SUPREME BLISS (Para Inbam)

It should be learnt that the Bliss arising out of the act of alleviating the sufferings due to hunger is the ultimate happiness (Para Inbam). This includes the enjoyment of all the worldly pleasures, Bliss of yogic power, bliss due to the power of having attained the true knowledge in the present life itself and the ultimate Bliss of getting liberation (Mukthi). Out of pity when food is provided to the human beings who are tired of hunger, intake of food gets their hunger satisfied. At that moment, they experience the outpouring of Bliss both from deep within their being and in their face. On seeing that Bliss, those who have given food also get the same kind of manifestation of Bliss, both within themselves and in their face. As the manifestation of this kind of Bliss is perfect both in the Soul and in God's domain, they are known as the Supreme Bliss (Para Inbam).

Those who suffer for want of clothes, place, land, woman, money etc., could endure those sufferings with the help of their strong mind, sustain their life and make whatever efforts they can. When there is suffering due to hunger, one should not endure that suffering and if they start enduring the same, they would lose their lives.

HUNGER IS UNBEARABLE

When people start suffering from hunger, parents will sell their children, the children will sell their parents, the husband will sell his wife, the wife will sell her husband and they will go to any extent to get their sufferings due to hunger satisfied. Hence, it is needless to say that they would sell their house, cattle, land, and other possessions which are not so important to them to get their hunger satisfied.

Even the Emperor ruling the whole world when affected by hunger, does not care about his powerful status, as Emperor and using humble words asks the minister nearby "I am hungry; what shall I do ?"

Even great soldiers who are courageous enough to hold the arrows of the enemies which have penetrated into their chest with one hand and conquer all the enemies they come across in a minute while feeling hungry, complain to those who are standing nearby. "I will be tired, so how to fight?

The Saints who hate and renounce all the worldly pleasures and of the celestial world (Indraloka), and treat them as insignificant and having acquired the true knowledge, get the existence of the knowledge in their experience, the Yogis who have complete control over the senses, mind and mental faculties, and are in the constant state of mediation (true nishtai), the Siththars who have unlimited super natural powers including the power to revive even those who are dead, and the men of austerity (Munis), and the ones known for doing penance all the time (Thapasis) while facing hunger, all of them give up their experience and goals and move to another place in search of food and in the event of non-availability of food they are distressed.

The sensitive and respectable People who will be prepared to lose their lives when something dishonourable happens to them even in dreams when suffer due to hunger, lose their self-respect and express their feeling even to worthless people.

The religious leaders (acharayas), who are very strict in following the discipline and the way of life of their respective religion and caste when they are hungry forget their discipline and expect food.

Even the great scholars, who have acquired very deep knowledge by way of learning and listening, who understand even complicated things which are normally non understandable, and are capable of doing great achievements when they are hungry, they lose their knowledge and the power of understanding and get puzzled.

The lustful persons, who indulge in the act of deriving sexual pleasure during day and night when they are hungry, forget coition and develop hatred for lust and are at pains.

Even the people who are very proud who think that they are only great and there are no other persons who are greater than them, when they are hungry, lose their arrogance and praise the one who offered them food as very great people.

Even the people, who indulge in the activities just for the sake of vain glories when they are hungry, lose their vanity and are perplexed. When all these people become like this because of hunger, how much suffering the poor people who do not have any kind of support will undergo when they happen to suffer due to hunger. At that time, if they are provided with food how much happiness will they get? How much benefit will those who created that happiness get!? It should be understood that it is too difficult to express by words.

THE PAINS DUE TO HUNGER (Pasien Avasthai)

When hunger gets increased,

The human knowledge (Jeeva Arivu) is not expressed but gets bewildered. Because of this bewilderment the manifestation of God who is in the form of knowledge of knowledge gets veiled, when it is veiled the principle of the Soul gets tired, when it gets tired, the primordial nature gets dimmed. When it gets dimmed qualities get differentiated. The mind gets puzzled and distorted. The intellect gets spoiled,

The decision-making ability (chitham) gets spoiled,
The ego gets destroyed
The life force gets unsettled,
The elements are uncomfortably placed,
The balance between the air, heat and coolness (vatham, pitham and slathamam) get dislocated.
The eyes become dim and go down from their original position,
The ears become deaf with humming sound,

The tongue gets dried,
The nose gets softened,
The skin gets thin and loses the sense of touch,
The arms, legs, get tired and hang loosely,
The nature of speech gets changed and stammered,
The teeth get loosened,
The anus and the urethra get burnt by heat.
The body gets scorched,
The hair becomes stiff,
The nerves lose their stiffness and get worn out.
The blood vessel loses their tensions and becomes soft,
The bones get scorched and the joints get loosened,
The heart burns,
The brain shrinks,
The semen becomes hot and gets dried,
The liver gets contracted and becomes smaller in size
The blood and the fluids lose their water content,
The flesh loses its nature,
The stomach gets burning sensation,

Afflictions and troubles continue one after another and more and more symptoms and experiences appear to indicate that the loss of one's life is imminent.

All these painful experiences due to hunger are common to all the living beings.
All the sufferings are removed when they get food and intake the same.

Once the hunger is satisfied, the physical aspects (Thathuvangal) of the body get strengthened, mind is cooled, the knowledge finds its expression and the effulgence of grace from within the living beings and that of God fully manifest both on the Soul and on the face leading to the joy and satisfaction of unique kind. Which act of virtue could be equated with this kind of virtuous act that creates this kind of Bliss?

With which God could we equate the doers of this kind of virtuous deeds? It should be understood as truth that their true nature is that of God of all the Gods.

Hence, it is to be learnt that the agony experienced due to hunger in to, is the outcome of all the three kinds of sufferings put together namely, the sufferings at hell, and the sufferings due to birth and death. The Bliss and satisfaction obtained by intake of food is indeed the everlasting Bliss of liberation that pervades in all the places viz. inside, outside, middle, below, above and on all sides.

HUNGER IS THE HELPPING INSTRUMENT

If there is no hunger at all, the human beings will not expect the help of one another for the sake of food, when there is no such expectation, the tendency to help each other will not exist. When this does not happen, compassionate life among them will not manifest. When it does not manifest, God's Grace cannot be obtained. It should, therefore, be understood that the hunger is also a helping instrument given by God.

Those who suffer due to hunger obtain happiness immediately when they see food and this kind of happiness they will never get even when they see their mother, father, wife, child, field, land, gold and jewels. If this is the case, what will be the nature of their happiness when food is taken? It should, therefore, be understood that the natural form, visible form and characteristics of the food are part of the natural form, visible form and attributes of the Grace of God.

COMPASSIONATE LIFE (JEEVA KARUNYAM)

A) When the fire called hunger, burns within the bodies of the poor, to get the fire extinguished by providing food to them is known as the act of showing compassion to human beings.

B) When the poisonous Wind called hunger, is about to blow out the lamp of knowledge of the poor, to provide them with food, and prevent the lamp from being put out, to switch on the light of the lamp, is known as the act of showing compassion towards human beings.

C) When the bodies of human beings which are the temples, where the natural manifestation of God takes place, are about to be destroyed by hunger, to provide them with food at that time, and get them strengthened is known as the act of showing compassion to human beings.

D) When the whole family consisting of the physical and the psychic principles of the human beings that dwell in the bodies for attaining divine Bliss get dislocated and are likely to be destroyed by hunger, to provide all the family with food and get the whole family well established, is known as the act of showing compassion to human beings.
E) When the tiger called hunger is about to pounce upon the poor and start killing them, to kill the tiger and save them is known as the act of showing compassion to human beings.
F) When the poison called hunger goes into the head of living beings, and they are about to faint, to bring down the poison by food and revive them from the faintness, is known as the act of showing compassion to human beings.
G) When the cruel scorpion called hunger enters into the stomach and stings, the pain due to stinging increases and the poor living beings are distressed, to remove the stinging pain with food and get remedy for their plight is known as the act of showing compassion to human beings.
H) The act of removing the anxiety of the poor human beings who are worried thinking "the sinner called hunger which had half killed and eaten throughout yesterday and night will come again even today. What can we do for this?" - is the act of showing compassion to human beings.
I) The removal of the perplexity of the poor human beings who are puzzled like the fly that has fallen into honey, saying "the sun is moving up, hereafter the pain called hunger will come up on us! What can we do for this event of fate?" - is known as the act of showing compassion to human beings.
J) When the poor human beings are deeply grieved saying "it is getting dark now, where will we go for food? Whom shall we ask? What shall we do?"- To get rid of their grief is known as the act of showing compassion to human beings.
K) By providing the necessary food to wipe off the tears of the poor people who are shedding tears saying, "the legs got tired by going on walking, mouth got tired by going on asking, the mind got tired by going on thinking, now what shall we do for this wretched stomach?"- is called the act of showing compassion to human beings.

L) By giving food to save the honour of the persons known for their self–respect, with their minds and faces looking tired like a dump person, who had an inexpressible dream, with their tongue tied and unable to express their feelings openly, but suffering in silence, "the day has also gone, hunger causes the pain, self-respect prevents from speaking out, shyness prevents from going to other places, stomach burns no way is known to lose this life, why have I taken this body?"- is called the act of showing compassion to human beings.

M) To give food to the poor human beings, to get them relieved from their sorrows, facilitate their sleeping when they are sleepless due to hunger and muttering, "In our previous birth, realizing the hunger of those who were hungry, if we had alleviated their hunger, in this birth somebody would have come forward to satisfy our hunger. We did not do so. Hence, there is no body to do so for us now-" is known as the act of showing compassion to human beings.

N) To satisfy the hunger of the wise men, who even when they are hungry and weak, with all the nerves visible all over the body, their life energy shrunk and still have no courage to ask other people to provide food, but think of God only repeatedly and go to sleep with cruel fire of hunger deep down their stomach, resembling people who lie down and sleep on fire, is the act of showing compassion to human beings.

O) "How to starve today as we had starved yesterday? - Though we dare to starve even today because of our youthfulness, what can we do for the stomach of the poor wife who will not tolerate starvation? Even if we do not take the starvation of this woman seriously, our parents who are already weak due to ageing process will die if they starve even today! What can we do for this? How can we look at the tired looking faces of our children who have become weary by weeping continuously because of hunger?". The act of removing the sorrows of those who think with pains like this again and again, with eyes full of tears, with their hand on their cheeks and with the fire of hunger, the fire of fears and the fire of anxiety always aglow inside, like the fire in the furnace of the blacksmith which always kept aglow by blowing - is the act of showing compassion to human beings.

P) To provide food to the suffering handicapped poor people who are worried and go on thinking repeatedly: "Here are the people lying helplessly due to hunger though they have organs like Eye, hand and leg without any deformity, and enough strength to earn their food; In what way can we who are blind, deaf, dumb and are crippled with defects in our limbs to get food? How to get rid of hunger?"- is known as the act of showing compassion to human beings.

Q) To alleviate the hunger of those people who suffer from hunger, according to their virtues and without enquiring and differentiating them based on their Country to which they belong, religion to which they belong, caste to which they belong, the activities they do and the way of human in their Country, religious way of living, caste way of living and kind of activities they do, realizing that the manifestation of God is common to all human beings and to treat all of them as one and the same kind is the act of showing compassion to human beings.

R) When the living beings like animal, bird, reptile and plant are hungry, to alleviate their hunger by providing sattvic food (pure food) to them which is in accordance with the food habits of the virtuous life (Sanmaarkkam) is known as the act of showing compassion to living beings.

Some people have the knowledge to acquire the necessary worldly pleasures and liberty to get their hunger satisfied, but they are not able to acquire the liberty due to their acts of sin in the past and carelessness, and thereby suffer from hunger. By providing them with food, to get them relieved from their suffering due to hunger, one creates the Bliss and satisfaction out of compassion to living beings. This, only by virtue of this act of compassion which is the cause for creating Bliss and satisfaction, and also the key to open the door of heavenly abode of salvation (Mukthi), one should open the gate and enter the house of salvation to experience the life of never ending happiness.

Hence, those who have earned the key to the house of salvation which is known as the acts of compassion (Jeeva Karunyam) in time, without the requirement of any assistance from the other kinds of spiritual activities such as controlling the mind (Sariyai), controlling actions (Kriyai), integration of body & mind (Yoga) acquiring true knowledge (Gnanam), will reach the house that was never reached and open the gate enter inside to live there as the eternally liberated ones.

S) The Devotees, Rishis and the Ascetics who practice austerities and rituals such as going on pilgrimage to holy places, taking bath in holy rivers, living in holy places, worshiping sacred Idols chanting mantras, conducting prayers, going on a fast (virudhamseithal), performing rituals, doing pujas etc., the Yogis who have forsaken food and sleep, renounced worldly affairs and three kinds of desires, controlled their senses, negated their minds. The Siththars who have acquired unlimited supernatural powers, the Saints who have realized what is eternal and what is transitory and have renounced all sorts of attachments and experienced Brahmam, the absolute, all of them unless they have earned the 'key' called the 'virtue of showing compassion to the living beings' will go up to the back and front of the 'supreme abode' wait nearby and return to earn that key but they will not open the door and enter the house to obtain the 'Bliss' and live there and this truth is to be understood.

T) It should also be learnt that for the people who possess Enlightened knowledge, only the act of practicing compassion to the living beings is the act of worshipping God. Moreover, the family men [Samusaris], who enjoy the worldly pleasures like eating and mating and at the same time leading the life of compassion towards all living beings, are fully eligible for the Grace of the all-powerful God.

U) Without practicing compassion towards all the living beings, the persons who are doing various kinds of spiritual acts, such as 'striving to acquire true knowledge (Gnanam), doing yoga, going on a fasting (Virutham), chanting holy mantras and practicing meditation, will not be deserving the grace of God even to a lesser extent. They should not even be considered as having the manifestation of soul. It should, therefore, be understood that the deeds done without compassion to the living beings are mere useless acts of magic & gimmick.

V) All living beings are a part of natural truth of God and the manifestation of grace gets expressed in each and every one of them. Hence, the Grace of God do not concur with the acts of those family men (samusaris), who in spite of having adequate resources to satisfy the hunger of their family members, like mother, father, children, life- partner etc., and still letting them suffer from hunger and going for satisfying the hunger of others and in a similar way letting other persons who are hungry and approach them for food starve and going for satisfying the hunger of their family members. They are, therefore, required to minimize their expenditure for their family as far as possible and alleviate the hunger of the people belonging to both categories.

W) The family men who are in possession of meagre resources which are not enough to get the hunger of their family members satisfied, should at least, get rid of the hunger of their family members. At the same time, they should have compassion for others who approach them with hunger, making the efforts to alleviate their hunger through somebody else. The capable and popular family men, according to their income should alleviate the hunger of their mother, father, life-partner, children, assistants, relatives, friends, guests, elderly people, servants, neighbours, enemies etc. In addition to this, they should also satisfy the hunger of their domestic animals like cow, ox, buffalo, goat, horse etc., that have been earned for their own use and the plants they have grown for the family to enable them to experience Bliss and satisfaction. Instead of spending material and financial resources lavishly on various occasions, various ceremonies and in various ways like marriage, birthday of a child, and rituals relating to worship of God, they should limit their expenditure in this regard and spend their resources in the glorious act of alleviating the hunger of the human beings with food, even on the occasions like marriage and thereby enabling them to experience bliss and satisfaction. If it is done so, the happiness gained by them will be many times greater than that of those human beings who got their hunger alleviated and it should be known as sworn truth.

The family men, on special occasions, such as marriage, decorate the pandal, perform various kinds of ceremonies, arrange a number of novel entertainments like dance, music, presenting expensive gifts, possession etc., and also serve extravagant food items like appam, sweet, pan cake and varieties of rice etc., and are immersed in the pleasures. At the time, they do not even care to look at the faces of the poor with hunger. During that moment of happiness, a disaster struck them, their children or their spouselose all their happiness and are grieved. When they are grieved like this, the decorated pandal, intentionally or unintentionally arranged ceremonies, novel entertainments like dance, vocal music, instrumental music, expensive gifts, procession etc. and the luxurious dishes like appam, varieties of rice etc., could not prevent the disaster and as a consequent they experienced grief. During that auspicious occasion, if they had provided food to the living beings who were really feeling hunger and got their hunger satisfied, thereby, revealing the manifestation of God and divine Bliss both within themselves and in their face, that manifestation and Bliss would have prevented the disaster at that time, and would have truly created the manifestation and Bliss in themselves. Isn't It? Hence, it should be known that according to one's capacity, it is important to alleviate the hunger of hungry people even on the special occasions like marriage and create Bliss and satisfaction in themselves.

i) If the family men suffering from incurable diseases like gastric ulcer, chronic stomach pain, leprosy etc., according to their capacity demonstrate the act of satisfying the hunger of the people, as a vow while living a simple life, It is true that, that compassionate act itself will serve as good medicine, and cure their diseases, making them exceptionally strong and healthy.

ii) If the family men who do not have descendants for a long time even after having performed so many rituals and observing austerities and are distressed, according to their capacity, demonstrate the act of satisfying the hunger of the poor, as a vow while living a simple way of life, it is true that, that compassionate act itself will enable them to have good and knowledgeable descendants.

iii) If the family men who come to know somehow that their life-span is very short and are afraid of facing death and are grieved, according to their capacity, practice the act of satisfying the hunger of the poor as a vow, it is true that, that compassionate act itself will enable them to have long life.

iv) If the family men who are very sad because of their lack of education, knowledge, wealth and pleasures, according to their capacity, do practice the act of satisfying the hunger of the poor as a vow while living a simple life, it is true that, that compassionate act itself will enable them to have education, knowledge, wealth and pleasures.

v) If the family men who is compassionate to all living being, satisfy the hunger of the hungry people as their only austere way of life, the extreme summer heat of the sun will not scorch them, the hot soil will not heat them, the natural calamities like torrential rain, strong wind, heavy snow, terrible thunder, great fire etc., will not harm them, the epidemic diseases like small box, plaque, cholera, infectious diseases etc., will not affect them, those compassionate family men will not be perturbed by floods in the river, dacoits and enemies, they will not be dishonoured by kings or Gods.

The yields in the fields of the compassionate family men will go on increasing without any effort, they will get unhindered profit in their business, and due recognition and promotion in their jobs, without any difficultly, they will be surrounded by relatives and servants, wild animals, poisonous creatures, evil spirits, harmful deities will not cause them fear.

It is a sworn truth that neither due to their carelessness nor due to the role of destiny, the family men who practice the act of compassion, will ever be endangered.

It is to be learnt that the act of alleviating the hunger of the people with hunger, and thereby creating Bliss in them, is known as the supreme path of showing compassion to all living beings, and it is the command of God that this practice is to be followed by all viz., Devars (Celestial beings), human beings, celibates, family men, Ascetics, Monks, Men, Women, Youth, aged persons and people belong to high class and low class.

The act of alleviating the hunger of hungry human beings, even if the wife prevents the husband, the husband prevents the wife, father prevents the children, the children prevents the father, the spiritual teacher (Acharya) prevents the disciple, God prevents His devotees and the king prevents his subjects, without getting obstructed even to lesser extent by those obstacles, and believing truly that the effects of good or bad acts, done by any one will reach only those who do the act(s), and it will not go to any other person, one should go on practicing the act of showing compassion to all living beings.

When thinking of providing food to those living beings who are really hungry, the mind of virtuous people gets detached from all other desires and consequently their mental faculties are purified. Since they think of providing food to the hungry living beings from this pure state of mental faculties, it is to be truly known that those virtuous people are Yogis. While feeding them as they had thought with kindness and hospitality and when they intake food because they feel they, themselves are eating the food and experience happiness, it is to be truly known that they are Saints (Gnanis). After having eaten the given food and getting their hunger satisfied at that moment, the manifestation of God and the Bliss of satisfaction which is also the divine Bliss fill up the Soul inside, outside, below and above, in the middle and in the sides, and cool all the principles such as subtle mental faculties and pervade all over the body with chillness, and gets expressed as effulgence in the face. It is, therefore, to be truly known that the virtuous ones, who have fed them, see and experience this manifestation of God and Divine Bliss, are the ones who have seen God, and they are the ones who are liberated (Mukthar) and experience divine Bliss. Since the hungry people who get their hunger satisfied after having eaten the food, really feel happy and consider these virtuous ones as God they themselves are God.

It is sworn, having God as witness that the virtuous men who follow the principle of showing compassion to all living beings and get them relieved from the danger called hunger are the glorious ones and are fit to be worshipped by Devars (celestial beings), Sages, Siththars and Yogis irrespective of their caste, religion or their deeds they do.

XV - COMPASSION – PART 2

BLISSFUL LIFE OF THE SOUL – AANMA INBA VAALVU

Those who have taken the superior birth as human beings in this world should as soon as possible, and within the available time span, know and attain the prime Joy of the bliss of soul (Thalaipatta AanmaInba Suham) which is attainable, in this birth itself.

How many are the kinds of that prime, blissful life of the soul?

It is to be realized that there are three kinds of bliss in life, namely
1) Blissful life pertaining to this world. (Inmmai Inba Vaalvu(
2) Blissful life pertaining to the other world. (Marumai Inba Vaalvu)
3) Life of absolute natural bliss of God. (Perinba Vaalvu)

1) BLISSFUL LIFE PERTAINING TO THIS WORLD:

It is to be learnt, that after having small body and mental faculties and by means of little efforts, enjoying little amount of worldly pleasures for few days, is known as the Blissful Life pertaining to This World.

Benefit of this worldly bliss:

It is to be known, that in the human birth after having the body, mind and subtle mental faculties that are free from disabilities, facing no dearth of wealth and enjoyments, possessing the right knowledge unhindered by obstacles such as hunger, disease and the pain of getting killed etc., surrounded by relatives, friends and others and with a good natured wife, who could give birth to worthy descendants, if one experiences the happiness arising out of these little things for a few days, it will be known as the benefit of this worldly bliss.

What is the glory of the one who has attained the bliss pertaining to this world ?

It is to be aware, that after having good characters like kindness, discipline, humility, patience, Truthfulness, purity etc., If one by striving experiences, the physical as well as the mental pleasures (Vizaya Inbangal), leading to the praiseworthy life, it will be known as the glory of the one who has attained this worldly bliss.

2) BLISSFUL LIFE PERTAINING TO THE OTHER WORLD.- (MARUMAI INBA VAALVU).

What is called the blissful life of the other world?

It should be known that having obtained higher birth with superior kind of body, mind and subtle mental faculties and by means of great efforts, if one experiences the bliss of great things (Periya Vizhayangal) for many days, that life will be known as the blissful life pertaining to the Other World.

What is the 'gain' of the bliss pertaining to the other world (marumai inba Laabam)?

It is to be understood that having obtained higher birth with all the good characters, which are denoted in the benefit of this worldly bliss, if one experiences the pure and spiritual bliss at an elevated level (Suththavizhayangal) for many days, it will be known as the Gain of the bliss pertaining to the other world.

What is the glory of the one who attained the 'gain' of the bliss relating to the other world?

It should be known that after possessing good characters like love, kindness etc., by virtue of their unhindered efforts and according to one's wish, if one experiences pure kind of bliss for many days and lead a praiseworthy life that will be the 'Glory' of the bliss relating to the other world.

3) LIFE OF ABSOLUTE NATURAL BLISS OF GOD. (PERINBA VAALVU)

Having obtained the perfect natural bliss of God who is in the form of perfect natural 'Truth', and who by his perfect natural manifestation, which is in the form of all pervading power of grace, create all the bodies, all the subtle mental faculties, all the worlds and all sorts of enjoyments, and get them appear, exist and enlighten, If one experiences the unique great bliss that is uninterrupted by any time, anyway, and by any limitation that life will be known as the life of absolute natural bliss of God.

What is the Gain of attaining the absolute natural bliss of God?

The Gain is one's existence in a state of perfect spiritual unity with all things in the universe without duality. (Yaavum Thamai Vilanguvathu).

What is the Glory of the one who attained the absolute natural bliss of God?

Their body made up of skin, nerve, bone, tissue, blood and semen etc., which are the products of the impure elements and the impure atom of illusory nature (Pragrathi - Maya), that act as the cause for the formation of the impure body, would have been transformed into high quality Golden body of immeasurable purity resulting in the creation of a pure body made of pure elements.

Apart from their appearance in the form of Golden body, they would have the pure body of sound (Pranava Theham), made up of pure elements and the same will not be felt by touching as it happens when the vast space (Aahash) is touched. In addition to that, they would also have body of true knowledge (Gnana Theham) resembling the wide space of the universe.

The thickness of the soil of the earth will not affect their inner body and even when stones and mud are thrown on them, their outer form will not be affected;

The cold water will not cool their inner body; Even if their outer body is immersed in water, it will not get submerged.

Their inner body will not get scorched by the fire; Even if the fire burns their outer body, the heat will have no effect on it and no scar will appear on the body.

Their inner body will not be moved by the force of the wind and the wind will not touch and move their outer body.

Their 'inner body' will not be made to float in the air due to its mingling with space (Aahash) and the space will not make their outer body to float.

Their body will move not only on the surface but also without any surface.

Normally, their sense organs like eyes etc., and the organs performing actions, like speech etc., will not perceive the thing that are seen and the things that are talked about. But out of compassion, if they intend to perceive those things, the barriers such as wall, mountain etc., will not hide their vision. From wherever they are, their eyes will be able to see all things that exist anywhere within the vast universe and outside the universe, and also within and outside the bodies.

Their ears will hear whatever is spoken from any place in the Universe and by anybody in the Universe.

Wherever he is, his tongue will taste all kinds of tastes that are available at any place.

Wherever he is, his skin will feel the sense of touch of anything that exists at any place.

Wherever he is, his nose will smell the fragrances which are present at any place.

Wherever he is, his hands could give to all the people who are at any place.

Wherever he is, his legs could walk to any other place.
Wherever he is, he could speak with the people who are present at any place.

Wherever he is, his other organs of sense could experience happiness enjoyed at any other place.

His mind and mental faculties etc. will not get attached to any kind of matters. In case he starts perceiving out of compassion, he will think, enquire and ascertain the nature and ways of thinking of all living beings in a minute.

His knowledge will not be specific about anything and in case he starts knowing anything specifically out of compassion, He will know about all the universes, all living beings, all characters, all experiences, all usefulness together in a minute.

He will not have any particular quality and he will not be affected within by the three qualities: viz Indolence (Tamasic), active (Rajasic) and peaceful (Sattvic). On the outside, their qualities will not get attached to the mind and subtle mental faculties.

He will not be covered inside by the illusory nature (prahirithi) and on the outside the illusory nature (prahirithi) will not get attached to any kind of his qualities.

He will not be differentiated by the principle of time within; on the outside, his sacred body will not be affected in anyway by time.

He will not be measured inside by the normal ways of measurements; on the outside, their sacred body will not get limited to any extent.

Moreover, they will not have other principles like time, Divine acts (Viththai), Desire (Raham), Divine qualities (Purushan) and their activities on them.

He will not be differentiated by the illusory nature of things (Maya). He will go beyond the pure great Illusion (Suththa Mahaa Maayai) and above that, he will be in the form of knowledge.

He will not be hindered by food, sleep, body's pleasures and fear etc....

His body will not have defects such as the shadows, sweating, formation of dirt, greying of hair, shrinking of skin, the process of ageing and death etc.

His body will not be affected by snowfall, rain, thunder, scorching sun, Giant (Paushadar), Demons (Asuras), Globling (Bhutham), Devils (Pisasu), Celestial beings (Devars), Ascetics (munis), Human beings, dwellers of hell, animal, bird, reptiles and plant etc., at any place and at any time.

His body will not get injured by the weapons like sword, knife etc....

His body has the natural tendency to minimize the big size like that of the universes, and make them appear like tiny atoms, and all the atoms of his body to get enlarged and make them appear as big as the universes.

In his presence, the Karma Siththis (Miracles) like reviving the dead, transforming the old into youth etc., Yoga Siththis and Gnana Siththis will always exist.

The acts of creation, protection, destruction, veiling and showering grace will take place the moment they think of those acts.

Their simple look at the Gods of the fivefold activities will enable them to do their respective work.

His knowledge will be the knowledge of God; his act will be the act of God; his experience will be the experience of God. He will be all powerful indestructible at any time and without three kinds of impurities like egoism, illusion and the deeds of the past (Karma) and the impact of these impurities on them and will exist as the one who has the characteristics of the supreme grace.

Even the lifeless thing will get life and perform the fivefold activities by his mere glimpse on it.

His glory will be in all the six kinds of philosophies (Aarantham) viz Vedantham, Sithantham, Kalantham, Pothantham, Nathantham, Yogantham and will also go beyond this six school of philosophies

It should be known that these are the glories of those who have gained the absolute natural bliss of God.

By which means these three kinds of happiness could be obtained?

It should be learnt that Grace is the natural manifestation of God and by obtaining the Grace, either partially or in full, the happiness could be obtained.

Out of three kinds of happiness, what kinds of happiness could be obtained by attaining the 'grace in part' and what kind of happiness could be obtained by attaining the grace in its fullness?

It should be known that both the bliss pertaining to this world and the bliss pertaining to the other world could be obtained by attaining a part of Grace, and the absolute natural bliss of God could also be obtained by attaining the Grace in its fullness.

What is the characteristic of the grace of god which is his natural manifestation?

It should be learnt that the Grace of God possesses all the characteristics of whatever the speaker speaks, the thinker thinks, one who knows, of one who experiences experience it, as a tiny part of its perfectly manifested existence, of all the characteristics, and enable the same to exist and enlighten in all of them.

Where does that grace exist?

It exists in all the places and at all times as it is in the cases of: **The place from | The place that will be seen**

By which means that Grace could be obtained?

It should be known that the Grace could only be obtained by the act of practicing compassion towards all living beings.

How, by the act of practising compassion towards all living beings, 'grace' could be obtained?

Grace is the mercy of God or it is the natural manifestation of God. The act of practicing compassion is the mercy of the souls or it is the natural manifestation of the souls. It is, therefore, to be learnt that it is like getting the great manifestation with the help of small manifestation and the great mercy with the help of small kind of mercy as both are the manifestations of one and the same characteristics.

Hence, it is to be learnt, that the act of practicing compassion towards all living beings, alone, is known as the supreme and virtuous path (Sanmaarkkam). When the act of showing compassion to all living beings is in existence, true knowledge and love will also co-exist, and thereby, all benevolent forces will exist, and because of the presence of the benevolent forces, all that are good and beneficial will come into being.

When the act of practicing compassion towards all living beings ceases to exist, true knowledge and love will disappear and thereby, the benevolent forces will also disappear, and because of the disappearance of the benevolent forces, all that are bad will emerge everywhere. Hence, it is to be known that the act of practicing compassion towards all living beings is the virtuous act (punniyam), and the lack of compassion towards all beings is the act of sin (paavam).

Moreover, it should be known as a sworn truth, that the manifestation arising out of practicing compassion towards all living beings is the manifestation of God, and the happiness gained out of that manifestation is divine happiness. The perfect and the fully qualified saints (Saathiyar), are only those who knew, attained and experienced this manifestation for a long period and are the liberated ones (Mukthar). They are the ones who gained the above mentioned absolute natural bliss of God, and will realize God by their knowledge, and attain a 'state of oneness' with God.

What is the basic principle of practicing compassion towards all living beings?

It should be known that it is the way of living by worshipping God, through the melting of the soul of the human beings, for the sake of the other human beings.

How can one worship God by means of melting of one's soul for the sake of the other human beings?

When the soul of the human beings goes on melting for the sake of the other beings, the Grace which is the manifestation of God within the soul get manifested and exist fully. Due to the existence of that Grace, the divine bliss becomes a full-fledged experience. It is to be known that the process of getting that experience perfected is called the act of worshipping of God.

When the soul goes on melting, the grace which is the manifestation of god within the soul gets expressed; how?

It is to be known that when the curd is churned by the wooden stick, due to friction, Butter and fire which are within the curd come out of it. In the same way, the Grace gets expressed due to the melting of one's soul.

How the divine bliss does becomes an experience and the experience becomes perfect due to the existence of grace of god?

When butter and fire come out of curd their true nature is experienced and that experience becomes complete. It should be known that the divine bliss also becomes perfect in nature in a similar manner.

When will the melting of the soul of the human beings for the sake of the other human beings get expressed?

The melting of the soul happens when the human beings see, hear and knows about the grief experienced by the fellow human beings due to hunger, the pain of getting killed, disease, danger, thirst, fear, poverty and desire.

a) Hunger:

When there is no food for the stomach, heat is generated inside the stomach and the heat pervades all over the body and burns the nature of the sense organs, mind and other mental faculties that are located within and outside the body, weakens the knowledge. Hunger is one of the variants of different kinds of Illusions, that generates fire in a part of physical body which act as the prime cause of expulsion of the soul from the body.

b) **Killing:**

killing is an act of cruelty; it is the variant of different kinds of illusions, and its impact on the body is to horrify and dislocate the various sense organs and the subtle mental faculties, which are located both inside and outside the body, disrupting their functions in violent manner and thereby, weakening the knowledge that results in the expulsion of the soul from the body.

c) **Disease:**

Disease is the variant of the illusions on the physical part of the body, and its various effects on the body are due to the variation of the impacts of three elements, such as air, fire and water on the body, and this condition of the body, impairs the sense organs and the subtle mental faculties, that are inside and outside the body, that results in the expulsion of the soul.

d) **Danger:**

Danger is a hindrance caused by one's ego, forgetfulness and doing various kinds of acts, by which one's physical enjoyments are prevented.

e) **Fear:**

Fear is the horrifying experience experienced by the mind, subtle mental faculties and the knowledge when the incidents that could harm the body, sense organs etc., happen.

f) **Poverty:**

Poverty is one's incapability of possessing the facilities such as education, wealth etc., by one's freedom.

g) **Desire:**

Desire is one's obsession with the things which one wants to have and enjoy but cannot get them as they are difficult to get.

THE PRIMARY, SECONDARY AND FINAL ONES:

Among these, hunger and killing are the primary hindrances, as they hinder all the three kinds of bliss namely: the bliss of this world, bliss of the other world and the absolute natural bliss.

Disease, fear, danger and poverty are known as the secondary hindrances, as they hinder little amount of the bliss of this world, and the bliss of the other world.

Desire is known as the last and final hindrance, as it hinders only little amount of this worldly happiness.

THE POWER OF PRACTISING COMPASSION TOWARDS ALL LIVING BEINGS;

What is the power of the act of showing compassion to all living beings?

Whatever cause among the causes, such as hunger and getting killed etc., evokes one's compassion towards other living beings, the act of making efforts to remove that cause, so that living beings do not suffer due to the same cause, is the power of showing compassion towards all living beings

What is the usefulness of practicing compassion towards all living beings?

It is to be known that the usefulness is to create happiness in the lives of all living beings.

ARUTPERUNJOTHI - ARUTPERUNJOTHI
THANIPPERUNKARUNAI - ARUTPERUNJOTHI

XVI - COMPASSION – PART 3

DISTINGUISHING FEATURES OF THE ACTS OF COMPASSION

Jeeva Kaaruniathin Saurubam

What is the right for getting one's soul melted, which is an act of showing compassion towards all living beings?

All human beings are a part of natural Truth of God (Kadavul Eyarkkai Ekadesa Wunmai), and they have the same characteristics. Since all human beings have been brought into existence in the bodies made up of basic elements by God's Power of Grace, they are of the same kind and all of them do have one and the same right. When a brother sees or hears or knows that one of his brothers is grieved due to a danger, he naturally considers the body of the other as the body of his own brother, and due to the right he has for the body, his soul gets melted for him. In the same way, when a human being is grieved due to a danger, his soul gets melted because he considers that living being are being made up of the same soul, as he is. It should, therefore, be aware that it is the right of the soul.

Some human beings are stony-hearted, and they do not display the quality of compassion to the fellow human beings, even after having seen them in distress; why don't these people have the right of the soul?

It should be known, that despite their 'right of the soul', some people do not show compassion to the human beings who are grieved, because of the knowledge of the souls (Aanmaarivu), which is the eye, that makes one understand that the suffering of humans are of the same kind of souls as they themselves are, they are grieved and will be grieved, has lost its brightness due to a disease called fallacy or untruth. Moreover, since the ancillary instruments to the soul such as mind etc., which function as the mirror, have lost their luster and have become thick, they are unable to perceive the truth.

But, where will the power of showing compassion to the human beings, which is the melting of one's soul, emanate?

Whatever hindrance among the hindrances such as hunger, getting killed and disease etc. that caused one to be compassionate, the place where the same hindrance is removed, there the power of showing compassion asserts itself.

The sufferings of the human beings due to hunger, the agony of getting killed and disease etc., are only the experiences of subtle inner instruments like the mind (karanam) and the sense organs like the eyes (indiriyam) etc., not of the soul; hence, there is nothing special about the usefulness of practicing compassion to the human beings; what is the answer to those who say so?

In this physical body, except the existence of the soul and God's manifestation in the form of knowledge of the knowledge, other principles like the mental faculties and the sense organs are merely inert instruments, and they are not the knowledge as the souls are. Hence, the Joys and sorrows will be experienced only by the souls. The other principles which are devoid of any knowledge will not be aware of experiencing the same. The subtle instruments like the mind etc. and the sense organs like the eye etc., are merely instruments in the small house constructed and provided by the Grace of God to the life of human beings. One who is within that house alone will experience the Joys and sorrows. The sand, bricks, wood, pillar fire and water etc., which are only the instruments of the house will not experience the same. Moreover, when the eyes which are diseased, and subsequently got the power of vision impaired, see sad things with the aid of the spectacles, only the eyes will shed tears not the spectacles. Hence, the inner instruments like the mind etc. that provide only the ancillary assistance to the soul's perception will not be aware of experiencing the happiness and unhappiness.

When the human beings are rejoiced, the mind is cheerful; when they are grieved, the mind gets weakened. Hence, it should be understood that the mind only experiences the happiness and grief; what is the answer to those who say so?

Just like the healthiness as well as the tiredness of the land lord who resides within the glass-house gets reflected within the house and appears outside through the glasses, just like the brightness as well as the fatigue of the eyes gets reflected outside through the spectacles one wears over the eyes, the joys and sorrows experienced by the soul caused by pleasure and pains gets reflected through the subtle instruments and the sense organs like the mind, eyes etc. and are visible outside.

Moreover, when the light of lamp which is kept inside a house is luminous, the house and the things within the house are very bright. When the brightness of the light decreases, the house and the things within the house also get their brightness decreased.

It should, therefore, be known that the happiness and grief are only the experience of the soul, not of the mind, and to experience the same, the subtle inner instruments and the sense organs are only helping instruments.

Why, many human beings created by god suffer a lot due to hunger, getting killed, disease etc?

Since those human beings were 'hard hearted', and had no intention to lead a life of compassion towards fellow beings in their previous bodies, and followed the vicious path of living, they suffer a lot due to hunger, getting killed, disease etc., in accordance with the Gracious order of God.

How is it said that the human beings did have previous bodies?

A family man who has come to reside in a rented house, should have lived in another rented house previously, he would not have lived without a house. If he faces any crisis in the present house, he will go and live in another house. In the event of building a house for himself, he would stop going to a rented house for residing as he was doing before. In the same way, the 'Life Force' (Jeevan) or soul, that has come to reside in the present body, by paying food as rent, should have lived in another body previously after having paid the same sort of rent, it will not exists without a body. In case of trouble in the present body, he will go and reside in another body. Hence, it is to be known that in the event of getting his own Eternal body of Grace, he (the Jeevan) will not go to reside in another body.

One never took a body previously and will not take body after the present one; if the present body gets destroyed, he who dwells in the body will also be destroyed; he will attain liberation (mukthi); he will experience the results of his sins and virtuous deeds; he will continue to be in the same place where his body has been destroyed without a body; why do some people argue like this in different ways?

It should be understood that all such persons are connected with the principles of the worldly religions, which believe that the body itself is the soul, and enjoyment of the worldly pleasures alone is liberation (mukthi). They have not realized the truth, that there is a soul who is the knowledge in itself within the body, which has no knowledge and the soul has. It will experience bondage and liberation until it gets liberated, it will go on taking one body after another, due to different kinds of attachments it had. They are not able to understand this truth by means of their right perception, by surmising or by evidences and for defending their own principles on their part there is no proof, inference and experience.

How is it said that it is "not"?

If it is true that the human beings have the freedom to acquire their bodies and enjoy pleasure as they wish, they should get the bodies and pleasures also as they wish. But it is not so. Some have bodies without deformities and enjoy the pleasures, whereas the others have bodies with deformities which are not fit to get their material desires fulfilled, and consequently, they experience grief. Hence, it should be learnt that Human beings do not get bodies and pleasures as they desire.
If it is said that everyone gets bodies like that due to 'nature', nature should always have the same characteristics without undergoing any change at any time; as it is not the same kind always, and that there are various kinds, it is not because of nature. If it is said that it is the will of God, as God is Gracious and always just, he would have made all the human

beings experience the enjoyments of one and the same kind, as he has not done so, It is not the will of God.

Ever since the First Creation created by the Grace of God, human beings had Failed in their efforts in following the Divine Laws that commanded them to experience 'His natural bliss', due to the age old impact of their acts connected with impurities (Malavasanai) in them. Consequent upon that beginningless impurities, that led to the differences in the efforts of the human beings, different sorts of bodies with different sorts of enjoyments came into existence in the Second Creation. This has to be concluded and understood in this manner.

If no other body is taken once the present body is lost, the number of bodies which were destroyed from the time of first creation to the present time are uncountable, and similarly the souls too are innumerable. Hence, the souls should not take any more bodies hereafter. But it is not so. They are going on taking bodies repeatedly. It is said that the souls are created a new, again and again, and bodies are provided anew for them. In this regard, it is to be known that only the bodies could be created anew again and again but the soul that dwells in the body could not be created anew again and again.

THE SOUL

The soul exists and manifests eternally. It has no birth and death and it is neither created nor destroyed. If souls are made like pot they will not be able to know and experience the pleasure and pain and they will not be affected by their acts of virtue and the acts of sin [punniyapavangal]; when the pot gets destroyed, the soul will also be destroyed along with the pot and if so destroyed, there will not be any Bondage and Liberation (Bandam and Mukthi), there will not be sinful deeds and virtuous deeds. But it is not so. Even the young children know that the air and the space that are within the pot will not get broken but remain intact even when the pot is broken. It must, therefore, be realized by drawing the right conclusion, that when the body is destroyed, the manifestation of soul and the manifestation of God within the body will not get destroyed, and it is true that the souls assume different kinds of bodies and experience various sorts of enjoyments, in accordance with the kinds of efforts they make.

At a specific time, twins are born from one parent. One among them is fair and the other one is dark; one child is with deformities and the other one is without deformities; one child drinks milk whereas the other one makes noise while drinking milk; one child is diseased and the other one is not diseased; one child is able to speak at the age of two and the other one does not know how to speak. When the cause for existence of different characteristics between the twins at this stage is thoroughly examined, it could be realized that this difference is because of different kinds of deeds which were done by them, by making different kinds of efforts while they were in the bodies they had in the previous birth.

At the age of three, when the twins play, their parents give food to each one of them. At that time, in addition to these two children, one more child comes there and on seeing that child, one of the twins give the food which is in its hand to the child, whereas the other one prevents the former one from giving it; one of them takes a book and reads like a young boy but the other one snatches the book and throws away saying that the former one should not read and starts beating it; one child is fearful and the other one is fearless.

If one starts analyzing how one among the two children has characteristics such as kindness, love, knowledge and activities etc., whereas the other one does not have the same, even at this stage of their lives, without having been taught by their father and mother, it will be concluded that the impacts of the qualities (Vasanai) of the body they had in their previous birth, have come into existence in their present body, without getting taught by anyone. If one starts learning this way, it will be clearly understood, that human beings had bodies before and will have bodies once the present body is lost. As it is not rightly comprehended in this manner some people say that there is no birth and rebirth.

Moreover, even when the present body is not destroyed, the soul takes various kinds of bodies and experience, so many strange enjoyments in the dream. It is, therefore, needless to say that when the present body is lost, the soul will take another body and experience various sorts of enjoyments, in accordance with the effect of its past deeds.

On leaving the present body, if a soul is able to enter another body by means of spiritual powers (Siththis), it is needless to say, that when the present body is destroyed, the soul existing within the body will enter another body according to the effect of deeds done in the past.

Moreover, if a bird reaches the body of a chick from its previous body as an egg in course of time, and due to charge in its qualities, it is needless to say, that the souls after leaving the present body will enter another body, according to the effect of the kinds of deeds done in the past.

Moreover, if a Germ, from the body of a worm, enters the body of a wasp because of wasp, it is needless to say, that a soul will enter from one body to another body because of the deeds of the past.

Moreover, even in one birth, if a soul that is in the body of an infant enters the body of a child, from the body of a child to the body of a youth and from the body of a youth to the body of an old man, it is needless to say that, the soul according to its different kinds of deeds of the past will enter another physical body.

Moreover, even in one birth, If the souls transmigrate from the body of a female to the body of a male, and from the body of a male to the body of a female, due to the effects of different type of rituals and prayers like chanting divine names (Mantras) and worshipping God in various ways (Tantras). It is needless to say that, the soul according to its different kinds of deeds of the past will take another body.

Moreover, the soul that is in the body of a plant enters the body of a worm called the Emerald Germ (Marahatha Kirini) form its present body itself; The soul that is in an ant enters the body of ant-bird (Pibilihapatchi), from its present body itself, and the soul that is in a snake, enter another body called snake-bird (Sarpapatchi) from its present body itself.

As the soul that are within the human being, animal, bird, reptile, aquatic creature and plant etc., take other bodies from their respective present bodies in a similar manner, it is needless to say, that the souls will take other bodies when their respective bodies get destroyed.

Some people ask "if it is true that there was a previous body who were you in the body and what was your history? Tell us" - what is the answer to this question?

When a seventy years old person is asked to tell the history of what happened in his life when he was at the age of five, he is puzzled and says, at present he is not able to tell his history of what happened even the day before, because of his problems and distractions (Avasthai). Hence, how he could recollect and narrate the history of whatever happened when he was five years old and how it could be asked.

It is, therefore, to be known that if he is unable to tell his history of what happened even in his present birth due to various troubles and distractions and gets puzzled, how we could, us who are confronting to so many problems and remain perplexed, tell the history of what happened in the previous body, is the answer to this question.

The sinful deeds as well as the virtuous deeds committed by the human beings in their previous bodies will come into existence in the present body also; How to know this?

If a family man had invited vicious people to the house where he lived previously, and entertained them, the same people will follow and befriend him even if he leaves the house and occupies another one. In the same way, if a human being had willingly committed the acts of sin while they were in the previous body, the sinful deeds will follow him even if he takes another body and will be with him. The same will be the condition for the acts of virtues, and this is to be known. If it is the will of God that makes those human beings, who in their previous birth had deviated from the life of showing compassion to human beings and followed the vicious path to be grieved in their present birth due to hunger, thirst etc., will it not be against the commandment of God to show compassion to those human beings and provide food etc., to alleviate their misery?

What is the answer to this simple question?

The king, through his servants, feeds even the criminals of the worst kind who were fettered and imprisoned for having disobeyed his orders. In a similar way, God feeds even the sinners who antagonized Him by being disobedient to His commandments and are kept as slaves in the hell in various ways, through his sub-ordinate deities. The king dismisses those servants who have disobeyed his orders by committing simple offences of various kinds, from service. He also prevents them from receiving any material gains and sends them from the place of service to any other place to enable them to acquire the right knowledge. Consequent upon their loss of job, they lose happiness and food etc., and move around the country in search of food etc. and suffer. On seeing their miserable condition, the kind hearted people provide them with food and other needful things. When the king comes to know about this or sees this happening, he will not be angry with the donors but will appreciate them as good and compassionate family men and hold them in high esteem.

Similarly, All powerful God by His power (Sakthi), precludes the human beings who have not acted in accordance with His will and committed simple crimes from enjoying physical as well as the material comforts of this world and with a view to enable them to acquire the right knowledge removes their 'Being' from the present body and brings into existence in another body. Since those human beings have lost their physical comforts and worldly enjoyments, they move from place the place in search of food etc. and suffer. If kind hearted people, on seeing their miserable state of existence, give them food etc., God will never be angry with them but will be too happy to know that they are merciful people and shower His Grace to make them happy and prosper more and more and will also hold them in high esteem.

Hence, the answer to this question is that the Gracious Law of God always acknowledges the quality of exhibiting compassion by human beings to fellow human beings and this truth is to be known.

The worldly discipline exists only due to the practice of showing compassion to the human beings. If it is not, not even a little amount of worldly discipline will exist. When there is no compassionate in the life of the human beings, True knowledge and love will not exist. When they do not exist, benignity, the sense of spiritual oneness and benevolent attitude will also cease to exist, and due to non-existence of these characteristics, the discipline of the weaker human beings will be obstructed and destroyed by the envy etc., of the stronger human beings. Later, even the conduct and discipline of the stronger human beings get changed to baseness out of their pride and be destroyed. In the jungles where the animals like Tiger,

Lion etc., live, the worldly discipline does not exist because they do not lead a life of compassion. It is, therefore, to be learnt that the worldly discipline will not exist in the place where people live without compassion.

The heavenly discipline too, exists due to the life of compassion of the human beings, and in the absence of the same, even the heavenly discipline will not exist. When there is no compassion to living beings, Grace will not find its expression. When Grace does not get expressed, the 'Divine state' is not attained. When the 'Divine state' is not attained, no one will enjoy the bliss of salvation (MukthiInbam), and in the event of non-attainment of salvation by anyone, heavenly discipline will not exist at all.

As compassionate life is not prevalent in wide-spread manner, only the beings who follow the 'vicious path' have increased, and this situation has led to the existence of immorality as a way of life everywhere. The human beings who had not practiced the act of showing compassion to living beings in their previous body, according to their sins, they committed have taken birth some as: dwellers of hell, some as inhabitants of ocean, some as inhabitants of forest, some as ferocious animals like Tiger, bear, lion, Yale, elephant, wild oxen, pig, dog, cat etc., some as carnivorous group of birds like vulture, crow etc., some as poisonous creatures like snake, scorpion etc., some as hard and vicious creatures like crocodile, shark etc., some as impure plants like strychnine tree, milk hedge etc. It is, therefore, to be learnt that only immorality as a way of life is prevalent everywhere.

It is to be known that the practice of showing compassion to living beings is not only an important instrument to obtain the grace of god but also it is the partial manifestation of grace itself. As the act of showing compassion to living beings is the natural manifestation of the souls, those human beings who do not have that natural manifestation will never get the manifestation of god from inside and outside themselves. What is the objective of practising compassion towards human beings?

The souls are the part of the Natural Truth (Eyarkkai Wunmai). They are also the rightful place for co-existence of Grace, which is the manifestation of nature (Eyarkkai Vilakkam), in the form of knowledge of knowledge.

For the souls to become human beings and multiply, the bodies made up of elements are the pre-requisite.

In case, the souls do not become human beings in the bodies and get multiplied, the manifestation of soul will be concealed and because of this concealment, the Grace will not manifest, and this kind of circumstance will lead to the state of nonexistence of knowledge (Moodam), and this situation will keep the souls in Bondage. Hence, The Bodies made of elements are absolutely necessary. As the primary cause for the bodies made of elements is Maya (Illusion), the Maya by its various illusory qualities such as hunger, thirst, disease, danger, desire, poverty, fear, getting killed will endanger the bodies frequently. The human beings, by the Grace of God, have been given enough freedom and knowledge to be extremely careful against those dangers, and try to avert the same, with the help of intelligence derived from mental faculties and sense organs. The human beings, by making use of this freedom, should get rid of those dangers to their bodies and make efforts to obtain the spiritual benefit. In the case of human beings who suffer because of their inability to safeguard themselves against the dangers caused by hunger, thirst, disease, danger, fear, poverty, desire and getting killed the human beings who are privileged enough to get rid of those dangers must take pity on them and eradicate those dangers.

The acts of kindness relating to the alleviation of sufferings caused by hunger and getting killed are known as the primary acts of compassion (Thalamaiyana Karunyam), whereas the acts of reliving the human beings from any other kind of suffering is called Abara Jeeva Karunyam, and this will lead only to a little amount of worldly happiness. But, the act of removal of suffering because of hunger and getting killed are known as Para Jeeva Karunyam, and the ones who practice this sort of compassion, by the Grace of God, will be provided with all the worldly pleasures unlimited bliss arising out of performing miracles (Siththis), and the eternal bliss of attaining liberation (Mukthi).

The human beings, who in spite of their having sufficient knowledge and freedom, to safeguard other human beings from the dangers mentioned above, but have not done so, and betrayed them, will lose their freedom to enjoy this worldly happiness, the happiness of the other world and the happiness of attaining salvation (Mukthi). Moreover, they will lose whatever worldly luxuries, pleasures and liberties they enjoy at present as stipulated by the Gracious order of God. Hence, in the case of human beings, who do not have enough knowledge and freedom to safeguard themselves against the dangers, those who have enough knowledge and freedom to safeguard them should alleviate their sufferings, without betraying them, and it should be known that, this is the objective of leading a life of compassion towards all living beings.

Even though the objective of practicing compassion towards all living beings is to safeguard them against the dangers caused by hunger, getting killed, thirst, disease, danger, fear, poverty and desire, only the act of averting the danger due to hunger and getting killed is mentioned here as the primary act of compassion ; Why is it so?

There are two kinds of compassionate activities. One is Abara Jeeva Karunyam, and the other one is Para Jeeva Karunyam. As the acts of averting hunger and getting killed are the acts pertaining to Para Jeeva Karunyam whereas the other acts of compassion are the acts pertaining to Abara Jeeva Karunyam, it is quoted with significance here. Besides this, the persons who are kind enough to alleviate the hunger of the human beings, who suffer from hunger, will not be reluctant to supply water to them to quench their thirst. Moreover, water is found in lake, pond, canal etc. and much effort is not required to supply water to those who are in need of it.

XVII –RAMALINGAM VALLALAR'S DEATHLESS LIFE & CHARITABLE TRUST

A R U T P E R U N J O T H I - A R U T P E R U N J O T H I
T H A N I P P E R U N K A R U N A I - A R U T P E R U N J O T H I

VAST SUPREME GRACE LIGHT - VAST SUPREME GRACE LIGHT - VAST SUPREME COMPASSION - VAST SUPREME GRACE LIGHT

THE GOAL OF THE TRUST

The trust in Chennai in partnership with the Association in Luxembourg:

"ARUTPERUNJYOTHI RAMALINGA VALLALAR'S DEATHLESS LIFE & CHARITABLE TRUST AND ASSOCIATION"

The purpose of the trust in Chennai, in coordination with the association in Luxembourg is to create a bridge between Europe and India, to bring full support for humanitarian activities and the establishment of an education for deathlessness to the poor, supported by the teachings of Ramalinga Vallalar (1823 - 1874).

The trust aims at creating open spaces for reflection, study, research and service, to all human beings everywhere, beyond any cleavage, religion, race, colour, ethnicity, language, belief, as a place of welcome, especially meant for the poorest, those without family, those in suffering and despair; through the free distribution of vegetarian food and clothing, the dispensation of free medical care, and by giving them true knowledge and experience, allowing them to reconnect with their true self, regaining their autonomy, and thus enabling them to be useful to society by becoming a lighthouse of wisdom to all.

RAMALINGA'S EDUCATION FOR DEATHLESSNESS TO ELIMINATE SUFFERING, POVERTY AND IGNORANCE

the understanding of education today, is to provide the student with information, facts and skills, neglecting the student's consciousness and values. Consequently, education has become a commodity shaped according to the common understanding of life, according to the market, the market's preference for the technical and natural sciences, neglecting a more comprehensive and holistic approach, adapted to the intellectual, physical, cultural, social and spiritual needs of the student, in its relationship with the world and the universe at large.

Ramalinga's Education is responding to the needs of today's world, by providing the understanding and experience of the origin, course and goal of existence. Thus, covering the entire scope of education, thereby, leading every student from the state of darkness and ignorance to the state of light, purity and truth.

As Thirumular, a Great Saint SIDDHA said:

"the soul is by nature intelligent, but it remains ignorant without even knowing its potency of intelligence"

Ramalinga says:

"Man is living in darkness, being ignorant about the true nature of god and the soul; every man has the capability of becoming full light, the Light that is within us, inside our soul; it just needs to be kindled."

The consciousness is already living inside us, it just needs to be awakened.

THE PATH TO IMMORTALITY – THE PATH TO TRUE AND COMPLETE KNOWLEDGE – THE PATH TO UNCOVER OUR TRUE DIVINTY

"It is a great privilege and a great opportunity to be born as a human being. by god's great mercy alone, the soul is getting a human body. therefore, the highest and unique purpose of being born as a human is to attain and lead a unique great life, a life that is transcending the barriers of time, places, limitations and all ways, after gaining the absolute natural felicity in the form of natural truth."
- **Ramalingam Vallalar**

Once we have recognized that we are part of the sum of a Great Principle of Energy and Intelligence, and know that this Great Universal Principle of Intelligence is nothing but God, we shall soon find ourselves conscious of the fact that all intelligence throughout the all Cosmic Universe is working with us. We also realize quickly that the Intelligence of all great genius, as well as the little mentality of each single cell of the body, is working with us in perfect harmony and accord. This is One Great Intelligent Cosmic Mind with whom we are requested to be positively aligned, on the Suddha Sanmarga Path; this because we are this very Mind; we are the self-consciousness of the Universe. The instant we feel this, nothing can keep us away from the Godhead.

TRUE LEARNING

From This Universal Consciousness, we can draw all knowledge, we can know everything, without studying and without process of reasoning, not going from one lesson to another nor from one point to another. The lessons are necessary only in order to bring us to the attitude in which we can step forth into this understanding. When we experience and understand that we are part of the whole, we move irresistibly with the whole. It is impossible for any condition to keep us from this accomplishment to realize the whole and become the whole. A drop of water is only weak when it is removed from the ocean; reconnect it again and it becomes as powerful as the whole ocean. It matters not whether we like it or whether we believe it. It is Intelligent Law and we are that.

The sum of all Truth is the Great Principle, God. Everything from Eternity to Eternity, whether we think it is a great truth or a little truth; every true word, thought or spoken, is a part of the Great Universal Truth. Being that Ultimate reality, when we realize this oneness of existence and stand absolutely with that Truth, we have the totality of Truth working for us and our irresistibility is increased. It is the power of the ocean backing the waves that gives the wave its power; that, too, it is but a portion of God - Force that move us towards our full realization.

EDUCATION THROUGH LOVE

The sum of all Love is the Great Principle, God. It is the sum of every affection, every fervent emotion, every loving thought, look, word or deed. Every attracted love, great or small, sublime or low, makes the one infinite love stand forth and nothing is too great for us. As we love unselfishly, unconditionally, we have the totality of the ocean of Cosmic Love with us. That which is thought least is greatest as it sweeps on to absolute perfection; thus, the whole universe of love is consciously with us. There is no greater power on earth or in heaven than pure love and compassion. Earth becomes heaven and heaven is Humanity's true home.

Finally, the sum of every condition, every form, every being is the One Infinite Cosmic Principle, God. Whether it be individuals, worlds, planets, stars, atoms, electrons or the most nano particles. All together they make One Infinite Whole, the body of which is the Universe, the Mind, Cosmic Intelligence; the soul, Cosmic Love. Woven together as a whole, their bodies, minds and souls are held together as a whole, their bodies, minds and souls are held together with the cohesive force of love; yet each one functions in eternal individual identity, moving freely in its individual orbit and octave of harmony, attracted, drawn and held together by the love that is The Supreme Grace Light of the Universe. We constitute that Great Being that nothing can thwart. It is made of every unite of humanity as well as every unit of the Universe. If a portion of one unit excludes itself from the whole, it makes no difference to the Infinite Cosmic Principle Being, but it makes a vast difference to the unit. The ocean is not conscious of the removal of the drop of water, but the drop is very conscious of the ocean when it is reunified with it.

SELF-REALIZATION BASED EDUCATION

It is not enough for us to say that we are close to the Great Cosmic Principle, God. We must know that we are one with The Great Cosmic Principle, God, and that we cannot be separated or apart from God. Thus, we work in perfect alliance with this Principle of Power, which is all Power, based on which, we live, move, and have our being. Thus, when we wish to meet God, we do not think of something away from us and difficult to attain. All that we need to know is that God is within us, as well as all about us, and that we are all included in God; that we are consciously within the presence of God and are present in God and in command with full power. Thus, we need not pause, we need not ponder; we take the path directly to God within us. Here "Arutperunjyothi" (The Vast Supreme Grace Light) stands steadfast and Supreme, and with God we endure forever.

IMMORTALITY – THE GOAL FOR A COMPLETE EDUCATION

Thus, we arouse our dead selves into the realization of the life within and that life resurrects us from the dead; we return to life immortal, unchanging. We are convinced of life and of our rights to live that life fully and perfectly. The Light within stands forth and says, "I come that you may have complete life and live more abundantly". That experience must be a true resurrection in our consciousness – an upliftment of our dead senses and body into a higher vibration of life, truth and love. As the all of nature is awakening about us, let us arouse ourselves and see the dawn of this approaching day. Thus, we get up and out of our grave flesh, up and out of all senses of limitation in which we have bound our bodies. We move the veils of our human egoistic nature completely from our soul, that heavy weight of thought that has separated the life within from the life without; and which has held the life form in death and led us in the deny of life, having not recognized its rights to life. Let us get up and wake up out of death – that is what the resurrection means. It is an awakening to the full realization of life here and now – and that life omnipresent, omnipotent, omniscient; nowhere absent, nowhere powerless, nowhere unconscious; but everywhere present, everywhere powerful, everywhere conscious, in fullness, in freedom, in gloriously radiant expressive, expansive action. When the flame of our soul is radiating its full glory and our all being glows with this life within, we can readily accomplish anything. Thousands of years of this awakening have been presented to humanity, yet too many are still sleeping. But their sleeping does not justify us in doing so. It is because of what great siddhas have done for centuries, and most recently Ramalinga Vallalar, who has revealed in its completeness what has been kept hidden for so long, that humanity is awakening to that rightful heritage.

OUR RIGHTFUL HERITAGE

As we awakened to our rightful heritage, we shall awaken to the beauty and purity of the age-old message that our bodies are eternally beautiful, pure and perfect. They are always beautiful, pure, spiritual bodies, most magnificent and divine, the true temples of God. This awakening also convinces us that our bodies have never descended from that high estate. We see that it was only a human concept wherein we thought they had descended. As soon as this thought is released, our body is released to its true inheritance of divinity. Then the fragrance of a warm summer evening diffuses all nature and our bodies begin to take on this effulgence. Soon pure rays of white light appear within our bodies and become aglow with this light; and this soft light, yet very brilliant living light, invades the clear atmosphere around us like a white gold vapor. This light increases steadily until it covers and permeates everything about us. Bathed in this radiance, there appears a pure crystal white light, dazzling and scintillating with a radiance much greater than that of the purest diamond, yet it is emanating from our bodies and they stand forth ablaze with pure light, radiant and beautiful.

THE BODY OF LIGHT

This is true body which humanity has always had, and which have today. Such a body always has existed and always will exist. It is a body so luminous that no germ of old age or decay can find lodgement therein. It is a body so alive that it cannot die. Such a body is eternally divine.

The message is that man of his own freedom shall leave the man-made kingdom and evolve to the God Kingdom.

God knows that in the great structure of the universe there is a splendid place for every human being and that each has his individual place. The structure can stand only because each is in his right place. Does not this message lighten the burden of everyone and adorn each countenance with a smile, even those of the weary ones who think they labour like dumb, driven cattle?

OUR TRUE MISSION IN THIS LIFE

You are an especially designed creation, you have a particular mission, you have a light to give, a work to do that no other can give or accomplish; and if you will open your heart, mind and soul wide to spirit, you will learn of it in your own heart. There you find that your very own Father speaks to you. No matter how wayward or thoughtless you have thought yourself, you will find that your Father loves you devotedly and tenderly the instant you turn your attention to God within. The anointing which you have of God abides in you and you need not the teaching of any man. Is this not a resurrection from the old thought? "Ye need not that any man teaches you." It is only necessary to receive the anointing from God that has always been yours. You may accept others as brother helpers, but you are always instructed and led from within; the truth is there for you and you will find it.

THE WHOLE IS MORE THAN THE COLLECTION OF THE PARTS

Truth always teaches that humanity is a complete unite; nor a unity, but a great unit; combined with God they are the Great One. Humanity is more than a brotherhood. It is One Man, just as a vine and its branches are one vine. No one part or one unit can be separated from the whole.

The truth is, all is One; One Spirit, One Body, the Great Lord Body of humanity. The Great Love, Light, Life of God completely amalgamates that body into One Complete Whole.

EDUCATION FOR DEATHLESSNESS TO THE POOR

Ramalinga's school for deathlessness is meant for the poorest young men and women, to receive a complete education, an education for deathlessness and charity, not merely for the accumulation of information, facts and skills, but for the development of the student's mind-soul and body. This, in order to think properly, to be able to give new directions to life, by developing life supporting ideas in full accordance with all the laws of nature; for the welfare, peace and harmony among the family of men and women, thus, creating a universal brotherhood on earth.

Education means to draw out that which is within you, to actualize your inner intelligence and inner capacity to love.

Ramalinga's education is preparing you to be yourself and not an imitator. It teaches you how to live in full accordance with all the laws of nature and to know how to live with others. This by offering to everyone the understanding and the experience of life and evolution, bringing thus, every student from a state of despair, confusion, doubt, fear and ignorance to a state of self-knowingness, truth and light. This, by exposing everyone to the Holy scriptures which have their roots in wisdom, love, compassion and kindness, to gain mastery over the most traditional disciplines as transmitted by the great saints and siddhas of the blessed land of India and Tamil Nadu, especially by Ramalingam Vallalar, who has revealed in its uniqueness, the knowledge of deathlessness in a very simple and practical way, for everyone to follow, in order to attain the highest pinnacle of human development.

THE DISCIPLINES TAUGHT AT RAMALINGA'S SCHOOL FOR DEATHLESSNESS

- The study of English, Tamil and Sanskrit languages,
- The study and practice of the 4 disciplines to gain control and mastery over all the 96 tattvas or principles of existence.
    1 – Discipline of the senses,
    2 – Discipline of the mind and its faculties
    3 – Discipline of Jeeva,
    4 – Discipline of Anma, the soul.

- The study of Siddha Medicine according to Ramalinga's Science of deathlessness: to restore the preventive approach to perfect health and longevity, for the annihilation of all diseases, ignorance and suffering everywhere.

- Vedic Astronomy and Astrology: to bring life in full accordance with all the laws of nature and prevent any obstacle before it arises.

- Ramalinga's vision on organic farming, diet, and sacred herbals: for the healing, rejuvenation and transmutation of everyone's body-mind and soul.

- The Science of Compassion and Immortality through compassionate service to the poor, the study and chanting of Thiru Arutpa, Agaval, Thiruvasagam, Thirumandiram, Thirukkural to gain the understanding and experience of Higher State of Consciousness and for the transformation of the human physiology in body of light.

The purpose of Ramalinga's Education is "to obtain deathlessness and live forever. Through his education, Ramalinga wishes to uplift the whole of mankind towards perfect bliss, free from hunger, disease, thirst, poverty, fear, decay and death, with full self-existent felicity. This by means of true knowledge, true love and compassion, without disparities of dogmatic rituals pertaining to any religions, philosophies, caste, colour, creed, clan, sex or nationalities."

Ramalinga's Education for Deathlessness Life, Research Centre and Charity is proposing his vision to every school, college and university who wishes to give to every student complete knowledge: 100% of relative and 100% of absolute Knowledge, knowledge of the self. Thereby, creating the foundation for a new paradigm on earth, shifting from an age of limited knowledge, ignorance, darkness, selfishness, conflict and war, to an age where truth, creativity, perfect health, light, love and compassion will become a living reality to all.

CALL TO WELL-WISHER

To achieve our trust main goal, to build a school for the poor, in which education for Deathlessness will be provided, as revealed by Ramalinga Vallalar, we are calling to all well-wishers who feel to be part of this divine project, to become sponsor.

Your contribution alone will permit the building of the school as well as ensuring the good functioning and continuity of the school on a yearly basis.

Your precious help will help providing a solid foundation for the eradication of suffering and ignorance everywhere.

As Albert Pine said:

"What we do for ourselves dies with us; what we do for others and the world remains immortal."

"The natural and inherent quality of the soul is compassion; if a soul realizes its ultimate sphere through compassionate service to all living beings, it will surely experience the union with God."

- **Ramalinga Vallalar**

ABOUT TRANSFERRING MONEY INTO THE TRUST - BANK ACCOUNT

Every potential sponsor is invited to contact:

Mr. Vinothkumar
Whatspp No. +91 8667555300 | Mobile No. +91 8608403333
Email: vinothkumar3333@yahoo.com

prior doing any transaction, this in order to follow a specific procedure to be in full accordance with the Laws of the country.

TRUST & ASSOCIATION INFORMATIONS

RAMALINGA VALLALAR'S TRUST – CHENNAI – INDIA
"Arutperunjothi Ramalingam Vallalar's Deathless Life & Charitable Trust"

Founder Trustee: V. Chithra
Co – Founder Trustee: R. Vinothkumar

Address: 1/1234 A, 8th Cross Street, Balamurugan Nagar, Balaji Avenue, Ponneri Taluk, Attanthangal, Tiruvallur, Sholavaram, Chennai – Tamil Nadu – 600 067 – India

Telephone: +91 8608403333, +91 908031299, +918667555300
E-mail: vinothkumar3333@yahoo.com, arvdlctrust@gmail.com
Website: www.ArutperunjyothiRamalingamTrust.org

Account Name	ARUTPERUNJOTHI RAMALINGAM VALLALARS DEATHLESS LIFE AND CHARITABLE TRUST
Savings Account Number	092588700000064
IFSC Code	YESB0000925
Customer ID	8129227
Swift Code	YESBINBB
Bank Name	YES BANK LTD
Bank Address	Door No 225/3, Ground Floor Mount Road Chennai, Tamil Nadu - 600002

RAMALINGA VALLALAR'S ASSOCIATION
LUXEMBOURG – EUROPE

"Arutperunjothi – Ramalinga Vallalar Deathless Life & Charitable Association"

President: Legras Alain Pierre - Aruludaiyaar
Treasurer: Colaux Virginie Marguerite
Secretary: Soboleva Ekaterina

Address: Rue Nicolas Braunshausen 2, 1257 Luxembourg – Europe
Telephone: 0033 6 95 85 16 19/ 00352 621 740 496/ 0091 76 95 99 24 29
E-mail: Arutperunjyothi.deathlesslife@gmail.com
Website: www.ArutperunjyothiRamalingamTrust.org

BIBLIOGRAPHY

- **ARUT PERUN JYOTHI & DEATHLESS BODY** Volume 1&2 – T.R. THULASIRAM – University of Madras 1980
- **TIRUMANDIRAM** Volume 1&2 – Babaji's Kriya Yoga and Publications, Inc.
- **THE YOGA OF SIDDHA TIRUMULAR** – T.N. Ganapathyn – KR. Arumugam Geetha Anand – Babaji's Kriya Yoga and Publications, Inc.
- **THIRUARUTPRAHAASA VALLALAR - HIS BIOGRAPHY AND TEACHING** – Translated and Published by the team of Sanmargam – Vadalur -607 303.
- **ARUT PRAKASA VALLALAR – THE SAINT OF UNIVERSAL VISION** – V.S. Krishnan.
- **PATHWAY TO GOD TROD BY SAINT RAMALINGAR** – G. Vanmikanathan – General Editor: DR. N. Mahalingam.
- **VALLALAR THE GREATEST SAINT AND MYSTIC** – volume 1 & 2 - V.Rajappa.
- **SAINT RAMALINGAM** – Swami Saravananda.
- **AN INTRODUCTION TO THE PHILOSOPHY OF RAMALINGA SWAMI** – Dr. C. Srinivasan – Published by Ilakkia Nilayam, Tiruchi (1968).
- **VEGETARIAN OR NON-VEGETARIAN – CHOOSE YOURSELF** – By Gopinath Aggarwal
- **VALLALAR MESSAGER OF GRACE LIGHT** By Dhaya Mesrobian
- **LIFE AND TEACHING OF THE MASTERS OF THE FAR EAST** - by Baird T. SPALDING - Volume 2 - De Vorss Publications, Camarillo, California

Printed in Great Britain
by Amazon